WHAT OTHERS ARE SAYING . . .

"This is the best self-publishing manual on the market."
—Judith Appelbaum, *How to Get Happily Published*

"This is by far the best book of its kind."
—Writing & Publishing

"The book is a must for those considering publishing as a business, for writers who want to investigate self-publishing, and is eminently useful for its new and old ideas to those who have already begun to do it. A fine and handy guide by a fine and successful publisher."
—Small Press Review

"With this book, you will learn how to speed write your book; copyright it yourself; bypass publishers; set up your own book publishing company; promote your books with book reviews, book signings, feature articles and radio/TV interviews; get your book into bookstores, specialty stores, catalogs and on the Web; and make spin-offs of your book."
—The Writer

"A handy, concise and informative sourcebook... Expertly organized and chock-full of hard facts, helpful hints and pertinent illustrations... Recommended for all libraries."
—The Southeastern Librarian

"Poynter is at his best when discussing such specifics as starting one's own publishing house; dealing with printers; establishing discount, credit and return policies; promoting, advertising and selling a book; and order fulfillment."
—Publishers Weekly

"A deeply researched how-to book on writing, printing, publishing, promotion, marketing and distribution of books."
—The College Store Journal

"Poynter is a self-publisher of considerable experience which he passes along in minute detail... There is real gold here."
—Quill & Scroll

The Self-Publishing Manual
The guide that has launched thousands of books

THE BOOK THAT STARTED
THE SELF-PUBLISHING REVOLUTION...

...by the man the industry turns to for publishing advice.

You *can* be in print. You *can* have a book you will be proud of. You *can* make it a successful seller. Most importantly, you *can* afford it!

The Self-Publishing Manual, more effectively and successfully than any other book, has turned writers with an idea into successful authors with books. Real books. Books to be proud of.

How? By providing solid, usable information in clear, concise, readable language. By covering every stage of the process from putting ideas into words and words into print, and print into books and books into the hands of readers. This is not the stuff of theory; it is the product of hard-earned experience written by a man who walked, then ran the path to success. More than 120 times.

Dan Poynter is *the* acknowledged expert in the field of publishing. He didn't get there by self-promotion. He got there by producing measurable results for countless authors who were turned down by or chose to turn away from established publishers.

From the very first edition through the 15th, *The Self-Publishing Manual* delivered insider secrets for creating a solid foundation in self-publishing. Each subsequent edition was updated to cover the latest development in the technology and realities of the publishing industry. However, unless you have the 16th edition, you don't have all you need to know to keep you on the fast track to success in the rapidly evolving world of publishing.

This is your single most important resource; it will lead you to publishing success.

> *I have never met an author who is sorry he or she wrote their book. They are only sorry they did not write it sooner.*
>
> **—*Sam Horn,* Tongue Fu!**

Dan Poynter's
SELF-PUBLISHING MANUAL

Dan Poynter's
SELF-PUBLISHING
MANUAL

How to Write, Print and
Sell Your Own Book

Dan Poynter

Sixteenth Edition
Completely Revised

Santa Barbara, California

DAN POYNTER'S SELF-PUBLISHING MANUAL

How to Write, Print and Sell Your Own Book by Dan Poynter

Para Publishing
Post Office Box 8206
Santa Barbara, CA 93118-8206 U.S.A.
Orders@ParaPublishing.com; http://ParaPublishing.com

Unattributed quotations are by Dan Poynter.

Edition ISBNs
Softcover	978-1-56860-134-2
Large Print	978-1-56860-135-9
LIT	978-1-56860-136-6
PDF	978-1-56860-137-3
Mobipocket	978-1-56860-138-0
Palm	978-1-56860-139-7
Audio, MP3	978-1-56860-140-3

First Edition 1979. Sixteenth Edition/Twentieth Printing 2007, Completely Revised
Printed in the United States of America

Library of Congress Cataloging-in-Publication Data

Poynter, Dan.
Dan Poynter's self-publishing manual : how to write, print, and sell
your own book / by Dan Poynter. -- 16th ed., completely rev.
p. cm.
Rev. ed. of: Self-publishing manual. c2007.
Includes bibliographical references and index.
ISBN-13: 978-1-56860-134-2 (trade pbk. : alk. paper)
1. Self-publishing--United States. I. Poynter, Dan. Self-publishing
manual. II. Title. III. Title: Self-publishing manual.
Z285.5.P69 2006
070.5'93--dc22

2006010649

CONTENTS

3 STARTING YOUR OWN PUBLISHING 81
COMPANY: BASICS FOR TAKING THE PLUNGE

4 PRODUCING YOUR BOOK: 109
DESIGNING BOOKS, TYPESETTING, LAYOUT, BOOK
PRINTING MATERIALS, THE PRINTING PROCESS

8   WHO WILL BUY YOUR BOOK?:   279
MARKETS, DISTRIBUTION CHANNELS

A common observation by those who use a highlighter to indicate the important parts of The Self-Publishing Manual is that their copy winds up completely yellow.

ABOUT THE AUTHOR

DAN POYNTER is the author of more than 120 books and a Certified Speaking Professional (CSP). He has been a successful publisher since 1969.

Dan is án evangelist for books, an ombudsman for authors, an advocate for publishers and the godfather to thousands of successfully published books.

His seminars have been featured on CNN, his books have been pictured in *The Wall Street Journal* and his story has been told in *U.S. News & World Report*. The media come to Dan because he is a leading authority on publishing and the Father of Self-Publishing.

His books have been translated into Spanish, Japanese, British-English, Russian, German, and others. He has helped people all over the world to publish.

Dan shows people how to make a difference as he makes a living by coaching them on the writing, publishing and promoting of their books. He has turned thousands of people into successful authors. His mission is to see that people do not die with their books still inside of them.

He was prompted to write this book because so many other authors and publishers wanted to know his secret to selling so many books. Now Dan is revealing it to you—the good life of self-publishing.

PREFACE—NOTE TO THE READER

This is an exciting time to be in the book business. Book writing, publishing and promoting are changing—for the better!

You will encounter pivotal stories of my own experiences and some from people like you who wanted to write books and perhaps now play a part in influencing what others think and do—to possibly even change the course of a reader's life. I hope you enjoy these stories. I have also included quotations from experts in the field of writing or publishing, related quotations from others and some of my own thoughts (they are the unattributed quotations).

There's not enough room in one manual to include everything you should know about self-publishing. Consequently, Para Publishing has prepared many supplemental reports (called Documents, Special Reports or Instant Reports), which are referenced in relevant places throughout this manual. You may not want or need these supplements right now, but when you do you can find them on our Web site (by typing in the document number in the search box) or can contact us by email or telephone about getting copies. Appendix 2 gives a comprehensive listing of these resources.

Dan Poynter, Santa Barbara

ACKNOWLEDGMENTS

I have not attempted to cite in the text all the authorities and sources consulted in the preparation of this manual. To do so would require more space than is available. The list would include departments of the federal government, libraries, industrial institutions, periodicals and many individuals.

Scores of people contributed to the earlier editions of this manual. Information and illustrations have been contributed to this edition by Jay Abraham, Bill Alarid, David Amkraut, Judy Appelbaum, Walter Becker, James Scott Bell, Susan Bodendorfer, Chuck Broyles, Jerry Buchanan, Dan Buckley, Gordon Burgett, Judy Byers, Jack Canfield, John Culleton, Jack Dennon, Dave Dunn, Robbie Fanning, Elizabeth Felicetti, Scott Frush, Alan Gadney, Bud Gardner, Barbara Gaughen-Müller, Eric Gelb, Peggy Glenn, Scott Gross, Bill Harrison, Don Hausrath, Ken Hoffmann, Sam Horn, Lee Ann Knutson, John Kremer, Paul Krupin, Michael Larsen, Andrew Linick, Terri Lonier, Ted Maass, Tess Marcin, Maggie Mitchell, John McHugh, Susan Monbaron, Jan Nathan, Christine Nolt, Terry Paulson, Raleigh Pinskey, Tag Powell, Bob Richardson, Ed Rigsbee, Joel Roberts, Joe Sabah, Ellen Searby, Dan Snow, Ted Thomas, Doug Thorburn, George Thornally, Jan Venolia, Liz Wagner, Dottie Walters, Mary Westheimer, Liz Zelandais and Irwin Zucker.

Special thanks go to Robin Quinn for editing, Patricia Bacall for interior design, Ghislain Viau for typography, Alan Gadney for technical editing, Robert Howard for cover design, Brookes Nohlgren and Arlene Prunkl for proofing and proofreading, Laren Bright for marketing copywriting and Ellen Reid for guiding the process to excellence.

I sincerely thank all these fine people. I know that they're as proud of the part they have played in the development of entrepreneurial publishing as they are of their contribution to this work.

WARNING—DISCLAIMER

This book is designed to provide information on writing, publishing, marketing, promoting and distributing books. It is sold with the understanding that the publisher and author are not engaged in rendering legal, accounting or other professional services. If legal or other expert assistance is required, the services of a competent professional should be sought.

It is not the purpose of this manual to reprint all the information that is otherwise available to authors and/or publishers, but instead to complement, amplify and supplement other texts. You are urged to read all the available material, learn as much as possible about self-publishing and tailor the information to your individual needs. For more information, see the many resources in Appendix 2.

Self-publishing is not a get-rich-quick scheme. Anyone who decides to write and publish a book must expect to invest a lot of time and effort into it. For many people, self-publishing is more lucrative than selling manuscripts to another publisher, and many have built solid, growing, rewarding businesses.

Every effort has been made to make this manual as complete and accurate as possible. However, there may be mistakes, both typographical and in content. Therefore, this text should be used only as a general guide and not as the ultimate source of writing and publishing information. Furthermore, this manual contains information on writing and publishing that is current only up to the printing date.

The purpose of this manual is to educate and entertain. The author and Para Publishing shall have neither liability nor responsibility to any person or entity with respect to any loss or damage caused, or alleged to have been caused, directly or indirectly, by the information contained in this book.

If you do not wish to be bound by the above, you may return this book to the publisher for a full refund.

YOUR PUBLISHING OPTIONS

WHY YOU SHOULD CONSIDER SELF-PUBLISHING

> *Books are the main source of our knowledge, our*
> *reservoir of first faith, memory, wisdom, morality,*
> *poetry, philosophy, history and science.*
> **—Daniel J. Boorstin, Librarian of Congress Emeritus**

Nearly everyone wants to write a book. Most people have the ability, some have the drive, but few have the organization. Therefore, the greatest need is for a simple system, a road map. The basic plan in this book will not only provide you with direction, it will also promote the needed drive and expose abilities in you that may never have been recognized.

Magazines devoted to businesspeople, sales reps and opportunity seekers are littered with full-page advertisements featuring people with fabulous offers. Usually, these people discovered a successful system of business in sales, real estate or mail order, and for a price they are willing to let the reader in on their "secret." To distribute this information, they have written a book. Upon close inspection, one often finds that the author is making more money from the *book* than from the original enterprise. The irony is that purchasers get the wrong information; what they need is a book on how to write, produce and sell a *book*!

Writing a book is probably easier than you think. If you can voice an opinion and think logically, you can write a book. If you can *say it*, you can *write it*. Most people have to work for a living and therefore can spend only a few minutes of each day on their book. Consequently, they can't keep the whole manuscript in their head. They become overwhelmed and confused, and find it easy to quit the project. The solution is to break up the manuscript into many small, easy-to-attack chunks (and never start at page one, where the hill looks steepest). Then concentrate on one section at a time and do a thorough job on each part.

People want to know "how to" and "where to," and they will pay well to find out. The information industry—the production and distribution of ideas and knowledge as opposed to goods and services—now amounts to more than one-half of the U.S. gross national product. *There is money in information.* To see how books are tapping this market, check the best-seller lists in *Publishers Weekly, USA Today, The Wall Street Journal* or *The New York Times*.

Your best sources for this salable information are your own experiences, plus research. Write what you know. Whether you already have a completed manuscript, have a great idea for one or need help in locating a suitable subject, this book will point the way.

Since poetry and fiction are very difficult to sell, we will concern ourselves with nonfiction. Writing nonfiction doesn't require any great literary style; it is simply a matter of producing well-researched, reorganized, updated and, most important, repackaged information. Some of the recommendations here can be applied to fiction, just as the chapters on promotion and advertising might be taken separately and used for other products and businesses. However, all the recommendations are written toward, and for, the reader who wishes to become an author or an author–publisher of useful information.

> *Writing ranks among the top 10 percent of professions in terms of prestige.*
> **—Jean Strouse, as quoted in Newsweek**

BECOMING A CELEBRITY AUTHOR

The prestige enjoyed by the published author is unparalleled in our society. A book can bring recognition, wealth and acceleration in one's career. People have always held books in high regard, possibly because in past centuries books were expensive and were, therefore, purchased only by the rich. Just 250 years ago, many people could not read or write. To be an author then was to be an educated person.

> *Books through the ages have earned humanity's high regard as semi-sacred objects.*
> **—Richard Kluger, author and editor**

Many enterprising people are using books to establish themselves in the ultimate business of being a celebrity information provider. Usually starting with a series of non-paying magazine articles, they develop a name and make themselves visible. Then they expand the series of articles into a book. Now with their credibility established, they operate seminars in their field of expertise, command high speaking fees and issue a high-priced newsletter. From there, they teach a course at the local college and become a consultant, advising individuals, businesses and/or others. They find they are in great demand. People want their information or simply want them around. Clubs and corporations fly them in to consult, because it is more economical than sending all their people to the expert.

Achieving this dream begins with the packaging and marketing of information. Starting with a field you know, then researching it further and putting it on paper will establish you as an expert. Then your expert standing can be pyramided with interviews, articles, TV appearances, talks at local clubs, etc. Of course, most of this activity will promote your book sales.

> *Recognition is everything you write for: it's much more than money. You want your books to be valued. It's the basic aspiration of a serious writer.*
>
> **—William Kennedy**

In turn, all this publicity not only sells books, but also opens more doors and produces more invitations, leading to more opportunities to prove your expert status and make even more money for yourself. People seek experts whose opinions, advice and ideas are quoted in the media. Becoming an expert doesn't require a great education or a college degree. You can become an expert in one small area if you're willing to search the Internet (the world's largest library), read up on your subject elsewhere too and write down the important information.

SAMPLE EXPERT BIO

Dan Poynter is a parachute expert who advises attorneys, judges and juries about what happened or what should have happened in skydiving accidents. He is not a lawyer or even an engineer, but has written seven books on related subjects. His technical books on parachutes and popular books on skydiving give him the expertise to be hired and the credibility to be believed.

A BOOK LASTS FOREVER

A book is similar to a new product design or an invention, but is usually much, much better. A patent on a device or process runs only 17 years, whereas a copyright runs for the author's life plus 70 years. Patents cost thousands of dollars to secure and normally require a lot of legal help. By contrast, an author with a simple two-page form and $30 can file a copyright. Once you write a book, it's yours. You have a monopoly on your book and there is often little direct competition.

Many people work hard at a job for 40 years and have nothing to show for it but memories and pay stubs. However, others take their knowledge and write a book; the result is a tangible product for all to see. A book lasts forever, like a painting or a sculpture, but there are many copies of the book—not just one. While a sculpture can only be admired by a limited number of persons at any one time in the place where it is displayed, books come in multiple copies for the entire world to use and admire simultaneously.

Another success secret is to cut out the *intermediaries* who are the commercial publishers and produce and sell the book yourself. You can take the author's royalty and the publisher's profit. You get all the rewards because you are both the author and the publisher. Now, in addition to achieving the wealth and prestige of a published author, you have propelled yourself into your own lucrative business—a publishing house. This shortcut not only makes you more money (why share it?), it also saves you the frustration, trouble and time required to sell your manuscript to a publisher. You know the subject and market better than some distant corporation anyway.

> *It circulated for five years, through the halls of 15 publishers, and finally ended up with Vanguard Press, which you can see is rather deep in the alphabet.*
> **—Patrick Dennis**

To clarify for those readers who might misunderstand, publishing doesn't mean purchasing a printing press and actually putting the ink on the paper yourself. Nearly all publishers leave the production to an experienced book printer.

YOUR OWN PUBLISHING BUSINESS

A business of your own is the great American dream, and it is still attainable. In your own business, you make the decisions to meet only those challenges you find interesting. This is not goofing off; it is making more effective use of your time by working smarter, not harder. After all, there are only 24 hours in a day. If you are to prosper, you have to concentrate on what will bring the most return.

Running your own enterprise will provide you with many satisfying advantages. You should earn more money because you are working for yourself rather than splitting your efforts with someone else. You never have to worry about a surprise pink slip. If you keep your regular job and moonlight in your own enterprise as recreation, it will always be there to fall back on should you need it. In your own company you start at the top, not the bottom, and you work at your own pace and schedule.

In your own small business, you may work when and where you wish; you don't have to go where the job is. You can work till dawn, sleep till noon, rush off to Hawaii without asking permission. This is flexibility not available to the time-clock punchers.

Before you charge into literary battle and attack your keyboard, review Chapter 11 of this book. It describes how your life will change once you become a published author. Being an author–publisher will sound like a good life, and it can be. However, working for yourself requires organization and discipline. Yet work won't seem so hard when you are counting your own money.

THE BOOK PUBLISHING INDUSTRY

To help you understand what's ahead, here are some definitions and background on the book publishing industry:

•◊ **To Publish** means to prepare and issue material for public distribution or sale or "to place before the public." The book doesn't have to be beautiful; it doesn't even have to *sell*; it needs only to be *issued*. Salability will depend upon the content, the packaging and the book's promotion.

•◊ **A Publisher** is the one who puts up the *money*, the one who takes the risk. He or she has the book assembled for the printer, printed and then marketed, hoping to make back more money than has been spent to produce it. The publisher might be a big New York firm or a first-time author, but he or she is almost always the investor.

•◊ **A Book** by International Standards is a publication with at least 49 pages, not counting the covers. Books should not be confused with "pamphlets," which have less than 49 pages, or "periodicals," such as magazines and newspapers. Periodicals are published regularly and usually carry advertising.

THE BOOK PUBLISHING INDUSTRY in the U.S. consists of some 82,000 firms (up from 3,000 in 1970), according to the R.R. Bowker Co., but there are many more thousands of publishers. Altogether, they publish more than 200,000 titles every year. The large publishers, based in New York, are consolidating, downsizing and going out of business; there are just six left. There are perhaps 300 medium-sized publishers and more than 81,000 small/self-publishers. Some 8,000 to 11,000 new publishing companies are established each year. Currently, 2.8 million titles are available or "in print" in the U.S.

YOUR PUBLISHING CHOICES

An author who wishes to get into print has many choices. You can approach a large (New York) general publisher or a medium-sized niche publisher. You can work with an agent, deal with a vanity press (a bad choice) or publish yourself. And there are also choices when it comes to printing (see Chapter 4).

If you publish other authors as you expand your list of titles, you may graduate to the ranks of the medium-sized publisher. You could one day even become a large general publisher. Here are the choices.

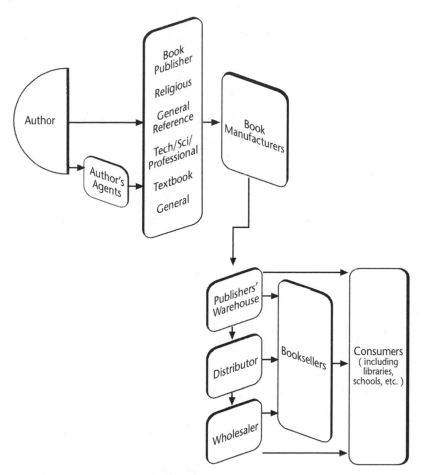

How books get from writer to reader

1. LARGE PUBLISHING FIRMS are like department stores; they have something for everyone. They publish in many different fields and concentrate on books that anticipate audiences in the millions. A look at the numbers in big publishing will help us to better understand their challenges.

It has been estimated that more than 2 million book-length manuscripts are circulated to publishers each year, and many of the large publishers receive 3,000–5,000 unsolicited manuscripts each week. Reading all these manuscripts would take an enormous amount of time, and a high percentage of the submissions do not even fit the publisher's line. They are a waste of editorial time. Consequently, many of the publishers refuse delivery of unsolicited manuscripts by rubber-stamping the packages "Return to Sender"; writers are being rejected without being read!

> *Authors do detailed research on the subject matter but seldom do any on which publishing house is appropriate for their work.*
> **—Walter W. Powell, Getting into Print**

The 12,000 bookstores in the U.S. don't have enough space to display all the 200,000 titles published each year, so they concentrate on the books that move the best in their neighborhoods. Consequently, most publishers figure that even after selecting the best manuscripts and pouring in the promotion money, only three books out of ten will sell well, four will break even and three will be losers. Only 10% of the New York-published books sell enough copies to pay off the author advance before royalties are paid.

Have you ever wondered why books in bookstores tend to have very recent copyright dates? They are seldom more than a year old because the store replaces them very quickly. Shelf space is expensive and in short supply. The books either sell in a couple of months or they go back to the publisher as "returns."

Large publishers have three selling seasons per year. They keep books in bookstores for four months and then replace them. Most initial print runs are for 5,000 books. Then the title remains in print (available for sale) for about a year. If the book sells out quickly, it is reprinted and the publisher dumps in more promotion money. If the book does not catch on, it is pulled off the market and remaindered (sold off very cheaply) to make room for new titles.

The financial demands cause publishers to be terribly objective about the bottom line. To many publishers, in fact, a book is just a "product." They are not interested in whether it is a good book; all they want to know is whether it will sell. Therefore, they concentrate on well-known authors with good track records, or Hollywood and political personalities who can move a book with their name. Only occasionally will they accept a well-written manuscript by an unknown, and then it must be on a topic with a ready and massive audience. A published writer has a much better chance of selling than an unpublished one, regardless of the quality of the work.

> *Few of the major trade publishers will take a chance on a manuscript from someone whose name is not known.*
> —**Walter W. Powell**, **Getting into Print**

Publishers, like most businesspeople, seem to follow the 80/20 principle: they spend 80% of their effort on the top 20% of their books. The remaining 20% of their effort goes to the bottom 80% of their line. Most books have to sell themselves to induce the publisher to allocate more promotion money.

Many publishers today suggest that their authors hire their own PR firm (at the author's expense) to promote the book.

A SAVVY SUCCESS STORY

There is a story about one author who sent her relatives around to bookstores to buy up every copy of her new book. The sudden spurt in sales excited the publisher, who increased the ad budget. The increase in promotion produced greater sales and her book became a success.

Royalties: The author will get a royalty from the large publisher of 6% to 10% of the net receipts (what the publisher receives), usually on a sliding scale, and the economics here are not encouraging. For example, a print run of 5,000 copies of a book selling for $20 could gross $100,000 if all were sold by the publisher at the full retail list price, but an 8% royalty on the net (most books are sold at a discount) may come to just $4,000. That isn't enough money to pay for all the time you spent at the computer. The chances of selling more than 5,000 copies are highly remote, because after a few months the publisher takes the book out of print. In fact, the publisher will probably sell fewer than the number of copies printed, because some books will be used for promotion and unsold books will be returned by bookstores.

Your publisher will put up the money, have the book produced and use sales reps to get it into bookstores. However, they will not extensively promote the book—contrary to what most first-time authors think. Authors must do the bulk of the promotion. Once authors figure out that very little promotion is being done, it is often too late; the book is no longer new (it has a quickly ticking copyright date in it) and is about to be remaindered. They also can discover, to their dismay, that their contract dictates that they must submit their next two manuscripts to this same publisher.

> *Whether you sell to a publisher or publish yourself, the author must do the promotion.*

Big publishing houses provide a needed service; however, for many first-time authors, they are unapproachable. And once in, an author doesn't get the best deal, and getting out may be difficult. In addition, these publishers often chop the book up editorially, change the title and take a year and a half to publish it. Authors lose artistic control of their delayed book.

Their publishing approach might be more acceptable if the big commercial publishers were great financial successes. They aren't, or at least they haven't been so far. One publishing house even admits that it would have made more money last year if it had vacated its New York office and rented out the floor space!

But there is a brighter side for the small publisher who understands who his or her readers are and where they can be found. Since the old-line, *big department store-like* publishers only know how to sell through bookstores, there's a lot of room left for the smaller *boutique-like* publishing house and self-publisher.

Be careful if you hang around with people from the traditional book industry. Learn, but don't let their ways rub off. Study the big New York publishing firms, but don't copy them. You can do a lot better.

> *To the smaller publisher, there is no front list*
> *or back list; it is an "only" list.*

2. MEDIUM-SIZED (NICHE/SPECIALIZED) PUBLISHERS are the smaller and newer firms that serve specific technical fields, geographic regions, categories of people or other specialized markets (business, hiking, boating, etc.). Some of these publishers are very small, some are fairly large, but the most successful ones concentrate on a single genre or subject area.

The owners and staff are usually *participants* in their books' subject matter. For example, I publish parachute books with a sense of mission—because I like to jump out of airplanes. Participants at these firms know their subject matter and where to find their reader/buyer because they join the same associations, read the same magazines and attend the same conventions the readers and buyers do.

The secret to effective book distribution is to make the title available in places with a high concentration of your potential buyers. When a niche publisher takes on your book, they can plug it right into their existing distribution system. For example, while some parachute books are sold in bookstores, more than 90% are sold through parachute stores, skydiving catalogs, jump schools and the U.S. Parachute Association for resale to its members. Usually three or four calls to major dealers can sell enough books to pay the printing bill—before the book is even printed!

Some writers may think a large New York publisher is more prestigious (good for impressing people at cocktail parties), but a small to medium-sized publisher will usually sell more books because they sell to nonbook trade accounts as well as to bookstores. Remember, most book buyers are interested in the subject matter of the book and want to know if the author is credible. Rarely does anyone ask who the publisher is.

> *Professionals sell then write, while amateurs write then try to sell.*
>
> **—Gordon Burgett**

Contacting a niche publisher: If you decide you want your book published by someone else, the secret is to match the manuscript to the publisher. To find the right publisher, check your own bookshelf or go to your nearby bookstore and consult the shelves where your book will be. Check the listings at an online bookstore such as Amazon.com. Look for smaller publishers who do good work. When you contact a niche publisher, you will often get through to the top person. They know and like the subject, and they are usually very helpful. They will be able to tell you instantly whether the proposed book will fit into their line.

Niche book publishers tend to be helpful and friendly. No two niche books are exactly alike; it is rare that two books on the same niche subject are published in the same year. Consequently, these publishers do not feel threatened by other publishers. In fact, publishers often promote other books and each other. This is why when you contact a publisher and they decide that your manuscript is not for them, they are eager to recommend another publisher. They know of lots of other publishing companies, and most relish being able to help you and the other publisher get together.

3. VANITY OR SUBSIDY PUBLISHERS produce around 6,000 titles each year; roughly 20 firms produce about 70% of the subsidized books. Subsidy publishers offer regular publishing services, but the author invests all the money. Under a typical arrangement, the author pays the full publishing costs (more than just the printing bill) and receives 40% of the retail price of the books sold and 80% of the subsidiary rights, if sold. (See a fuller explanation of subsidiary rights in Chapter 8.) Many vanity publishers charge $10,000 to $30,000 to publish a book, depending on its length.

Vanity publishers claim that they will furnish all the regular publishing services including promotion and distribution. All this might not be so bad if they had a good track record for delivery. But according to *Writer's Digest*, vanity publishers usually do not deliver the promotion they promise, and the books rarely return one-quarter of the author's investment.

A CAUTIONARY TALE

Soma Vira, Ph.D., paid $44,000 to have three of her books produced by a well-known subsidy publisher. She received 250 books but could not verify how many were printed and suspects they made very few for stock. The books were not properly edited, typeset, proofed or manufactured. Distributors, bookstores and reviewers refuse to consider books from this and other vanity presses. The books she received cost her $176 each and she had to start over.

Legitimate publishers don't have to look for manuscripts.
—L.M. Hasselstrom

Since binding is expensive, the subsidy publisher often binds just a few hundred copies; the rest of the printed sheets remain unbound unless needed. The "advertising" promised in the contract normally turns out to be only a tombstone ad that lists many titles in *The New York Times*. Sales from this feeble promotion are extremely rare.

POD publishers also provide a subsidy service; *the author pays*. Most of them make more money selling books to the author than to the public. Most of their marketing efforts are aimed toward the author. (See discussion of printing options in Chapter 4.)

The ads reading, "To the author..." or "Manuscripts wanted by..." easily catch the eye of the writer with a book-length manuscript. Vanity presses almost always accept a manuscript for publication and usually do so with a glowing review letter. They don't make any promises regarding sales, and usually the book sells fewer than 100 copies. Vanity publishers don't have to sell any books because the author has already paid them for their work. Therefore, subsidy publishers are interested in manufacturing the book (as few copies as possible), not in editing, high-quality cover design and typesetting, promotion, sales or distribution. Since they are paid to publish, they are really selling printing contracts, not books. They are simply taking a large fee to print unedited and poorly reproduced manuscripts.

Review copies of the book sent to columnists by a subsidy publisher usually go straight into the circular file (trash can). The reviewer's time is valuable, and they do not like vanity presses because they know that very little editing has been done to the book. They also realize that there will be little promotional effort, that the book has not been distributed to bookstores and that the title will not be available to their readers. The name of a subsidy publisher on the spine of the book is a kiss of death.

One major vanity press lost a large class-action suit a few years ago, but they are still advertising in the *Yellow Pages*; they are still in business.

4. LITERARY AGENTS match manuscripts with the right publisher and negotiate the contract; 80% of the new material comes to the larger publishers through them. The agent has to serve the publisher well; for if he or she submits an inappropriate or poor manuscript, the publisher will be reluctant to consider anything more from that agent in the future. Therefore, agents like "sure bets" too, and many are disinclined to even consider an unpublished writer. Their normal commission is 15%.

Agents are 85% hope and 15% commission.

According to *Literary Market Place*, about 40% of the literary agents will not read manuscripts by unpublished authors, and a good 15% will not even answer query letters from them. Of those agents who will read the manuscript of an unpublished author, 80% will charge for the service. Eighty percent of the agents will not represent professional books; 93% will not touch reference works; 99% will not handle technical books; 98% will not represent regional books, satire, musicals and other specialized manuscripts. Although most agents will handle novel-length fiction, only 20% are willing to take on either novellas or short stories, and only 2% have a special interest in literature or quality fiction.

> *It's harder for a new writer to get an agent than a publisher.*
>
> **—Roger Straus, president Farrar, Straus & Giroux**

On the fringe, there are people who call themselves agents who charge a reading fee and then pay students to read and critique the manuscript. They make their money on these fees, not from placing the manuscripts. For a list of literary agents, see *Writer's Market, Literary Agents of North America* and *Literary Market Place*. Also see the directory of agents on the Writers Net Web site at http://www.writers.net and the Association of Authors' Representatives, Inc., an organization of independent literary and dramatic agents, at http://www.publishersweekly.com.

5. SELF-PUBLISHING is where the author bypasses all the intermediaries, deals directly with the editor, cover artist, book designer and printer, and then handles the distribution and promotion. If you publish yourself, you'll make more money, get to press sooner and keep control of your book. You'll invest your time as well as your money, but the reward will be greater.

Self-publishing is not new. In fact, it has solid early American roots; it is almost a tradition. Well-known self-publishers include Mark Twain, Zane Grey, Upton Sinclair, Carl Sandburg, James Joyce, D.H. Lawrence, Ezra Pound, Edgar Rice Burroughs, Stephen Crane, Mary Baker Eddy, George Bernard Shaw, Edgar Allen Poe, Rudyard Kipling, Henry David Thoreau, Walt Whitman, Robert Ringer, Spencer Johnson, Richard Nixon, John Grisham, Tom Peters, Stephen King, Ken Blanchard, L. Ron Hubbard and many, many more.

These people were self-publishers, though today the vanity presses claim their books were "subsidy" published.

Years ago, authors might have elected to go their own way and self-publish after being turned down by regular publishers. However, today, most self-publishers make an educated decision to take control of their book—usually after reading this manual.

Do self-publishers ever sell many books? Here are some numbers (at last count): *What Color Is Your Parachute?*, 22 revised editions and 5 million copies; *50 Simple Things You Can Do to Save the Earth*, 4.5 million copies; *How to Keep Your Volkswagen Alive*, 2.2 million copies; *Leadership Secrets of Attila the Hun*, over 0.5 million copies; and *Final Exit*, over 0.5 million copies. These authors took control and made it big. For an expanded self-publishing success list, see Document 155 at http://parapublishing.com/sites/para/resources/allproducts.cfm.

Self-publishing is not difficult. In fact, it may even be easier than dealing with a publisher. The job of the self-publisher is not to perform every task, but to see that every task gets done. Self-publishers deal directly with the printer and handle as many of the editing, proofing, cover and page production, promotion and distribution jobs as they can. What they can't do, they farm out. Therefore, self-publishing may take on many forms, depending on the author–publisher's interests, assets and abilities. It allows them to concentrate on those areas they find most appealing and use outside services for the rest.

Properly planned, there is little monetary risk in self-publishing. If you follow the plan, the only variable is the subject of the book. Unlike poetry and fiction, most nonfiction topics sell relatively easily, especially to their target markets.

Because the big publisher tests a book only for a few months and then lets sales dictate its fate (reprint or remainder), the first four months are the most important to them. The self-publisher, on the other hand, uses the first year to build a solid market base for a future of sustained sales. While a big publisher may sell only 5,000 copies in total, the self-publisher can often count on 5,000 or more each year—year after year.

Para Publishing's *Is There a Book Inside You?* has a self-paced quiz to help you decide between a large publisher, a medium-sized niche publisher, an agent, a book producer, a vanity press and self-publishing.

> *Do you realize what would happen if Moses were alive today? He'd go up to Mount Sinai, come back with the Ten Commandments, and spend the next eight years trying to get them published.*
>
> **—Robert Orben, humorist**

EIGHT GOOD REASONS TO SELF-PUBLISH

1. **To make more money.** Why accept 6% to 10% in royalties from a publisher when you can have 35% from your bookstore distributor (or 100% if you sell direct to the reader)? You know your subject and you know the people in your field. Certainly you know more than some distant publisher who might buy your book.

Although trade publishers can get your book into bookstores, they don't know the nonbookstore possibilities as well as you do, and they aren't going to expend as much focused promotional effort. Ask yourself this question: Will the trade publisher be able to sell four times as many books as I can?

2. **Speed.** Most publishers work on an 18-month production cycle. Can you wait that long to get into print? Will you miss your market? The 18 months don't even begin until after the contract negotiations and contract signing. Publication could be three years away! Why waste time shipping your manuscript around to see if there is an agent or publisher out there who likes it?

NIXON & THE SPEED OF SELF-PUBLISHING

Richard Nixon self-published Real Peace in 1983 because he felt his message was urgent; he couldn't wait for a publisher's slow machinery to grind out the book.

Typically, bookstores buy the first book published on a popular subject. Later books may be better, but the store buyer may pass on them since the store already has the subject covered.

3. **To keep control of your book.** According to *Writer's Digest*, 60% of the big publishers do not give the author final approval on copyediting; 23% never give the author the right to select the title; 20% do not consult the author on the jacket design; and 36% rarely involve the author in the book's promotion.

The big New York trade publishers probably have more promotional connections than you do. But with a huge stable of books to push, your book will most likely get lost in the shuffle. The big publishers are good at getting books into bookstores, yet fail miserably at approaching other outlets or doing specialized promotion. Give the book to someone who has a personal interest in it—you, as the author.

4. **No one will read your manuscript.** Many publishers receive hundreds of unsolicited manuscripts for consideration each day. They do not have time to unwrap, review, rewrap and ship all those submissions, so they return them unopened. Unless you are a movie star, noted politician or have a recognizable name, it is nearly impossible to attract a publisher. Many publishers work with their existing stable of authors and accept new authors only through agents.

5. **Self-publishing is good business.** There are many more tax advantages for an author–publisher than there are for just authors. Self-publishers can deduct their lifestyle.

6. **Self-publishing will help you think like a publisher.** A book is a product that comes from you, somewhat like your own child. You are very protective of your book and naturally feel that it's terrific. When someone else publishes you, you think the book would sell better if only the publisher would pump in more promotion money. The publisher will respond that they are not anxious to dump more money into a book that isn't selling. So if you self-publish, you gain a better

understanding of the arguments on both sides. It is your money and your choice.

7. **You'll gain self-confidence and self-esteem.** You will be proud to be the author of a published book. Compare this to pleading with people to read your manuscript.

8. **Finally, you may have no other choice.** There are more manuscripts than can be read. Most publishers don't have time to even look at your manuscript.

The greatest challenge facing the smaller and newer publisher today is finding a system for *managing the excitement*. Nonfiction book publishers in their how-to books provide valuable information that readers willingly buy because it is going to save them time and money. We send out review copies, draft articles, make email solicitations and circulate news releases on our books—and customers respond. That is exciting! Publishing is an easy business, a profitable business and a fun business. The publishing business is truly *excitement-driven*.

SHOULD YOU SELF-PUBLISH?

Would-be author–publishers should be cautioned that self-publishing is not for everyone. Writing is an *art*, whereas publishing is a *business*, and some people are unable to do both well. If you are a lovely, creative flower who is repelled by the crass commercialism of selling your own product, you should stick to the creative side and let someone else handle the business end.

On the other hand, some people are terribly independent. They will not be happy with the performance of any publisher, no matter how much time and effort is spent creating and promoting the book. These people should save the publisher from all this grief by becoming their own publisher and making their own decisions. Fortunately, most of us fall somewhere in between and can handle both the creative and promotion sides of publishing.

SELLING OUT TO A BIG PUBLISHER: Many self-publishers find that once they have proven their books with good sales, they're approached by larger publishing houses with offers to print a new edition. If you're considering selling to a large publisher, see the related discussion in Chapter 8 along with my noted precautions and recommendations.

$4.2 MILLION PAID!

Richard Paul Evans took six weeks to write the 87-page Christmas Box. He did so well selling it for two holiday seasons that Simon & Schuster paid him $4.2 million for it. Now it is in 13 languages. Sometimes authors begin as self-publishers, get attention and then sell to a larger publisher.

THE FUTURE OF PUBLISHING

Packaged information is becoming increasingly specialized. More and more books are being printed in smaller quantities. The information in books is going out-of-date faster. Books are being produced more rapidly. Computerized equipment allows people to rapidly write, edit, lay out, print and deliver books. The customer wants more condensed and targeted information, *faster.*

The chapters that follow describe in detail an alternative to traditional publishing. This self-publishing route will enable you to get your book into print at minimum cost. This book could be your second chance. It will show you the way to publication, fame and extra income—a new life.

Obviously, your success cannot be guaranteed, but many people are doing very well in the writing/publishing business. This isn't a get-rich-quick scheme; there is work involved. Even though you are working for yourself, at your own pace, it is still *work*. You won't get rich overnight. Building a sound business venture takes several years.

> *Make effective use of your most valuable asset—*
> *your time.*

The secret is to invest your labor. Your time is precious. Like gold, there is a finite quantity. You have only 24 hours of time each day. You can use your time in several ways: you can throw it away, sell it or invest it. For instance, you can waste your valuable time in front of the television set; time is easy to lose that way.

Most people spend their lives punching a clock, going to work and getting a check. They trade their labor for money on a one-to-one basis. If you don't punch in, you don't get paid. But isn't it better to invest your time in a book that will sell and generate income while you are away doing something else? Your labor becomes an investment that pays dividends for years while you are playing or working on another investment. Don't throw away your time; invest it. It is up to you.

You have all the ingredients it takes to be a successful published author. This book is your recipe.

2

WRITING YOUR BOOK

GENERATING SALABLE MATERIAL

Write on a subject you love. Your profit center should also be your passion center.

What are your talents and what do you want to do? Do you enjoy writing, or do you want to become a published author but find writing painful? Analyze your abilities, motivations and overall agenda. Do you want to write, publish or sell books, to pursue any combination of these activities or even do all three?

I love being a writer.
What I can't stand is the paperwork.
—Peter De Vries

In this chapter, I'll cover areas to help you make an educated, personal choice about who will do the writing part of the equation. First, I will discuss how to get your thoughts on paper yourself. Then I will look at avenues for obtaining writing from others. The second part of this discussion will also take us into areas of publishing.

PICKING A SUBJECT

This is the first step. Consider the elements necessary for selling nonfiction:

- **The subject is interesting to you.** What topic do you want to be talking about two years from now?

- **You have the expertise** (education) **or experience** (you have been there, done that).

- **The subject interests others; it must be salable.** If you build it, will they come?

- **The subject matter is tightly focused.** Readers want specific, narrowly targeted information today.

- **The market is easy to reach.** You will be able to determine *who* your potential customers are and *where* your customers are. You'll know what stores they visit, what associations they join, what magazines they read and what events they attend.

- **The market of potential buyers is large enough.**

> *There are three rules to successful writing:*
> *(1) have something to say, (2) know how to say it,*
> *and (3) be able to sell it.*
> **—David Hellyer**

The book should be on a subject that you're interested in and on which you are an expert—or on which you would like to become an expert soon. Perhaps you've spent years working at, specializing in and learning about something, and there are thousands of people out there willing to pay good money to get the inside information from you. Or if you select your hobby, there are a number of advantages—

(1) you know what has been written in the past, (2) you have the contacts for gathering more information and (3) your further participation in that hobby will become tax deductible.

If you need help evaluating your project, contact author–publisher Gordon Burgett at Gordon@sops.com. He will read your manuscript and make recommendations on market targeting, manuscript rework (if necessary), publishing and marketing; he will report on readability and salability.

FICTION VS. NONFICTION

Nonfiction is information that people buy because it will save them time or money. It is much easier to convince people to buy nonfiction than fiction. Unfortunately, the unknown fiction writer or poet is at the same point as the unknown painter or musician.

Nonfiction. Most often, the subject of a book—not the name of the publisher or the comments of a reviewer— is what sells nonfiction. Every new national craze requires how-to books. Don't be discouraged if your subject has already been covered. That just proves someone else thought it was important. Using your own experience and the latest information, you can do it better. The how-to subjects with the best sales potential are money, health, self-improvement, hobbies, sex and psychological well-being. Find a need and fill it. Remember, most people buy nonfiction to learn something or to solve a problem. You can help them.

130,000 SOLD!

One specialized book that sold for years was my title *Hang Gliding*. It went through the press 10 times for 130,000 copies in print. And the printings sold out.

Fiction is related to all other books of fiction in its category. A reader who buys one mystery is a prime candidate for another mystery. Fiction must compete for a person's leisure time too. He or she must choose not only between reading this book of fiction and reading other books, but also between reading this book and engaging in other forms of entertainment, such as going to a movie, renting a video or walking on the beach.

Poetry is even more difficult to sell than fiction. But since we receive so many requests for this information, we have assembled the Instant Report 606, *Publishing Fiction and Poetry*; find it at http://parapublishing.com/sites/para/resources/allproducts.cfm.

At Para Publishing, we specialize in coaching nonfiction book publishers to sell more books. We do not claim to have any expertise in magazine or newsletter publishing, fiction or poetry. There are many kinds of publishing. Some of our programs, ideas, leads and resources will work for creative literature, but that is not our specialty.

There may be more money in publishing your information in short monographs than in longer books. Timely monographs usually command a higher price, can be published in shorter runs and take less time to produce. You can even sell them on the Web as downloadable information. Don't overlook well-researched short reports.

WRITING IT YOURSELF

Creating your own material is easy if you have a system; all it really takes is organization and discipline. When you follow my system, creating copy becomes challenging fun, and you see the progress you're making—which is encouraging.

Although writing a book is not difficult, it's not for the lazy. As with joining Alcoholics Anonymous or going on a diet, you'll have to change your lifestyle. This means waking up one morning and making a decision to do it now. Getting into the system and developing good habits will provide you with a sense of purpose and a feeling of accomplishment. Once you have selected a topic, only the decision to start stands between you and the finished book.

For more detailed, step-by-step instructions on how to write your book, see my book *Writing Nonfiction* at http://parapublishing.com/sites/para/resources/allproducts.cfm.

> *Writing has to come first.*
> **—Sue Grafton**

Time,—that is,—a lack of it, is the most frequently heard excuse for not completing a book. But somehow we always find time for those things that are important to us. We just naturally put them first. Often we can fit in an hour of writing time each day by completing our other chores faster. Another way is to get up one hour earlier. This is perfect scheduling, because the house tends to be quiet, the telephone doesn't ring and you are refreshed; most writers find the early morning to be their most creative and productive time. But you must put this daybreak hour first and not let anything interfere with it. Once you gather momentum in your project, you'll find that rising early will be easy; you won't even miss that hour of sleep. Or, like some other writers, you may prefer to write at night after work, in the wee hours after other people in your household have gone to bed or on the weekends.

Set up a writing area in a spare room or in a corner of the living room. Keep your computer and research tools there. Your creative-writing time is precious; don't waste it trying to get organized in a new location each time.

CHOOSING A TITLE

Spend time on your title. A good title is essential; in fact, it's half your sales package. If you have a poor title, your potential customer may never recognize the book as being valuable to him or her.

Start with a short, catchy and descriptive title and add a longer, explanatory subtitle. If the first word of the title is the same as the subject, it will make the book easy to find in the alphabetical book directories.

Brainstorm the title and also come up with a good one-liner that tells a complete and compelling story about your subject. Write down all your ideas for both. Your title may evolve and change as you write the book. The title is the single most important piece of promotional copy you will draft for the book.

If you need more explanations, see Document 630, *Selecting a Book Title that Sells*, at http://parapublishing.com/ sites/para/resources/allproducts.cfm.

DEVELOPING THE BOOK'S COVERS

FRONT COVER: Your front cover will feature your title and subtitle. In the planning stages, list the most important person in your field (association or industry) for the Foreword (and please note the spelling of *Foreword*). You will try to get him or her to pen the Foreword later.

SPINE: If you stack the title on the spine, it will read more easily on the shelf. (See the spine of this book.) An image is also a nice touch to grab attention. I often use the logo for my publishing company.

BACK COVER: Write your back-cover sales copy before you write your book. This exercise will help you focus on your audience and what you plan to give them. You have to draft the back-cover copy eventually, so you might as well do it *before* you write the book.

DRAFTING YOUR BACK-COVER SALES COPY

Stores have tens of thousands of books displayed with their spines out. With all this congestion, it's hard to get attention. Initially, all that buyers see is the book's spine. If they take it down, they will gaze at the cover for about four seconds and then flip it over to read the back cover. On average, they will spend just 14 seconds here, so the trick is to keep them reading longer. Your back-cover copy has to be punchy and laden with benefits; it has to speak to the potential buyer.

Your cover designer will lay out the packaging of your book and incorporate the illustration, put it all on disk and send it to you ready for the printer; however, you must draft the sales copy. The back-cover layout shown above will take you step by step through the sales-copy drafting process. Use your computer so you'll be able to move the copy around once it has been entered.

Here are explanations for each area of the worksheet.

➡ **CATEGORY:** Visit a bookstore and check the shelf where your book should be displayed. Note the categories on the books and the shelves. Listing the proper category on the back cover of your book will ensure that your book will be easier to find, because the bookshop personnel will place it on the right shelf.

•❖ **HEADLINE:** Now you need an arresting headline addressed to potential buyers. You want them to relate to the book and find themselves in it. Do not simply repeat the title here; do not bore the potential buyer. You have already printed the title on the front. For an example of a strong headline, look at the back cover of this book.

•❖ **DESCRIPTION:** Concisely (in two to four sentences) state what the book is about. What will the reader gain by reading this book? Get to the point—many times. This section is all the potential buyer will read before skimming the rest to make a buying decision.

•❖ **BENEFITS AND HIGHLIGHTS:** Focus here on the specifics of what the reader will get from your book in terms of benefits and coverage. Concentrate on the most valuable and most important items.

Say, **"You will discover:"** and then present the list:

- 1   [item]
- 2   [item]
- 3   [item]
- 4   [item]

•❖ **TESTIMONIALS AND ENDORSEMENTS:** Dream up three different quotations from people you would *like* to quote. Use *names* or *titles* recognizable in your field, sources that might impress potential buyers. This is just a draft; dress it up. You will secure some of these endorsements later.

Category

H E A D L I N E

Description plus promises and benefits:

You will discover:
- (1)
- (2)
- (3)
- (4)
- (5)
- (6)

Testimonials:

(1)

(2)

(3)

Author's bio.:

Sales closer:

ISBN & bar code
80% magnification with
.5" high bars

Price

Back cover layout

•• **AUTHOR:** Show that you, the author, are the ultimate authority on the subject. Just two or three sentences will do.

•• **SALES CLOSER:** End with a sales closer in bold type. Ask the browser to buy the book. Use something like "This book has enabled thousands to..., and it will show you the way too."

•• **PRICE:** Bookstores like a price on the book. The price is a turnoff, so place it at the end of the sales copy. Never locate the price at the top of the back cover. If this is a hardcover book, place the price at the top of the front flap.

•• **BAR CODE** with the International Standard Book Number (ISBN) and price. The bar code on a book identifies the ISBN, which in turn identifies the publisher, title, author and edition (hardcover, etc.). Make room for, but do not worry about, the bar code and ISBN now.

Your *title, subtitle,* back cover *headline* and *benefits/highlights* may be swapped. Once you have written them, you may wish to move some of them around. For example, one of your benefits might actually be a better subtitle.

The back-cover copy on most of the books you see in bookstores is weak and uninspiring. The title is repeated and then is followed by several quotations and a bar code and that's it! Haphazard copy is the sign of a lazy (or maybe inexperienced) copywriter. This lack of effective competition on the shelf will give you the upper hand. Work on drafting mouth-watering, action-producing, customer-stampeding, riot-provoking, wallet-grabbing sales copy.

Years ago I said, "Write your ad before you write your book." This was to help writers focus on their audience and what they were going to give their readership. Then I realized that the most important "ad" you will ever write is your back-cover copy. Now I say, "Write your cover copy before you write your book."

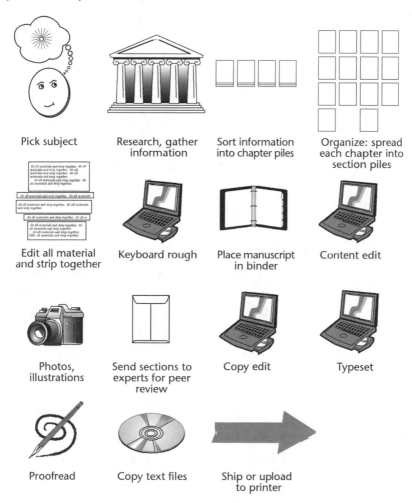

Pick subject	Research, gather information	Sort information into chapter piles	Organize: spread each chapter into section piles
Edit all material and strip together	Keyboard rough	Place manuscript in binder	Content edit
Photos, illustrations	Send sections to experts for peer review	Copy edit	Typeset
Proofread	Copy text files	Ship or upload to printer	

The flow of the manuscript

Unfortunately, many nonfiction books are written without a specific market in mind, and since the book does not provide what the potential buyers want, it does not sell. The book-cover writing will help you focus on who your customer really is.

For more information on covers, see Document 631, *Covers That Sell Books*, at http://parapublishing.com/sites/para/resources/allproducts.cfm.

RESEARCH: FINDING MATERIAL FOR YOUR BOOK

Research is simply reading, making notes, condensing and rearranging the gathered pertinent information. All research should begin with the Web because you'll pick up more current information there than at any library or bookstore. Register your information needs with Excite and Google. They will send you clippings from several sources.

Search online bookstores such as Amazon.com. Research what has been written in your field. Then study actual copies of the related books. What's missing? What could you do better? Use the Internet search engines and library resources to find more information.

> *The greatest part of a writer's time is spent in reading in order to write.*
>
> **—Samuel Johnson**

Be a detective. Gather everything ever written on your subject. Load yourself up with so much material that you'll have to decide what to leave out. Overdo it, and you will be proud of the result—secure in the knowledge that you have covered the subject completely.

You'll want your readers to know about all the books, magazines, newsletters, tapes, software and other references available on your subject. List them in the Appendix of your book.

As an author and opinion-molder, you may not have to buy some of these resources. Ask the publishers for free reference copies, and discuss the possibility of permissions and attributions for used information. Now that you are researching, you're a member of the print media and will be able to attend a lot of related events for free. Use your new business card to get a press pass, media packet and preferential treatment.

COPYRIGHT: WHAT YOU CAN LEGALLY USE

Copyright is a subject that interests potential authors. They want to know how to protect their precious material from others and also how much they themselves can borrow.

Copyright does not cover facts or ideas. Copyright covers only the *expression* of ideas in a sequence of words. Copying ideas is research; copying words is plagiarism. So copy ideas, copy facts, but do not copy words. Make it a rule never to repeat any three words in a row.

GETTING PERMISSION

If you find material that you wish to use as is, contact the author for permission. Type out exactly what you wish to use and email: *"I would like to quote you in my book. The wording is below. Since it has been some time since you wrote it, I am wondering if you would say it exactly the same way today. Please look it over, make your changes and let me know how you wish to be credited at the end of the paragraph."*

The 1987 Copyright Act was amended by the Sonny Bono Copyright Term Extension Act in 1998. Your copyright will last for your life plus 70 years. See the Copyright Office Web site for details and see the charts at http://www.unc.edu/~unclng/public-d.htm and http://www.copyright.cornell.edu/training/Hirtle_Public_Domain.htm.

Many documents are not copyrighted. If you want to find out whether some material is protected under either the current or pre-1978 law, the U.S. Copyright Office at the Library of Congress will conduct a search for you. Send them as much information as possible, such as the author, title, publisher and publication date. The easiest way is to photocopy the title page and copyright page of the book. The Copyright Office charges for the time spent, and they should be able to make two searches per hour. Get a copy of Copyright Office Circular 22, *How to Investigate the Copyright Status of a Work*, by calling the Copyright Office at 202-707-3000 or the forms hotline at 202-707-9100, or print out the circular from the Copyright Office Web site at http://www.copyright.gov/forms/.

Government and military publications are in the public domain. Even if they were not, the Freedom of Information Act would probably cover them. If you really need some material, military or civilian, ask for permission. It is safer and cheaper than hiring a lawyer later to prove you had a right to use it.

Your copyrighted material is valuable property, or it may become so one day. File copyright forms on all those magazine articles you write but don't get paid for. You may need an article for inclusion in a book someday, and the expenditure on fees for your copyright application will justify to the IRS that you really are in the word business.

If, on the other hand, you are asked for permission to reprint some material from your book, you might consider limiting the permission to a section or two and stipulating that an editor's note must indicate that the material was used with your permission and came from your book. This will show, once again, that you are an expert; it is also good publicity for the original work. A copyright on your book is not only for protection—it carries prestige because it shows you are a professional. Copyright is discussed in several other places in this book. See the Index. For more information on copyrights, see the Copyright Office Web site at http://www.copyright.gov/.

ORGANIZE YOUR MATERIAL WITH THE "PILOT SYSTEM"

Start by drawing up a preliminary Table of Contents; just divide your notes into 10 or 12 chapters. Then sort all your research material and "pile it" as required.

SORT, SHUFFLE AND MARK: Decide on your chapter titles. Now, using scissors when necessary, sort all your research material into the applicable chapter piles. During your research, you must have written down a number of interesting observations and many of your own experiences. Make sure these notes are added to the piles.

Now spread out the individual chapters. They could completely fill your living room. Pick an interesting pile—any one, not necessarily the first—and go through it, underlining important points and writing in your additional comments. Write out longer thoughts on a tablet and place those sheets of paper in the pile in the order you plan to write that chapter.

Your notes ensure that you will not leave out any important points. And you will be entertained as you compare what other authors say about the same item. The similarities are often remarkably coincidental, sometimes to the point of including the same words and phraseology (which is why you should explain the information differently). This experience also emphasizes the importance of being accurate. Others will research and refer to your work in the future.

This floor spread will enable you to see the whole interrelated project, lending excitement and encouragement—a great incentive. Move the chapter piles around to ensure a good, logical flow of thought and to avoid duplication of copy. Condense the material by discarding unnecessary and duplicate material.

As you read what others say on a particular point, your memory will be jogged. You will have additional points, a clearer explanation or an illustrative story. Where you disagree with another author, you can always say, "Some people believe…" and then tell it your way. You have the advantage of the most recent information, since you are coming later.

MAKE NOTES: Carry paper and pen with you at all times, especially when running or engaging in any solo activity. This is a time to think, create, compose; this is when there is no one around to break your train of thought. Some authors keep a writing tablet in their car and compose away from home. I know of a detective-writer who outlines his stories while on stakeouts. When you are confined, captive or isolated, you have nothing else to do but create. Make use of any available time. Good material could develop while attending a dull meeting, for example.

Some people like to work with a small pocket tape recorder, but remember that someone must transcribe your dictation. It all depends on how you perform best. If you regularly dictate material and have someone transcribe your tapes, this may be the most comfortable and efficient method for you.

When a particularly original thought or creative approach hits you, write it down or you may lose it. Keep on thinking and keep on taking notes. Add your thoughts and major pieces to the piles. As you go along, draw up a list of questions as they come to mind, so that you'll remember to follow up on them for answers.

There is nothing to writing. All you have to do is to sit down at the keyboard and open up a vein.
—Red Smith

INPUT: GETTING IT INTO THE COMPUTER

Keyboard (or dictate with speech recognition software) your sorted notes. Write as you speak; relax and be clear. Don't worry about punctuation, grammar or style. You will edit the work later, and it is always easier to edit than it is to create. Right now, all you want to do is get your thoughts and research material onto the hard disk. Make notes where you are considering illustrations, graphics or tables.

Read a whole section of notes to grasp the overall theme. Then boil it down and use your own words. Think about the section and how you might explain the basic message better. Can you say it more clearly with fewer words? For organization, list the main points and rearrange the pieces. If you're having trouble with a section, skip ahead and come back to it later.

WHERE TO START: NONLINEAR WRITING

Don't start your writing with Chapter 1—to do so makes book writing feel like an impossibly steep climb, and it is hard to get started. Select the chapter pile that looks the smallest, easiest or most fun. Once you have drafted it, take the next most interesting chapter and so on. Skip around. Soon you will be past the halfway mark and the going will be downhill. You will be encouraged and will gather momentum. Using this approach, you will probably find you are writing the first chapter last. This is as it should be, because the first chapter is usually introductory in nature to the overall book, and you cannot know where you are truly going until you have reached the end. Many authors wind up rewriting and re-slanting the first chapter because they wrote it first. They may never proceed to Chapter 2. By the end, you may have drawn some new conclusions, which you will want to allude to in the introductory chapter.

> *The last thing one discovers in writing a book is what to put first.*
>
> **—Blaise Pascal**

Don't be concerned with what goes into the computer the first time around. The important thing is to get it down. Often these first impressions are the best; they are complete, natural and believable. In any case, later you'll go through the draft making corrections, additions and deletions. It's called "editing."

As you keyboard the rough first draft, and later as you review it, you will decide that whole paragraphs are misplaced and belong elsewhere. With your computer, it is an easy matter to move and modify material. Writing on a computer with all the capabilities of word-processing software will allow you to create in a nonlinear (random) fashion. You can easily move paragraphs, add, delete, change words and thoughts—much like the mind works.

If you lack a certain piece of information, a number or a fact, put a note in the text to remind yourself and move on. Don't lose momentum. Some authors use three asterisks (***) as a marker, because asterisks are easy to see (or find with a computer search). Similarly, if you find yourself repeating material, make a note with three asterisks so you can compare it with the other material later. Keep on writing.

CONCENTRATED WRITING

If possible, keyboard one whole section at a time. One whole chapter at a time is even better, and the entire book straight through is the best way to go. Most beginning authors are working at other jobs and can devote only a short period each day to their writing. But the more time you can put into each piece of the book the better, because there will be greater continuity, less duplication and clearer organization. If you can do only a small section at a time, try arranging the pieces in the evening, reviewing them in the early morning, thinking about them while commuting, etc., and then after you have formulated the section in your mind, come home to keyboard it.

HOW I'VE WORKED

My first book, on parachutes, took eight years to produce. I worked on this labor of love without guidance or direction. The huge, steady-selling manual became the foundation upon which I built my publishing company. My second book was a study guide for an obscure parachuting rating; it sold better than expected. In 1973, I became interested in the new sport of hang gliding. Unable to find any information at the library, I wrote the first book on the subject. I foresaw a trend and cashed in on it; the book sold 130,000 copies over 10 years, allowed me to move back to California and buy a home in Santa Barbara. Total writing time: two months.

By this time, I had developed a writing system. My fourth book took less than 30 days from idea and decision until I delivered the typesetting to the printer. And most of this time was used in waiting for answers to my many letters requesting information. The first draft took only five days.

From there, I concentrated on several high-priced, low-cost course pamphlets, turning out most of them within a week. My ninth book took all of two weeks to first draft, and it was typed clean. Very few editing changes had to be made to the original copy.

Using a word processor, I took 31 days to write, edit and typeset a book on computers. The actual time spent working on the book was just 18 days. Lately, my books have been longer and have required more time, but I still produce manuscripts efficiently. Writing a book is easy if you know the formula.

If you can, take a few weeks off from work, shut out all distractions and become totally involved in the manuscript. Do not pick up the mail or answer the telephone. Eat when hungry, sleep when tired and forget the clock except as a gauge of your pace. Keep up the pressure and keep on keyboarding. Focus on, say, one chapter per day. You should not have to force yourself to write, but you will need organization and discipline. After a couple of books, you will find yourself making very few major changes to your original draft.

Writing from notes is much easier than composing from thin air. Thin air produces writer's block. Incidentally, many writers say the hum of a computer—knowing the electricity is on—prompts them to work.

Don't throw out your materials and notes once your draft is typed. Put them in a cardboard carton. Someone may ask where you found a particular piece of information and you may want to trace it. Traceability is especially important with photographs and artwork.

USING STORIES

Stories make your points memorable; note how stories are used in this book. Solicit them from your colleagues. You can also submit your request for stories to the readers of my *Publishing Poynters Marketplace* newsletter. See http://parapub.com/sites/para/resources/newsletter.cfm.

Clean up the submissions; add the name and URL (most people want to drive traffic to their Web site) and email the piece back to the contributor for approval. Set the stories in a different typeface or indent them to make them easier to find and set them off from the main text.

LAY OUT THE BINDER

Now that you're generating copy, you need a place to store it. Find a wide, three-ring binder and add dividers corresponding to the chapters you've selected. Punch and insert the rough draft pages as you complete them. As the piles come off the floor, move across the desk and flow through the computer into the binder, you'll gain a great feeling of accomplishment.

Inserting the front matter of the book into this binder will further encourage you. As well, as you encounter resources, add them to the Appendix in the back. Soon you'll have a partial manuscript, the book will be taking shape and you'll have something tangible to carry around. The binder will make you feel proud and will give you the flexibility to proofread and improve your manuscript when you're away from home.

Write your name and address in the front of the binder with a note that it is a valuable manuscript. You do not want to misplace and lose your future book. With your binder in one place and your hard disk in another (and your book also on a backup CD), you won't have to worry about the financial and emotional disaster of losing your work in a fire, theft or computer crash.

Carry that binder with you everywhere you go; busy people often have trouble finding the time to return to their desk and their book. With the binder system, the book is always with you. As you go through the day and find a minute here and there, open the binder—to any section— and write in your changes, notes and comments. Periodically enter your changes into the computer and print out new pages. The binder is an anti-procrastination crutch, and it works! With the binder under your arm, the book will be continually in your thoughts. Your work and your manuscript will improve.

UNANTICIPATED BINDER BENEFIT

Ed Rigsbee agreed the binder was helping him stay on his project, but he also found an added benefit. His wife became much more supportive of the project once she saw the tangible evidence!

THE ORDER BLANK

The last page of your book should contain an order blank; place it on a left-hand page—facing out. Some readers will want to purchase a copy for a friend, and others may want a copy for themselves after seeing your book at a friend's home or in the library. Make ordering easy for them by listing the full price of the book, including sales tax (if applicable) and shipping. This order-blank system works. Several orders on the form are received for *The Self-Publishing Manual* each week.

WRITING STYLE

Before creating an article for a magazine, a professional writer will always read one or more editions of the periodical thoroughly to absorb the style and subconsciously adapt to that magazine's way of writing. The same technique can be used in writing a book by reading a couple of chapters of a book by a writer you admire.

Writing is a communication art. Write as you speak, avoiding big words where small ones will do. Most people regularly use only 800 to 2,000 English words available to them. Use simple sentences and be precise with words. Vary sentence and paragraph length, and favor the shorter ones. Try to leave yourself out of the copy; avoid the word "I." Read Strunk & White's *The Elements of Style*, which revolutionized writing in the 20th century.

> *I just sat down and started all by myself.*
> *It never occurred to me that I couldn't do it as well*
> *as anyone else.*
> **—Barbara Tuchman**

Relax, talk on paper, be yourself. Explain each section in your own words as you would to help a friend who is new to the subject. Keep your writing short. You are paying for every word that will be printed, so edit out the junk.

Like a speech, every paragraph of your book should have a beginning, a middle and an end. The first sentence of the paragraph either suggests the topic or it helps the transition from the preceding paragraph. Stay with one subject per paragraph. Each paragraph should tie in with both the preceding and following paragraphs (use good transitions).

If a reader doesn't understand a paragraph, don't blame the reader.

Be a professional and give the readers their money's worth. Your material will be used by others in coming years and you'll be quoted. If you're accurate and correct now, you won't be embarrassed later by the written legend you have created. As a published author, you have the responsibility of being a recognized expert. Use proper terms; don't start a new language. Steer away from jargon (words that are unique to a certain audience), coinages (words that aren't in the dictionary) and buzzwords (words that move in and out of vogue); you will only turn off your reader.

CHOOSE WORDS WISELY

In the early 1970s, hang gliding was a hot new subject. It was the rebirth of aviation, using a wing made in the sail industry, and the participants were kids off the streets. The terms for flying and parts of the glider could have come from the aviation community, the sail industry, or popular (new) jargon could have been used. Aviation terms became the choice. This was impressed upon the early book and magazine writers; aviation terms were used almost exclusively, and this usage aided the introduction of hang gliding into the community of sport aviation.

One technique for educating your readers in the correct terms is to use the proper term and then follow it with the more popular word or explanation in parentheses. Educating the reader as you progress through the book is preferable to making readers wade through a glossary.

You are finished when the manuscript is 95% complete and 100% accurate. Don't wait for one more photo, one more statistic, one more piece of information. Get your book to press and to your buying public. Hopefully, you will sell out in a few months, make corrections, add some updated material and return to the press with a revised edition.

> *Don't let perfection interfere with possible.*
> **—Keith Cunningham**

And your book will still be just 95% complete. Our society is evolving too rapidly, our technology is progressing too fast—your book will never be 100% complete. As soon as you put words on paper, the clock starts ticking. Get over it and go to press.

OTHER WAYS TO GENERATE A MANUSCRIPT

Help is available to those who still cannot write even after learning the tricks mentioned previously.

1. **HIRE A WRITER (Work-for-Hire):** If you cannot get your thoughts on paper, try the team approach. There are a lot of writers out there—people who love to put good thoughts into words. Look for a moonlighting newspaper reporter.

They are trained to listen and put your thoughts down accurately. Once they have your material written out, you may edit the work for rewriting. Plus, his or her media contacts could be invaluable.

Make sure your contract has a **work-for-hire** clause, or you may wind up not owning what you have hired the person to write. For more information on collaborating, responsibility charts, an explanation of work-for-hire and a sample contract, see *Is There a Book Inside You?* in Appendix 2 under Para Publishing Books & Reports or at http://parapublishing.com/sites/para/resources/allproducts.cfm.

AUTHORING, BUT NOT WRITING

Joe Karbo sold millions of dollars worth of *The Lazy Man's Way to Riche$*, and although he "authored" the book he did not write it. He gathered his original thoughts and materials and hired a writer to put it all on paper.

To find a ghostwriter or advanced editor, see http://parapub.com/sites/para/resources/supplier.cfm.

2. HIRE AN EDITOR: All savvy authors hire editors. Get someone who can take your information, restructure it, rewrite where necessary and put energy into it.

A DOCTOR SELECTS AN EDITOR

Dr. Rick Hartbrodt wrote a medical book about a common disease. The manuscript contained a lot of solid, helpful information but it was hard to read. He contacted writers' groups, editorial services and secretarial services listed in the *Yellow Pages* and located four people who were willing to help. He gave each a copy of the first chapter and asked them to edit a couple of sample pages and to quote their fee. Some editors only wanted to dot the i's and cross the t's, whereas others wanted to do complete rewrites. Using this method, he was able to compare their work and select the type of work he wanted, the editor he liked most and the best fee.

See the list of editors in the Suppliers section of our Web site at http://parapub.com/sites/para/resources/supplier.cfm.

Many people who are not professional writers get into print. If they cannot pick up the skills, they ask for help. You can too.

3. COMMISSIONED WRITING: Some of the more successful book houses approach publishing from a hard-nosed marketing position. They know what their clients want; what they have been able to sell in the past. They often stay in their field of expertise by hiring writers to produce more of these types of books.

Once you decide on the category for your books, you too can approach others to write for you by paying cash outright (work-for-hire) or using modest advances and royalties (a share of the proceeds) as an inducement. The accounting is simpler and the arrangement is often more cost-effective when you pay outright for material rather than paying royalties. Flat fees for shorter books are often $5,000 to $15,000, half on assignment and half on acceptance. Moonlighting advertising copywriters might wrap up these books in fewer than 60 days.

4. AUTHOR SUBMISSIONS: Another source of material is the traditional one of unsolicited author submissions. If you are concentrating on a certain genre or interest area and selling books to a select market, you are also in contact with those people best qualified to generate new material for you. Once you publish something they like, they will come to you. Many people have always cherished the dream of becoming an author, and they will seek you out once they recognize your publishing success.

> *Publishing is an active life while writing is a quiet life.*
> **—Linda Meyer**

You can always wait for manuscripts in your interest area to come to you, but you will save time and a lot of useless manuscript reading by soliciting manuscripts yourself. Prepare one-paragraph outlines of the books you need to round out your catalog and send the summaries to writing magazines such as *Writer's Digest* (http://writersdigest.com). Also, fill out a form for a publisher listing in *Writer's Market*. Make it easy for qualified writers to find you. The quickest response will come from a listing in my *Publishing Poynters Marketplace* newsletter. Subscribe to *Publishing Poynters*, and you will receive both newsletters. See http://parapublishing. com/sites/para/resources/newsletter.cfm.

5. CO-AUTHORSHIP (Multiple authors): Consider co-authorship if you have a book you want to write yourself, but recognize that you lack the required technical expertise. Find an expert in the field to write part of it while you write the other part, and then each of you can edit the other's material. This approach has many advantages, including the endorsement of an expert, more credibility for the book and another body to send on the promotional tour. The disadvantages are smaller royalties, extra accounting and author hand-holding (which can require a lot of time as you teach them the business and explain what you are doing and why).

FRISBEE BOOK PARTNERSHIP

I shared the responsibilities for the *Frisbee Players' Handbook* with disk expert Mark Danna. Danna wrote the throwing and catching chapters, and I wrote on history, record attempts and competition, and also assembled the Appendix. I came up with the unique package and marketing idea (a circular book packaged in a Frisbee), but did not have enough expertise or credibility as a Frisbee player. Mark Danna rounded out the team well.

Spouses may choose to co-author a book if one is an expert in the field and the other is a better wordsmith. A project like this gets both of them published, provides the couple with a common project (which may do great things for the marriage) and elevates their job stature.

6. GHOSTWRITERS: Lee Iacocca did not write those two best-sellers by himself. Iacocca is the author (it is his material), but he is not the writer. He does not have time to write. If you don't have the time or inclination to write, but you do have material recorded in articles, on tape, in lecture notes, collected in files, mapped out in your head, etc., you can hire a ghostwriter to put it all in book form. If you decide to work with a ghost, see *Is There a Book Inside You?* at http://parapublishing.com/sites/para/resources/allproducts.cfm for details and the contacts in Appendix 2.

7. REPUBLISHING ARTICLES: Many author–publishers have gone the easy route by simply editing the material of others after they had researched a subject they were interested in and found that many fine experts had already written about it. The collection of these articles, one per chapter, can form a book called an anthology. To pursue this course, contact each author for permission to use his or her material, send a copy of the article and ask each to update their piece with any new information or changed views. This makes your chapter better than the original article. If the chapter must be shortened, ask the author to do it. This is faster and easier than doing it yourself and then negotiating your changes with the author.

8. OUT-OF-PRINT BOOKS: Sometimes you can find good books that large publishers have let go "out of print." Normally, the copyright has reverted to the author. These authors are usually thrilled to have a new publisher put their books back into print. See the R.R. Bowker directory called *Books Out of Print*, available at your library.

MAKING THE OLD NEW

Bill Kaysing discovered an out-of-copyright book called *Thermal Springs of the World*. He abstracted just the data on hot springs in the western U.S., added some original comments and reprinted it as *Great Hot Springs of the West*. Review copies sent to several major magazines resulted in an entire column of flattering coverage in *Sunset*. Some 3,000 copies were sold in a little over a year.

---

9. TRANSLATIONS: Look for foreign language titles online and at U.S. and overseas book fairs that you can acquire, have translated and then publish. Contact publishers in other countries that specialize in books that interest you. See *International Literary Market Place* or the PMA Foreign Rights Virtual Book Fair Web site at http://pma-online.org/programs.cfm.

A good translator is a highly skilled artist whose writing does not read like a word-for-word translation. He or she will spend time searching for the single right word or phrase to convey the original meaning. Translators must be bilingual. English (the destination language) must be their first language, and they must be good writers. To find translators, see the American Translators Association Web site at http://www.atanet.org.

The English language rights to foreign language books are rarely expensive, so this is another interesting source of material.

NEGOTIATING AND CONTRACTING WITH AUTHORS

The object of an author–publisher contract is to clarify thinking and positions by laying all the details on the table and arriving at a mutually beneficial agreement. There will never be a second book if one side takes unfair advantage of the other; it pays to keep the future in mind. Small publishers should not offer less than the industry norm unless they will be satisfied with just one book per author—and there is no need to offer more.

Each contract will be somewhat different, but you can start with a standard one. For sample contracts ready to load into your computer, see Para Publishing's *Publishing Contracts* in Appendix 2 under Para Publishing Special Reports and on our Web site at http://parapublishing.com/sites/para/resources/allproducts.cfm. It is easier to edit form contracts than to create them from scratch.

First-time authors will be eager to become published and may not be terribly concerned about the contract initially. Many creative people are not business- or commercially-oriented. It is imperative that contract negotiation and signing be taken care of first to avoid misunderstandings later. Print out the contract and ask the author whether it is generally acceptable. If he or she has made any other commitments, such as for some subsidiary rights, this information must be added to the contract. Include a work schedule and a clause allowing you to cancel if he or she fails to meet deadlines; always keep the pressure on writers to perform. (See *Is There a Book Inside You?* at http://parapublishing.com/sites/para/resources/allproducts.cfm.)

Unless you have a narrow field of interest or the writer has very strong feelings about a particular aspect of the contract, you want a contract that gives you all possible rights and territories. Once you have published the basic book, you want to entertain the possibilities of translations into other languages. Then there are book club adoptions, film rights, magazine excerpts, newspaper serializations and mass-market paperback rights. You will also want to sell through bookstores, other types of stores, through the mail, to associations, over the Internet, etc. Your promotion will rub off on all areas, so take advantage of it by taking control of the complete project. Remember that people who write contracts slant them their way. Take control. Use the Special Report *Publishing Contracts* (at http://ParaPublishing.com) to create your own contract.

> *Many first-time authors are not concerned about the advance or royalties; they seek the notoriety. They get smarter on their second book and look for the money.*

ADVANCES, ROYALTIES AND FEES

ADVANCES (money paid "in advance" by the publisher) depend on the proposed retail selling price, the projected print run and the sales potential of the book. An advance seals the deal, which is an important legal consideration, and it puts pressure on both the author and the publisher to perform. The advance makes the author feel accepted and has great psychological value; it does not have to be large to work as an incentive.

Advances generally range from $100 to $10,000, and small publishers often keep them low as that is all they can afford. A good rule of thumb is to offer an advance equal to the projected first-year royalties (the author's share of the book's proceeds). One way to create an incentive, or at least make the author feel morally obligated, is to make progress payments. One-third can be paid on signing the contract, one-third when the writer submits the first draft and one-third when he or she completes the proofreading.

Advances are paid against royalties—that is, royalty payments are first deducted from any advances issued to the author before royalties are actually paid out. Ordinarily, advances are nonrefundable; the author keeps them even if he or she fails to deliver the manuscript or the book is never published. This is another good reason for publishers to protect the investment with progress payments and a written contract.

Authors may demand high advances from publishers in order to commit the publisher to push the book. The publisher, with a lot already invested in a book, has to bring it to market quickly and promote it well. The advance is the publisher's gamble.

FLAT FEES OR ROYALTIES: Should contributors get a percentage of the book or be paid a flat fee? Obviously, flat fees are simpler, and they are occasionally cheaper (you avoid semiannual accounting). An illustrator creating a major portion of the book should get royalties, whereas someone doing basic research or contributing a drawing should be paid a flat fee. Everyone must understand clearly what is in it for him or her. If you require a few drawings, go to a graphic artist to have them drawn to order. Then pay the bill and be done with it. With children's books, however, where the illustrations are considered to be equally as important as the text, the royalty split is typically 50/50.

THE ROYALTY FORMULA traditionally has been to pay the author 10% of the *list* (cover) price for each *hardcover* book sold through "trade book" channels, such as book wholesalers, bookstores and libraries. Graduated royalties for the *hardcover* edition might be 10% of the list price on the first 5,000 books sold, 12.5% on the next 5,000 and 15% on sales over 10,000. Often *softcover* authors command 7% for the first 12,000 sold and 9% above that number.

In the late 1980s, most of the larger publishers changed their terms by offering authors 6% to 10% of the *net* on books. They amended their contracts with some generous-sounding wording such as "We will pay you 6% of the net receipts." What they don't say is that many of the books are sold at varying wholesale discounts of 40% to 66%, so authors receive roughly half of what they used to receive.

Accounting for sales on the net is very time-consuming; every sale has to be calculated. A percentage of the list price is preferable to both author and publisher because it is much easier to calculate.

Royalties for college texts range from 10% to 18%, and those for heavily illustrated elementary and secondary school texts run from 4% to 10%. Royalties for children's books range between 10% and 15%, to be split between the author and illustrator.

Mass-market paperback publishers usually pay 4% to 7.5%, but they print in much greater quantities.

Most traditional contracts call for the author and publisher to split the subsidiary rights (films, book clubs, etc.) at some percentage. Many of the big publishers barely break even on the book itself and hope to make their money on the subsidiary rights.

Before going on to Chapter 3, turn to Appendix 1, "Your Book's Calendar." Before you start, it's nice to know where you're going. For more information on publishing choices, you can take self-evaluated quizzes to help yourself make a decision; see *Is There a Book Inside You?* at http://parapublishing.com/sites/para/resources/allproducts.cfm.

My hobby is writing. Fortunately, I have found a way to turn my avocation into my vocation.

SHARING WHAT I'VE LEARNED

I have operated and worked for large firms, but I opted to go it alone in 1969. It was 1983 before I decided to take on my first employee. In terms of both dollar volume and books sold, I was probably the world's largest one-person publishing company during those early years. Now Para Publishing is larger than it was then, but I have help.

Because I had committed myself to the "luxury" of a one-person enterprise, I had to operate efficiently. I concentrated on those areas that provided a maximum return on my investment of time and money—the highest profit and best results for the time and energy expended.

I know small business and small publishing inside out because I play both roles; I set policy as management and implement it as labor. Consequently, I have developed simple systems to handle every task. In this book, I share my experience with you.

If the large publishers are doing so well, why do they require authors to send return postage with their submitted manuscripts?

3

STARTING YOUR OWN PUBLISHING COMPANY

BASICS FOR TAKING THE PLUNGE

Forming your own publishing company is not difficult, and many of the requirements can be postponed until you are ready to send your manuscript to the printer. But you do need a system and must get into the habit of using it. Publishing your book is, after all, a business.

> *Writing a book is a creative act.*
> *Selling a book is a business.*

Having a business is just good business. Tax laws favor businesses because owners can deduct goods and services that the wage earner must pay for with after-tax dollars. If you don't have a business, you don't get to deduct very much.

Gross ➢ Taxes ➢ Net
Job
Gross ➢ Expenditures ➢ Net ➢ Taxes
Business

If you own a business, a lot of what you're already buying becomes deductible because it's part of maintaining your business (car washes, membership dues, magazine subscriptions, travel, taking people out to dinner, the business portion of your home, etc.). Having your own business will improve your lifestyle.

> *My take-home pay won't take me home anymore.*

BUSINESS STRUCTURES

There are three forms of a business—(1) the **sole proprietorship,** (2) the **partnership** and (3) the **corporation**—and each has advantages and disadvantages. You don't have to make the choice right now. If you do not file for corporation status, you'll be operating as a sole proprietorship or partnership anyway. All you have to do is say, "I am a business," and file a Schedule C (Profit or Loss from Business) with your tax return. Schedule C is where you list your deductions.

Here are a few things to keep in mind while you're focusing on your most important concern—*your manuscript.*

•◦ As a **sole proprietor,** what the business earns is yours to keep; what the business borrows is money you owe. The business is *you.*

In a book-publishing sole proprietorship, you have the choice of keeping your financial records on a modified *cash basis* or an *accrual basis.* The cash system is easier to understand, allows you to defer more income and requires less bookkeeping, which makes more sense for a small business. You can always switch to accrual when you grow larger. Once you use the accrual system, you cannot switch back to cash. Most accounting software programs, such as QuickBooks, operate best in the accrual system.

•• Many business consultants discourage the formation of a **partnership** because its success rate is not much better than that of marriages—for a lot of the same reasons. It's a rare pair who complement each other well enough to divide the work so that both are happy. If two or more people want to form a company, they should consider a corporation.

•• In a **corporation,** you are an "employee" of the corporation. This results in more accounting, payroll deposits, taxes, paperwork, annual meetings with published minutes, corporate taxes and possible annual registration fees. Incorporation may lend an air of permanence, but it can also be expensive to form, plus saddle you with unwanted paperwork, meetings and legal bills.

Incorporation limits liability. Although the corporation can be sued, the individual stockholders, employees and officers are normally protected. However, the attorney for the plaintiff will name both the publishing company and the author as defendants, so incorporation may not protect all of those with interests in the book.

There's a recently popular business structure that also limits your liability—a **Limited Liability Company (LLC).** This may be less expensive to form, less complex to manage, and offer better tax aspects than a corporation, yet provide many of the same benefits.

There is also a corporate structure called a **Sub-S Corporation (S-Corp)** that allows corporate income and deductions to pass directly to the individual shareholders, who then pay only their individual taxes rather than also being taxed at the corporate level.

All these business structures offer benefits and drawbacks and should be discussed with your lawyer and accountant.

WHERE TO LOOK FOR HELP

The Small Business Administration (SBA) provides a toll-free answer desk at 800-827-5722 to provide information on free counseling, pre-business workshops and many other SBA services. The national office is in Washington, D.C., and can be reached at 202-205-6665. You may find your local office more helpful, however. Look for its number in the U.S. Government section of the white pages of your telephone directory under Small Business Administration. The Web site is also helpful: http://www.sba.gov. The SBA has numerous educational, business-development and loan-guarantee programs.

SCORE (Service Corps of Retired Executives) is the Small Business Administration's volunteer network of experienced men and women who you can call or email for counseling. There is no charge for this service except for occasional out-of-pocket traveling expenses. There are several hundred SCORE chapters around the country. Call the SBA office nearest you to see if there is a local SCORE chapter. Look in the U.S. Government section of the white pages under Small Business Administration. Tell them what you need, and they will find someone tailored to you and your business. Naturally, it's always best to get this advice before you get into trouble; do it sooner, not later. SCORE's Web site is http://www.score.org.

PUBLICATIONS: *Publishers Weekly* magazine will teach you about the book trade, provide many stimulating ideas and generate enthusiasm. Purchase a copy of *Literary Market Place* (the LMP); it is *the* resource of the book industry. Due to its price, I used to recommend using a library copy whenever it was needed, but it has become too important for just occasional use. You can also subscribe to it online at the LMP Web site, http://www.literarymarketplace.com. Some areas of the site are free.

Writing references—such as dictionaries, writing style and usage manuals, and a thesaurus—can be purchased inexpensively in used bookstores. Also, get the free InfoKits from Para Publishing. See http://parapub.com/sites/para/resources/infokit.cfm.

SETTING UP YOUR BUSINESS

YOUR COMPANY NAME will have to be selected before you go to press, so keep thinking about it. You could name it after yourself, such as Sam Horn Enterprises or Gail Gardner Publishing Company, but these choices don't make your company look as "big" as if you used a fictitious name. (By the way, the use of the word "enterprises" is often the sign of a rank beginner and may give the impression that you don't know yet what your company is going to do.) If the business succeeds and one day you decide to sell out, the name will be sold with it. What is the value of Gail Gardner Publishing without Gail Gardner? A different name will have more value. For instance, toward the end of the 20th century, any company name with a dot com in it got a lot more attention and had a lot more value. A year later, that changed. Appearing to be larger may be important when applying for credit from your vendors (suppliers) or asking a paper mill for samples. A fictitious company name will create the impression that you have a going business.

GETTING TOP BILLING

Starting your company name with an A will place your business high in alphabetic listings. Peggy Glenn changed her PiGi Publishing to Aames-Allen to ensure top billing in directories.

Non-English names can pose cataloging problems. Would you list La Cumbre Publishing under L or C? If people don't know where to catalog you or where to look for you, you may not be found—and you could lose business.

Geographical names can be limiting. Which makes you sound larger, East Weedpatch Press or North American Publishing? Which company would you rather run? What happens if you move to West Weedpatch?

To find a new name, one that isn't being used in the publishing industry, you can go to the library and look through *Books in Print* and several other directories. But start with a Google search. This exploration is fun, and you will find that the newer publishing companies have some pretty interesting names. As a new, small outfit, it does not hurt to have a "handle" that attracts attention.

Pick a name that isn't being used by anyone else. If you select a name that has already been taken (or is even close), you will receive some of their mail, some of their returns as well as calls from confused customers. No name is worth that hassle.

After you select a name for your new publishing company, you will probably be required to file it as a fictitious business name with your city or county and also to run a notice in a local newspaper. This Doing-Business-As (DBA) notice is your way of letting the public know that you and the publishing company are the same person.

▀▄▀▄▀ Para Publishing

YOUR LOGO is a graphic image, an easily recognizable symbol; it may consist of a drawing or just the company name in a distinctive style of type. If you can dream up something clever and easily recognizable, start putting it on all your letterhead, labels, business cards and brochures. If you look carefully at the Para Publishing logo, you will see a parachute canopy.

YOUR PLACE OF BUSINESS will be your residence for a while. Initially, you will not need a lot of space to write—or to store and ship books. When you have several titles, need more space and have employees, you may need to move your business elsewhere. But for now, a home location has many advantages. Working at home (in your house, apartment, mobile home, camper, etc.) can save money on gasoline, clothes, additional rent and utilities, plus allow you to avoid the headaches of a second property. Operating the business at home requires some organization and discipline, but for many it is very comfortable working in an atmosphere with less stress.

Almost 40 million people in the U.S. work out of 35 million households, and they can measure their commute with a yardstick. According to *The Wall Street Journal*, many states are now realizing that home-based businesses are more stable than large companies.

Before you begin sorting, shipping and selling books in your living room, quietly check the zoning ordinances. Local regulations may allow only certain types of businesses to be run from residences in your area. The publishing business will be small at first, and as long as you don't have employees and large trucks aren't pulling into the drive every few minutes, no one is likely to complain. Avoid walk-in traffic and refer to yourself as an "author" or "writer" rather than a "publisher," and you shouldn't encounter any difficulty.

Working from your home should not be confused with an "office" in the home. The IRS has cracked down on offices that are *in addition* to one's place of business outside the home. If you use 50% of your home for your business activities and don't have another office, you may deduct 50% of most of the house expenses—for example, mortgage or rent payments, electricity, gas, water, insurance and cleaning. If you use more of the home for business, you may deduct proportionately more of your expenses.

If you're worried that a visiting vendor or client might not be favorably impressed with your home setup, make a lunch appointment in a restaurant. Actually, the visitor will probably envy you. Working out of your home is more comfortable, more efficient, less expensive and safer—you don't have to commute at night.

I never said starting your own publishing company would be easy. I just promised it would be worth it!

RENTED POSTAL BOX VS. STREET ADDRESS: There are many good arguments for each of these choices. Some people feel quite strongly that a street address is more effective in a mail-order ad or sales brochure because the location reflects more substance and stability. But, today, even the big firms are using boxes. This is probably the result of the higher incidence of urban crime. There was a time when the mail was sacred, and no crook would dare to touch it—but not anymore.

If you rent a box from a private company, make sure the firm is stable. If it goes out of business or loses its lease, you will have to change a lot of business cards and you will lose a lot of mail-order business. Incidentally, you may not call your mailbox a "suite" in Pennsylvania. In 1991, Attorney General Ernest D. Preate, Jr., said it is misleading to call a 5" x 3" cubbyhole an "office" or "suite." Check the ordinances and laws in your area.

Long street addresses ("1234 Northwest Whispering Valley Parkway, Suite 1701" vs. "Box 3") could cost you more in classified ads where you are charged by the word.

Box mail can be available earlier in the day than home-delivered mail. Another advantage of a box is that you can maintain the same address even if you move to a new home in the same area. With most boxes through private firms, someone is there during office hours to receive deliveries such as FedEx packages. Perhaps the most important reason to maintain a box is to keep your excited, loyal readers from dropping by at all hours to meet their author.

Apply for a box now, and consider getting a large one. In some areas, boxes are in short supply and there is quite a waiting list. It may take you months to get one. Write your name, your company name and the title of your book on the box registration card, so you will get your mail from the post office no matter how it is addressed.

TELEPHONE: Fortunately, telephone service is becoming less expensive. I suggest that you retain your present line for the family and get a new one for your company. Get a third line for your fax and perhaps your modem. If the business gets large enough, get a fourth line just for outgoing calls so you will not block incoming orders. Call-waiting can help on the company line for a small business, especially when combined with a voice-mail answering service. However, don't fool with fax/phone switches.

Shop around for the best phone package, including long-distance flat rate plans. The savings can be considerable.

YOUR COMPUTER is your most important piece of machinery; spend the money and get a good one. You are a wordsmith now and require the best and fastest word-processing equipment you can afford.

Your computer will speed up your writing, and it can be used for email, other correspondence, mailing-list maintenance, typesetting, order entry and bookkeeping.

INTERNET ACCESS: As soon as possible, you will need DSL, cable or wireless access to the Internet.

LICENSES AND TAXES

The legal requirements of operating a business are covered in many parts of this book, just as you will encounter them in every facet of your daily publishing life. The following is what you need to run your business, but remember that most of this can be postponed until you are ready to go to press, move out of the house or hire employees. These tips, of course, are food for thought—not a substitute for legal counsel or accounting help.

Interview a friend or acquaintance who has recently set up a small business in your community. He or she will be able to tell you about his or her experience and who you must deal with at city, county, state and federal levels. In some areas, you must register your business with local authorities, but not in all. Do not volunteer. Most registrations come with a fee or tax.

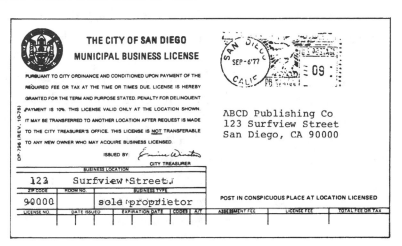

Business license

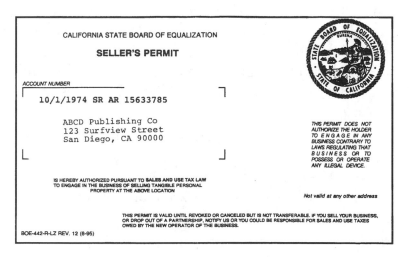

Resale permit

As a sole proprietorship your business will not need a separate bank account, and until you hire employees you will avoid Employer Identification Numbers (EIN) and special accounts.

SALES TAX: Most states have a sales tax. If your state does, you're required to collect it only on those books sold and shipped to end-users at destinations within the state. The sales tax is collected only once at the retail level from the ultimate purchaser. It's not collected from dealers such as bookstores or wholesalers within your state who will in turn "resell" the book to an end-user. The reseller will collect the sales tax from the end-user purchaser.

> *We do not charge sales tax here;*
> *we just collect it for the state.*

As a commercial firm, you must either collect the sales tax from a sale within your state, show by the shipping address on the invoice that the goods are going out of state or claim to be selling the books to another dealer in your state "for resale." Many states require you to maintain a file of customer resale numbers. Some dealers list their resale number on purchase orders, but usually you have to request it. Type "for resale" on the invoice.

In some states, shipping supplies, such as cartons and tape, are not subject to the sales tax. Be careful what taxes you pay. Other states exempt certain nonprofit or public institutions, such as libraries and schools, from paying sales tax. Be careful what you collect.

Before you go to press, obtain your resale permit. Then if your books are printed in your state, you won't have to pay sales tax when you pay the printing bill. Many of the larger book printers require a copy of your resale permit no matter what state you live in, because they have sales offices (a presence) in numerous states.

Find the sales tax office in the telephone directory. In California, it is called the State Board of Equalization; in Massachusetts, it is the Sales and Use Tax Bureau of the Department of Corporations and Taxation. Check the posted resale permit posted at a nearby store; the name of the controlling agency will be on it.

When you apply for your sales-tax license or resale permit, tell them you are just starting out as an author and hope to sell a few of your books. Tell them that most sales will be wholesale to bookstores or shipped out of state. This way, you may be able to avoid giving the tax agency a deposit and you may be allowed to report sales-tax collections annually instead of quarterly, thus saving both money and paperwork. As your business grows and you collect more sales taxes, the taxing authorities will require you to report more often. When you apply, the tax office will supply you with an explanatory sheet detailing your responsibilities for sales-tax collection in your state.

THE LAWS YOU MUST KNOW

As an author–publisher, your legal concerns are copyright, defamation (libel), right of privacy, illegal reproduction and negligence.

•❖ Copyright works both ways: (1) it protects your work from others, and (2) it protects their work from you. Take pride, do your own original work, and make your book better than the others. For a detailed explanation of the copyright, see Chapters 2 and 5.

•◆ **Defamation** is "libel" in the printed word and "slander" when spoken. *Black's Law Dictionary* defines defamation as "the offense of injuring a person's character, fame or reputation by false and malicious statements." Libel may take the form of either words or pictures. The offense is in the "publication" of the matter, so you are not excused just because you read it somewhere else first. You are safe if the statement is true; this is the perfect defense, but check the source. The best practice is never to say anything nasty about anyone. You will need all the support you can get to sell your book. If you disagree with another authority, leave his or her name out and write, "Some people will argue…" or "Many authorities believe…" and then tear up this position with your view. If you don't like someone, the worst thing you can do to them is to leave them out of your book altogether. Cover yourself and stay out of court; the legal game is expensive.

•◆ **Right of privacy** is another area of law you may face. Unless people are part of a news event, they have a right to keep their photo out of publications. Most people love to see their photo in a book and in fact are prime customers for the finished product. However, to protect yourself, it's smart to get a written release signed.

•◆ **Illegal reproduction** covers the promoting of lotteries, financial schemes, fraudulent activities, printing of securities, reproducing postage stamps, etc. In other words, don't print money. If you're writing about these subjects, you probably already know about the challenges and the postal and other laws relating to them. If not, seek legal advice.

•◆ Negligence. Readers could sue you, claiming your book misled them, to their great damage.

NOT SO SAFE

Warner Books recalled 115,000 copies of *First Love* when Dr. Ruth Westheimer and Dr. Nathan Kravetz mixed up the "safe" days for the rhythm method of birth control. Suits have been brought against the publishers of a diet book and a cookbook, but so far the courts have sided with the publishers.

In most cases, the courts have not found books to be "products," so publishers are not strictly liable for their content. It must be proven that the publisher knew or should have known of the inaccuracies. Books are not the reader's only source of information.

See Document 636, *Insurance for Publishers,* at http://parapublishing.com/sites/para/resources/allproducts.cfm.

Today, many books contain **disclaimers** warning readers not to exclusively rely on the text. See the disclaimer in the front of this book and paraphrase it.

KEEPING RECORDS AND PAYING TAXES

TAXES are one place an author–publisher gets a big break. Not only are the costs of printing your book deductible, so are all the direct expenses incurred while writing, producing and promoting it. If you are writing about your favorite hobby, you may deduct the expenses of pursuing that too. For example, if you are writing on aviation, you can probably deduct flying lessons and trips to the national convention since you are also conducting research as you pursue your avocation. With detailed records, the IRS will have a hard time declaring your business a "hobby."

Assuming you're already employed and Uncle Sam is withholding 30% or more from your weekly check, that withheld money amounts to thousands of dollars a year. The game is to see how much you can get back. How much did you pay to the IRS last year? Would you like to get a full refund? Getting money back is fun and rewarding. Of course, if your book is a great success, you will make more money and have to pay taxes on it. For complete details, get a copy of publication 334, *Tax Guide for Small Business*, from your nearest IRS office or from your Enrolled Agent or other tax professional. See "What You May Deduct" below for possible deductions.

"Profit" is not a dirty word.

RECORD-KEEPING must be done from the beginning of your writing, because it is difficult to justify deductions you have not recorded. In starting a new business, many people are so involved with their great idea and the process of pursuing it that at year-end they find they have not kept good records (or any at all). The best thing to do from the beginning is to write checks for, debit or charge every possible deductible expense and keep receipts so that you have a paper trail. Legally, these are called "contemporaneous records," as they are written as they occur.

Open a separate business checking account (the bank will require that you have filed a fictitious business name statement). Select one charge card to use exclusively for business, using only that card for writing and publishing expenses. Always record the category of expense on the check or on your charge-card slip (for example, office supplies, rent, printing, advertising, etc.). That way, at year-end you have already done most of the work.

Be sure to report all your income. If you're audited, the IRS will probably ask about all your bank deposits. If $50,000 went through your bank account yet you reported only $35,000 in income, you'll have some explaining to do. If the extra cash flow is from gifts or loans, be prepared to prove this.

No one takes better care of your money than you do.
—Cliff Leonard, License to Steal

While most business failures are due to poor marketing and pricing decisions, some occur because of poor record-keeping. If you don't know your costs, you won't know the prices you must charge to make money. If you don't know you're spending more for something than you should, you won't realize that changes in operations, procedures or suppliers should be made. You also need past information about income and expenses to serve as a guide to future projections and business planning.

Start right now by ordering an accounting program. For example, Quicken has invoicing, accounts payable and a general ledger. This is all you need to start. QuickBooks has these features, plus inventory and accounts receivable; it is a full accounting program. These and other programs are listed under Order-Entry Software in Appendix 2.

You can't prove the deduction if you don't record it.

WHAT YOU MAY DEDUCT: Label the accounts in the accounting program as follows: meals (ME), travel (TR, with subheadings if you like for lodging—LO, airfares—

AF and other incidentals—TI), car expenses (CE, with sub-heading recommended for car lease—CL, gas—CG, repairs and maintenance—CR and car insurance—CI), equipment purchases (EP, which you also need to itemize individually to depreciate or take an "expense deduction" on your return), equipment repairs (ER), shipping and postage (SP), advertising and marketing (AD), cost of goods sold (GS, with subcategories for cost of printing—GP and other such costs, which can be written off only as the books are sold), dues and licenses (DL), subscriptions and books (SB), telephone (TL), refunds and allowances (RE) and office supplies (OS). Minimize use of the category called "miscellaneous" since the IRS likes to inquire about such expenditures. If there are other categories or expenses you regularly incur, add those to your account list.

The best way to get into the habit and to learn what's deductible is to list EVERY cent you spend the first year. Get receipts whenever possible—at the post office, for parking, tolls, meals, motels, etc.

You've already decided to carry pen and paper at all times to record your thoughts for your manuscript, so carry one more sheet for recording expenditures. Any money spent in the pursuit of income is deductible, so write down every cent. As you learn what's deductible, you'll find that you become generous where an expenditure can be written off and stingy where it can't. This is good discipline and good business.

Keep an envelope in the car. Each day, as you get in and start the car, let the engine warm up while you record the date, odometer reading and places you intend to go. Use the envelope to hold the receipts you acquire during the day. Start a new envelope every month.

At the end of each month, post the petty-cash expenses from your pocket notes and car envelope in your accounting program.

At the end of the year, take the printout with totaled figures to your accountant. The accountant will do the rest, and the charge will be reasonable. Record-keeping is so easy, and yet many people think there is some great mystery to accounting.

You don't even have to make money to claim deductions. You can claim a loss for at least three years in a row before the IRS questions whether you are a hobbyist rather than an author–publisher. Chrysler lost money for years and still took deductions. Keep good records and you will be able to prove you are in business.

High cash flow means taking in lots of money but often being unable to find much of it.

FINANCING YOUR BUSINESS

Raising the money you'll need to pay for the production and promotion of your book will take you into the world of finance, unless you have a lot of loose, ready cash lying about. Insufficient capitalization is one of the greatest challenges facing most new businesses. Money won't come looking for you. You have to find it by selling yourself and your book. But the money is there; it is available.

According to *The Wall Street Journal*, most entrepreneurs spend their own money to start their business. Roughly 48% rely on savings, 29% borrow from banks, 13% shake down their friends, 4% look for individual investors, less than 1%

strike deals with venture capital firms or government agencies and 5% are successful with other sources.

Do not expect the large national book printers to be interested in postponing the printing bill. They are printers— not publishers or lenders.

FINANCIAL PARTNERS: Don't take in partners on your book. Partners are rarely "silent." They want to know why the book is not selling better, why it is not in the airport bookstore, why you're spending money to attend a book fair, etc. You will spend more time explaining the publishing business to your partner(s) than you will spend promoting the book. Going to family or friends for a straight-out loan is a better choice for funding. See the "Family and Friends" section below.

Only two people make money on a book:
the printer and the investor.

SELF-FINANCING: In the beginning, you won't run up bills by hiring help or renting space, so you will not have any immediate needs for large sums of cash. Many people have more money than they need for necessities and throw away their disposable income on frivolous purchases. As you will need to find time to work on your book, the elimination of some movies, dining out, recreational activities and extended trips will give you new blocks of time for writing that you thought you didn't have and gain you some money in the process.

Some people advise the use of OPM (other people's money) rather than your own. Then if your business goes bust and you lose all the borrowed funds, you still have your own money in reserve. But as you tuck your prized manuscript under your arm and venture off, you're going to find that locating OPM often takes some searching.

WHY BE SELFISH?

Bernard Kamoroff found seven friends to participate in the first and second printings of his *Small Time Operator*. He reasoned: Why be selfish; why not let your friends share in the project? His best-selling accounting book has been through dozens of revised printings in the past 30 years.

THE SMALL BUSINESS ADMINISTRATION used to prohibit financial assistance to book publishers, bookstores, movie theaters, news operations, filmmakers and other "opinion-molders." This was to avoid financing radicals who might promote seditious activities and then file for bankruptcy, which would leave the taxpayers with a social problem and the bill for starting it. The "opinion-molder" rule was overturned in mid-1994. Contact your local SBA (in the U.S. Government section of the white pages under "Small Business Administration") or visit the Web site at http://www.sba.gov. They have numerous loan-guarantee programs available.

BANKS don't seek loan applicants in the start-up publishing industry. They like successful firms with upbeat balance sheets; like everyone else, they are in business to stay in business. Banks look on manuscripts and books as speculative. Even armed with a detailed market-research report on your product, you may find that you can't even get an appointment with the loan officer. A stack of books is not considered good collateral to a bank; if you default, they would not know how to turn the books back into money to pay the debt. If you ask for money to go into the publishing business, the bank probably won't be interested.

You know you have arrived when you don't have to check the balance before writing a check.

Basically, there are two ways to borrow money from a bank. The first is the term loan, which is normally used to finance purchases such as a car. Term loans are paid back monthly and are usually limited to 36 months. The second is an ordinary signature loan with interest at the prime rate plus about 5%. A signature loan runs for a period of months and you pay it off at the due date. But although the loan is written for a stated period, it is common to pay just the interest and renew it. Many authors have been successful in acquiring money by leaving the manuscript at home and asking for a vacation loan instead.

You may need collateral, perhaps a second mortgage. If you have enough real and personal property, you will be able to get the money on your signature alone. Don't think small; large amounts are often easier to borrow. An SBA loan guarantee can substitute for some of your collateral requirements.

All banks are not the same; shop around not only for loans, but also for checking account charges. Banks are not doing you any favors; you're doing them a favor by storing your money with them and paying interest on any loan. Stop by several banks and pick up pamphlets on their checking account and loan policies. Take the brochures home—compare them. Do they pay interest on personal or business checking accounts, and, if so, what is the minimum required balance? What are their fees for check printing, stop payments, etc.? Is overdraft protection available in some form? Don't just think of your present needs; think of the future.

When choosing a loan, don't pay interest rates comparable to credit-card interest. Shop for mortgage-level rates.

You may be better off working at your new publishing company part-time initially. Then if it fails, at least you are not out of a job too.

CHANGING YOUR W-4 FORM by decreasing the amount of your income tax "withholding" is advocated by some people as a way to have the IRS lend your withholding back to you. If you have a regular job, and a lot of money is being withheld from each paycheck, you can change the exemption from withholding by making out a new W-4 form with your employer early in the year. If you are in the 30% tax bracket, this is like getting a 50% raise. Of course, you must be serious about starting your business, keep good records and take full deductions. Done correctly, you should be able to spend and deduct as a business expense the formerly withheld money and zero out at tax time. Once you are working for yourself full-time, you will file estimated tax forms rather than W-4s.

PREPUBLICATION OFFERS are often used to raise money. As the book goes to press, send out an email announcement to all who might be interested in the book and offer to pay the postage for a prepublication order and/or autograph the copies (but never offer to discount a brand-new book). Emphasize that the manuscript is complete and that the book is on the press. Tell them you won't cash their check or process their credit-card number until the book is shipped. Mention a shipping date, but give yourself an extra month or two. Make a different special offer to dealers. Prepublication sales sometimes bring in enough money to pay the printing bill.

THINKING AHEAD

Alan Gadney and Carolyn Porter made far more in advance than just their printing costs. They started promoting their first book, a unique reference directory, a year before it was printed. They offered free shipping on advance orders, periodically notified all purchasers of the book's progress, and by the time it came off the press they had collected more than $10,000 in advance orders. And nobody ever asked for their check back... they all wanted the book hot off the press.

FAMILY AND FRIENDS will often lend on a book. They have faith in you and want to see your name on a book as much as you do. But if you do borrow from friends or relatives, make the same presentation to them that you would to a bank. Talk figures and do not get emotional. Then write a loan contract and pay them the same interest that you would pay the bank. Put the loan on a business basis and keep the good relationships, or things may get testy later when you attend a social gathering.

GRANTS are available from many foundations for worthwhile publishing projects. Check your state arts agency and the National Endowment for the Arts at http://www.arts.gov/grants/apply/index.html. Additional listings may be found in *Literary Market Place*. There are several magazines for fund-raisers. Ask your reference librarian. Make a search for *grants and awards* on the Web. Many large cities and educational institutions have grant centers (such as the Grant-manship Center in Los Angeles and The Foundation Center in New York and elsewhere), all stocked with excellent information.

Most grants and fellowships are for fiction and poetry. If your book qualifies, it can mean a large amount of money, but there will be a lot of paperwork to go along with it. If your book project deals with a special subject, you might look for grants available in your subject area rather than general writing grants open to all. You might also bundle your book with related product(s) and apply for a grant covering both.

WRITERS' COLONIES often supply free room and board to support budding authors. Some have rigid rules limiting the length and number of stays. For a list, see *Writer's Market*, *Writer's Digest* and *The Writer* magazine.

OTHER POSSIBILITIES include credit unions, retirement plans, the Veterans Administration (if appropriate) and the Farm Home Loan Association, which may consider some applicants as fitting its definition of a "farm community."

More information can be found in Document 626, *Raising Money to Publish Books*, at http://parapublishing.com/sites/para/resources/allproducts.cfm. All these suggestions for funding assume you have a good, salable book to begin with.

HOW MUCH DOES IT COST TO PUBLISH?

Asking this question is like asking how much a car costs. All books are different. If you are planning to print 3,000 copies of a 144-page, 5.5" x 8.5" softcover book with a few photographs, black ink on white paper with a four-color cover, the printing will cost less than $1.50 per book, so your printing bill will run around $4,500. Then there is typesetting ($1,000–$1,300), book cover design ($1,800 for softcover, a hardcover dust jacket will be more because of the larger size), professional editing ($1,000–$3,000 depending on the length of the book and the quality of the writing), other prepress expenses and trucking from the printer. Printing 3,000 hardcover books of the same dimensions with a dust jacket might cost about $3 each.

After the book is printed, it has to be promoted with book reviews, news releases, flyer mailings, co-op marketing and some email advertising. Money will not be coming in right away. There is a lot of lead time for writing, printing and promotion, and bookstores are notorious for paying slowly. For a book like the one described here, you should budget about $10,000 to get started (cover and page production, printing and initial marketing and promotion). If you print 500 according to the New Book Model, you should budget about $6,000 for production, printing and initial marketing.

A book with fewer photos, fewer pages and a one-color cover could run much less. However, without a good-looking book and some promotion money, the book is not likely to sell. For details, see Chapters 6 and 7 on pricing and promotion.

On your first venture, the printer will probably want payment in installments: one-third to start, one-third when the plates are made and one-third on the completion of the printing. After a book or two, they will no doubt give you normal 30-day terms and want their money a month after they deliver the books to you. If they want installments, agree, but request a 2% discount for cash (2% of $6,000 is $120).

LEAN AND MEAN: Run a streamlined, efficient operation. Do everything yourself and buy only those services you cannot perform. Avoid employees initially; they cost you management time, money and paperwork. Print in small quantities to keep the inventory low. Once you have learned the business by doing every part of it yourself, farm out the repetitive and least enjoyable tasks. When contracting for services, remember that although most businesses are ethical, everyone is in business for himself or herself first; you come second. Some of the subcontractors you hire may try to sell you more than you need. They don't care about your business as much as you do, because they have less to lose. Be careful taking advice from someone who is trying to sell you something.

Keep on top of costs. If you can save $1,000 per year by streamlining procedures and your net profit is normally 3%, the effect is the same as if you increased sales by $30,000.

Don't waste anything. For example, save the unusual stamps from the incoming mail. Stamp collecting is big business, and years from now you may be able to sell them to stamp companies. Check the *Yellow Pages* and call several local stamp dealers for prices. Recycle your shipping supplies, sell used printer cartridges to refillers (you can get $10 or more for some models), reuse scrap paper and cardboard and price-shop the Web.

EQUIPMENT YOU'LL NEED

As your publishing company grows, look for labor-saving machinery to multiply your efforts. Personal computers, photocopy machines, color printers, cordless telephones and package scales will save you time. They are much better buys than an employee, and you will find that with depreciation, machines are not very expensive. As machinery accumulates, you will begin to understand the advantages of owning your own business.

For more information, see Document 624, *How to Set Up & Run a Successful Book Publishing Business*, at http://parapublishing.com/sites/para/resources/allproducts.cfm.

> *Fortune assists the bold.*
> **—Virgil (70–19 B.C.E.), Roman poet**

4

PRODUCING YOUR BOOK

DESIGNING BOOKS
TYPESETTING
LAYOUT
BOOK PRINTING MATERIALS
THE PRINTING PROCESS

Now we'll go into what you can expect when your book enters the production stage. This explanation of the design, typesetting, layout, materials and printing process is meant to be brief and yet provide you with enough information to turn your words into an attractive product. Also see my book *Writing Nonfiction* for a prepress system (composition, layout, editing and design) and the Special Report *Buying Book Printing*, in Appendix 2 or at http://ParaPublishing.com.

Book production is entering its third evolutionary change in modern times. The first was the migration from hot-lead type to offset printing in the late 1960s. The second was the increasing availability of computer typesetting in the 1980s. The third was the entry of digital printing in the 1990s. All the evolutions saved a great deal of money and speeded the process. Also in the '90s, the Internet provided an alternative to the public library, and Web sites were replacing the brochure.

INFORMATION PACKAGING

Don't think of yourself as just a book author or book publisher. You are an *information provider*. People want your information but may not have the time or desire to read a book. They will gladly pay more to get the same information presented in a form that's most convenient to them. That's why you see the exact same information sold as a $20 printed book, a $10 eBook, a $60 audio series, a $100 non-credit course, a $150 video set, a $200-a-year newsletter, a $300-an-hour consultation or a $600 seminar. Each client learns best in different ways. Some people need to read, some prefer to listen, some require a classroom setting, and so on.

The information in each edition is the same; only the format is different. You'll provide your core information in any form your customer wants and needs. Wring maximum value out of your information. Let's start with printed books.

PRODUCTION AND PRINTING TIME

For a 144-page book, the final typesetting and layout should take a couple of days if you do it yourself on a computer, and about three to five weeks (depending on the complexity of the book's design) if you give the work to a typesetter. Copyediting may take a week and proofreading will take a few days. I recommend that you write in a layout format, and then turn the ultimate look of your book over to a professional typesetter. More on this as the chapter progresses.

Proofread. It is less expensive to put ink on paper than to take it off.

You can figure on about five weeks to offset print, bind and deliver softcover books to your location (slightly longer for hardcover books because of the binding process), but the work may take longer if your printer can't do all the work in-house and has to farm some of it out. Digital printing usually takes a couple of weeks. Softcover reprints usually take about three weeks. Trucking may take two to six days in the U.S. depending on the destination. Overseas color printing and shipping to the U.S. can take up to 10 weeks.

BOOK DESIGN

Go to a bookstore to search for a book that you can use as a *model*. Look for books in your category. If you can't find a book in your subject area that you like, try other subject areas that would appeal to your intended audience.

You'll find that most books in each category have a similar look and feel. Give your customers what they want, expect and deserve. If this is a business book, it should be in hardcover with a dust jacket. If it's a professional reference book for doctors, lawyers or accountants, it should be in hardcover without a dust jacket. If it's a children's book, it should be oversized, in four-color, hardcover and have a dust jacket.

Consider paper, binding, layout—*everything.* Buy that model book and place it above your desk. You'll use it as a guide for typesetting, layout, printing and binding.

If you want your book to sell like a book, it has to look like a book.

BOOK DESIGNERS will plan, typeset and lay out the interior of your book and the cover. Unless you're operating on an extremely tight budget, you'll want to hand the final design of your book over to one of these professionals. For a list of book designers, see Book Designers & Cover Artists in Appendix 2.

Often designers will provide design samples of their work for book interiors and covers on their Web site. See if you can find a designer whose style matches the feeling of your manuscript. If a designer you like does not have layout samples on his or her Web site, ask him or her to mail or email you samples for projects similar to the one you're working on.

In addition to considering his or her past work, see how you feel interacting with the designer during your initial contacts. Is this someone you'll want to keep working with as you develop your book? You want someone who is responsive to your questions and requests, and who can translate the idea behind your book into an appealing visual image.

BOOK FORMAT

Now let's consider various elements of book interiors that you'll want to know to proceed intelligently. For a more in-depth discussion of book design—both interior and the cover—see the guide *Book Design and Production* by Pete Masterson, which is available from Amazon.com. Masterson covers the basics beyond what is here, and he walks you through all the steps while explaining why they're done.

Note that the first page of each chapter of a book ordinarily begins on a right-hand page. If this leaves a blank on the left, the space can be filled with a photograph, chart or quotation. Each page should be used for something, even if it is just for a page number. The only exceptions might be your front and back matter.

Type can be set to *wrap around* illustrations, but it's simpler and cheaper to make a break in the text and insert the photo or drawing full width, from margin to margin.

RUNNING HEADS or "headers" are lines of type that appear across the top of the book page. Usually the title of the book appears on the left-hand page, and the chapter title is on the right.

FOLIOS are page numbers. Folios may be placed at the top outside corner (or somewhere else in the header), page bottom in the middle or even on the side of the page. However, the folio is usually part of the running head. Traditionally, pages received Roman numerals in the front matter and Arabic numbers in the text, because the text was set separately, and then the front matter was expanded or contracted to use up leftover pages in the printing signatures.

Today, many publishers take a tip from the magazine companies and start the count (though not the printed numbering) from the initial page. This makes the final page count higher and makes the reader feel he or she is getting more for the money. The argument goes, "I paid (the printer) for those pages, so I'm going to count them." See this book, for example.

If all publishers thought alike, all books might look alike.

STANDARDIZE AND SAVE MONEY: Generally I recommend going with a traditional book format. If you move away from the norm, your creativity may cost you sales. Occasionally, however, variations can be justified and the book will still be successful. For example, the photograph is of a die-cut, circular book on Frisbee play that comes nestled and shrink-wrapped in a custom 119 Frisbee disk. The unusual design feature contributed greatly to the sales of the book.

Remember that libraries and bookstores have standardized shelving. You want your book to fit. Most books are 5.5" x 8.5", perfect bound (glued spine) paperbacks, with or without photos and drawings, on a 50- or 60-pound paper stock. The cover is four-color on a 10-point C1S (coated one side) cover stock. Beyond this basic specification, a number of variations are possible.

TRIM SIZE: There are many standard book page trim sizes, and you want to give your customers what they expect. If it's a cookbook or computer book that is usually in a wide format so it will open and lie flat, you must provide the same wide format for your customers.

The conventional 5.5" x 8.5" size is suitable for both hardcover and softcover. It's one of the most economical, fits a library shelf well and by far has become the most popular. A book with 144 (5.5" x 8.5") pages has a much nicer feel than 77 larger (8.5" x 11") pages. The only good reason to go oversized is if you have too much material or if your sort of book demands a larger size (children's, art and coffee-table books). If you have a few large illustrations such as charts, consider foldout pages. The printer can insert them between signatures; specify where you want the foldouts.

Some digital and web presses will not yield a full measurement. Instead of 5.5" x 8.5", the finished trim will be 5.375" x 8.375". If you require a full trim size, specify it in your Request for Quotation (RFQ) for printing.

Whatever size you select, make all the books you publish measure the same to standardize your inventory of shipping bags and cartons. Nonetheless, if some books were 5.5" x 8.5" and others were 8.5" x 11", they would still stack well together. On the other hand, if some were 6" x 9", you would have packaging challenges.

NUMBER OF PAGES: Your book will be printed on several very large sheets of paper that will be folded down into *signatures*. (Originally, the person who sewed the pages together *signed* the work.) The number of book pages in each signature will depend on the size of your printer's press. The sheet-fed press usually works in multiples of 32; 16 pages are printed on the top side of the sheet (16 up) and 16 are put on the underside (16 down). Web presses usually work in multiples of 48.

To visualize a signature, take a sheet of paper and fold it *in half four times*. The folding results in 16 panels on each side of the sheet (16 up and 16 down), for a grand total of 32 pages in the signature. You will save money using the faster web press with 48-page signatures.

Aim for 144 to 288 total interior pages to be economical. A book of just 96 pages (2 x 48) will not command the price you want. A book of 720 pages (15 x 48) will be very expensive to produce because of the cost of paper.

More than 100 pages is psychologically good and will help to justify your price; so if you have just 90 pages, set the book in larger type, widen the margins, put more leading (space) between the lines, expand the Appendix or add some illustrations.

Aim for even signatures or even signatures with a single half signature of 24. The last signature will be shot twice and run side by side, but the press will be stopped at half the count.

In order to finally "page out" your book, you'll need to select a printer and know if the book will be printed on a press using 32- or 48-page signatures or some other page combination. You can then construct your final page count in full, half and even quarter-signatures (groups of 32, 16 and 8 pages or groups of 48, 24 and 12 pages).

Include all pages in your total count and move any leftover blank pages elsewhere in the book so they don't gang together at the end. Leaving blank pages at the back is bad book design. Instead, move them forward and fill them with quotations or illustrations; you might turn them into section dividers. You can also expand or condense the back matter and index to compensate for a couple too many or too few extra pages.

LAYOUT: In the layout stage, your word-processing file will be poured into a page layout program such as PageMaker, InDesign, QuarkXpress or Ventura Publisher. Next, the text file will be converted into a PDF image file to send to your printer.

MANUSCRIPT FORMAT: Many authors like to write their books in book layout format. The advantages to a book format are that the text looks like a book, you always know approximately how many pages you have and the book is closer to typeset.

To make your manuscript look like a book page, set your margins so that the text block will be about 4.2" wide and about 7" tall.

To set your margins in Microsoft Word, click *File\Page Setup* and change the Margins tab to *top* to 1.8", *bottom* to 2.3", *left* to 2.5", *right* to 1.9" and on the Layout tab, the *header* to 1.3".

To make a header with the book title and page number at the top of the page, click *View\Header and Footer*. Type in the tentative title for your book, then insert and place your page number using the header and footer box. Then set this in a sans serif font such as Tahoma or Arial, bold, 12-point type.

For your text, select a nice serif type font such as New Century Schoolbook (also Century or Schoolbook). Click *Format\Paragraph* and set the line spacing for *Single*. Set the type size to 12 pt. Serif fonts feature decorative lines at the ends of character strokes. (See Century examples below.)

With your manuscript laid out as it might look in the book, you will see how many pages you have. Now you can adjust the margins, type size, etc., and add or subtract resources in the Appendix to achieve the desired number of pages. You have some typographic control and your design will be more economical.

TYPE FONTS: Here are some examples of various type fonts (that is, typefaces and their various styles—i.e., regular, bold, italic and bold italic), their characteristics and how they can radically change the inside look of your book.

Read each of the following paragraphs. They not only show what the various type fonts look like; they are also a continuation of the text of this book.

CENTURY Regular   ARIAL Regular
CENTURY Italic   *ARIAL Italic*
CENTURY Bold   **ARIAL Bold**
CENTURY Bold Italic   ***ARIAL Bold Italic***

Century is a serif font; Arial is sans serif.
Notice that at the ends of character strokes,
serif fonts feature decorative lines.

Arial

TYPE FONTS are many and varied. Your word-processing or page layout program will have a selection. Pick a *serif* type font such as Century for the body copy and a *sans serif* font such as Tahoma for headlines. Serif type fonts have little "feet" on the vertical parts, and they are easier to read than sans serif fonts.

Garamond

Four type factors affect legibility: *font type* such as serif or sans serif, type size (make it large enough), *leading* (rhymes with "heading" and is the space between the lines) and the *column width* (the human eye has been trained to read narrow newspaper columns).

Times New Roman

To give your book some type style variation, you can use *italics,* **boldface,** ***bold italic,*** SMALL CAPS and larger sizes for chapter heads, captions, subheads and for lending emphasis.

Bookman

Here are some more type terms. *Point size* is the height of a capital letter (and its mount), as in

"10-point type." There are 72 points to the inch. A *pica* is the printer's standard measurement for the length of a line and the depth of a page. There are 12 points to a pica and six picas to the inch. Therefore, 24 picas means a 4"-wide column. *Leading* or *slug* is the space between the lines. Printers used to use a strip of lead, hence the name. If you have ten points of type plus two points of leading, the specification would be written out as "10/12."

Century

Nine on eleven leading is about as small as you should go for a legible book. Ten on twelve is very common, though children and older people with failing eyesight prefer 12 on 14. Most page layout programs will set your leading automatically at single spaced unless you specify what you want.

Goudy

Some type fonts, such as Goudy, are "condensed." They allow you to get more words on a page. On the other hand, if you want to fill up more pages, use an expanded font such as Bookman. (See above.)

Courier

For a successful book, don't venture too far from the common type fonts, such as Times Roman, Palatino, Baskerville, Caledonia, Bookman and New Century Schoolbook.

Read the above and compare the various type fonts.

6 Arial

8 Arial

10 Arial

14 Arial

18 Arial
20 Arial
22 Arial
24 Arial

**Character heights are measured in points.
There are 72 points to the inch.**

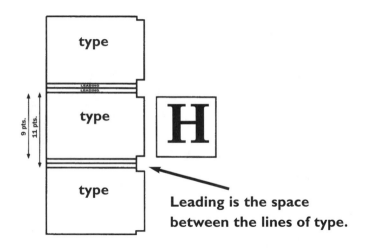

**Leading is the space
between the lines of type.**

HEADLINES, such as chapter titles, are usually set in a larger type, often in a sans serif typeface.

ILLUSTRATIONS will augment the text, enhance the appearance of the book and foster the salability of your words. Don't be cheap with illustrations. If a photo or drawing will make the book more attractive, readable or useful to the buyer, include it. Also consider charts, graphs, tables and sample forms to make your book as user-friendly and as valuable as possible.

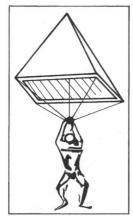

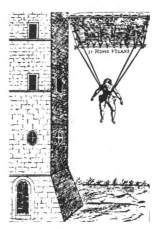

Line drawing   **Extra lines were crowded into this line drawing to give it the appearance of shading.**

LINE ART may consist of sketches, charts or type. Line art differs from photographs that must be screened. See halftones, below.

CLIP ART is often a type of line art that may be inserted into your book. Sometimes called "click art" today, it may consist of line drawings, cartoons, woodcut, icons and even stock photos. See http://www.ClipArt.com.

HALFTONES must be made of any artwork, such as a photograph, which is not solid black and white, but instead has "gray scale" (shades of gray). To make a halftone, the original photo is converted to dots by your computer. The eye blends the dots together into a continuous tone.

Screens come in several values and are measured in dots per linear inch (dpi). The more dots, the crisper the printed halftone. Newspapers commonly use a 65- or 85-line screen

(85 dots per inch), and books are commonly printed with 120-, 133- or even 150-line screens.

Photo printed unscreened

**Same photo screened.
Study with a magnifying glass
or loupe to see the dots.**

Photos taken from magazines and other books have already been screened. Reshooting or rescreening usually makes them muddier, or they will pick up a moiré (ripple or wavy) pattern.

With both photos and drawings, reductions are preferable to enlargements. Reductions become sharper, but enlargements only magnify flaws, causing a loss of clarity. Start with larger illustrations. Reduce and scan them into your manuscript so you can size and crop them to fit.

For photographs, a digital camera could be used, and the images easily inserted into your manuscript. Images can be imported into the word-processing file or linked (a technical approach used by professional typesetters). If linked, it will be easier to extract the photo for making adjustments such as to the light/dark level. The printer will screen the photo when going to film or plate. Using digital photo files will make the whole process faster, easier and cheaper.

COLOR PRINTING

Four-color printing should be used on covers but is normally too expensive for inside pages. For most color printing, the paper is run through the press four times, for each of the primary colors and black. Naturally, four-color printing is more expensive because of the additional camera work and press time. Even digital color—which is a different process—is still prohibitively expensive, except perhaps for a very short run of up to 10 sample books (say for children's books).

With very few exceptions, covers today must be four-color. We live in a color world. Our magazines, television and newspapers are in color. Buyers for both chain and independent bookstores are looking for books with good package design that will inspire a purchase.

Some publishers have found considerable savings on color processes outside the U.S. They have color separations made in Singapore, printing done in Hong Kong, etc. If you have a lot of inside color work for a children's book or coffee table book, get prices from the Far East. For more information on foreign color printing, see *Buying Book Printing* under Special Reports in Appendix 2 or at http://ParaPublishing.com.

> *Anyone who says you can't judge a book by its cover has never met the buyer from Barnes & Noble.*
>
> —*Terri Lonier*, **Working Solo**

PRINTING MATERIALS

PAPER choices can be confusing, and although you should know what to look for, you will need the guidance of your printer to make a final choice. Book printers typically stock

6 to 10 types of paper. They can provide these papers at a good price because they purchase them in huge quantities. If you want a paper they don't stock, they have to make a special small order and the cost will be considerably higher.

Basically, you have four general paper choices:

•❖ **Newsprint:** inexpensive, but it looks cheap, it yellows quickly and the photo reproduction is poor.

•❖ **Uncoated book stock:** looks good, photos OK. Most common.

•❖ **Coated book stock** (matte or gloss): looks great, photos great, more expensive.

•❖ **Fancy textured papers:** may be hard to print, especially photos. Expensive.

Unless you're doing an art book, an uncoated book stock is what you need. A printer would probably suggest a 50-pound or 60-pound "white offset book."

Paper comes by the sheet (for the sheet-fed press) or the roll (cut into sheets after printing on the web press). You must consider many criteria when selecting paper:

•❖ **Weight** is expressed in pounds per 500 sheets, but the measurements of the sheet vary according to the category to which the paper belongs. For example: 16-lb. bond office paper = 40-lb. book paper; 20-lb. bond (common photocopy paper) = 50-lb. book; 24-lb. bond = 60 lb. book; and 28-lb. bond = 70-lb. book. Cover stock is rated in point sizes, with 10-point (10/1000" thick—similar to the thickness of a business card) being very common. However, 12-point cover stock will provide a slightly more substantial cover. Dust jackets for hardbound books are usually 80- or 100-pound gloss enamel.

DELTA LITHOGRAPH COMPANY

TEXT PAPER COMPARATIVE COST FINDER

Many of our customers are interested in cost comparisons of the various weights and shades of text papers. The reasons for this are varied: weight savings, bulking, shade preferences and others. The cost trade-offs involved are often significant in reaching a decision. This Text Paper Comparative Cost Finder will help in these decisions.

The use of this chart is very easy. Using 50# Delta White offset book rolled stock as the base, or 100%, compare the other shades and stocking to calculate the comparative prices.

For example, if you have an estimate based on 10,000 copies of a book printed on 60# White sheets and want to calculate the approximate savings if printed on 50# White rolls, compare the 50# rolls listed below to the 60# sheets, or 100 vs. 130. Paper savings on the job would be 30%.

Text paper costs run between 28% and 50% of the total printing costs, depending on total pages in the book and the quantity of books produced. Therefore, in the example given, the overall cost savings would probably be about 15% (50% of 30%).

These figures cannot be used to calculate exact figures. They are only intended to give you a guide in figuring the comparative costs and specifications for your book.

STOCK	AVAILABLE IN	COMPARABLE PERCENT
50# Delta	Rolls	100
50# Delta	Sheets	112
60# Delta	Rolls	115
60# Delta	Sheets	130
45# Delta	Rolls	92
45# Delta	Sheets	105
70# Delta	Sheets	185
30# Omega Book	Rolls	78
35# Alpha Workbook	Rolls	65
50# Theta Natural Text	Rolls	115
50# Theta Natural Text	Sheets	130
50# Litecoat Beta Book	Rolls	110
60# Pica Matte	Sheets	215
60# Kappa Coated Book	Sheets	195

Paper comparison chart
(# = weight in pounds)

Most books are printed on 50-, 55- or 60-pound stock. Generally, heavier paper is more expensive, although some of the newer lightweight papers (developed to combat postal rates) are even higher in price. If the paper is too thin, the book will look and feel cheap; if it is too heavy, the pages may be too stiff as you turn them. In either case, you've wasted your money.

In the metric system used by overseas printers, the weighing technique is easier; paper is simply weighed in grams per square meter (gsm) of paper. There are no historic categories.

•• **Texture:** Some highly textured porous paper does not accept ink well; the ink diffuses into the paper. This spreading of the ink lowers the quality of halftones. Use a smooth paper such as 50-lb. white offset book.

•• **Color or shade:** Most informational books are printed on white stock. However, if you want a warm feeling for your fiction book, you might consider an off-white stock (called cream, antique or natural). Some of these papers are higher bulk and will add thickness to your book.

•• **Opacity:** You don't want the type on the other side of the page to show through. Lightweight paper can be very opaque, especially when coated. You can test opacity by placing a printed sheet under the sample sheet to see how much type shows through.

•• **Bulking factor** is expressed in pages per inch (ppi). A 45-pound paper may have a bulking factor of 640 pages per inch, while a 55-pound higher-bulk stock might be 370 ppi and a firm 60-pound stock might bulk at 444 ppi. Thus, heavier weight does not always mean thicker paper. Bulking depends on the fiber content of the paper and the milling process used. Whipping air into the paper during manufacture, which produces a thicker paper without increasing weight, can also produce a high bulk. However, this fluffed-up paper allows ink to diffuse more, so halftones are not as crisp. PPI is measured by the even inch. Once you know the bulking factor of the paper you plan to use, you can calculate the width of the spine for your finished cover.

FORMULA FOR DETERMINING SPINE WIDTHS

To determine the spine width, you must know the final page count and the pages per inch (PPI), or thickness, of the text stock being used. Paper is a fluctuating commodity constantly changing. PPIs used are averages for house brands currently used.

The formula for figuring your spine width is as follows:
Divide the page count by the PPI, and then add .03 (1/32 of an inch) to allow for the cover stock and the glue and air between the signatures.
Example: 176 (page count) ÷ 400 (PPI) = .44 + .03 = .47

You can use a ruler that measures in 100ths or use a ruler that measures in fractions and use a "Decimal Equivalents of Fractions Chart," which will convert the decimal reading from your calculator to fractions.

DECIMAL EQUIVALENTS OF FRACTIONS

1/32	.03125	17/32	.53125
1/6	.0625	9/16	.5625
3/32	.09375	19/32	.59375
1/8	**.125**	**5/8**	**.625**
5/32	.15625	21/32	.65625
3/16	.1875	11/16	.6875
7/32	.21875	23/32	.71875
1/4	**.25**	**3/4**	**.75**
9/32	.28125	25/32	.78125
5/16	.3125	13/16	.8125
11/32	.34375	27/32	.84375
3/8	**.375**	**7/8**	**.875**
13/32	.40625	29/32	.90625
7/16	.4375	15/13	.9375
15/32	.46875	31/32	.96875
1/2	**.5**	**1**	**1.0**

Courtesy of Central Plains Book Manufacturing

Spine width calculator

•● **Grain** in paper is similar to the grain in wood—it has a direction. Grain affects the way the text and cover lie. If the grain of the text is not parallel to the spine, the book will want to snap shut. Grain is also important if you plan to fold the paper for a foldout page, since it will fold cleaner with the grain. Printing presses are grain specific. The press used for 5.5" x 8.5" books should not be used for 8.5" x 11" books because the grain will be 90 degrees off.

If the cover grain is perpendicular to the spine, the cover will tend to pop up. Sometimes the cover will even crack on the spine folds. The challenge is that some automated book machinery trims the books cleaner when the grain is perpendicular to the spine than when it is parallel. But when the grain is parallel, the trimmer may make small tears in the cover stock where it folds around the spine of the book. With such machinery, the choice is between cover curl and cover tear. See the discussion of cover coatings and lay-flat laminate later in this chapter.

•● **Grade** refers to the type of paper, be it writing grade, book, cover stock, envelope, gummed, blotting, chipboard, etc.

•● **Coating** is done with a clay-like material and produces a smooth, shiny finish. On clay-coated stock, the ink dries on the clay surface, rather than down in the fibers of the paper, so the printed pages look crisper and cleaner. Coated stock, while more expensive, makes halftones look much better; it is essential for art books. Smooth finishes can also be produced by drawing the paper over a blade edge, or through calendering (a heat and pressure-roller process). The result will be a duller finish that is easier on the eyes.

•◆ **Acid-free paper** lasts longer and should be used for books of long-term interest. Sixty percent of the university presses (which sell primarily to libraries) and 21% of other publishers produce their hardcover books on acid-free paper. You may wish to specify *acid-free paper.*

•◆ **Recycled paper** is becoming increasingly popular, but the price is still higher than for new paper. The price is expected to drop as more publishers use it.

PURCHASING PAPER: If you attend one of the many publishing seminars, you may be advised to purchase your own paper and "save about 15%." This makes about as much sense as taking your own oil to the gas station when you want it changed. Printers aren't happy about losing their markup and sometimes charge you a handling fee if you bring your own paper. Or they may raise your price later, claiming the job was "hard to print."

If you buy your own paper, you will have to pay for it sooner, will be faced with storage and transportation charges and might lose it all if the printer botches a press run. It's far safer to obtain several quotations on the finished product and let the printer worry about the materials. After all, what you want is the least hassle and best price.

Incidentally, printers and paper salespeople continually use the same pressure tactic, claiming there will soon be a paper shortage. Expect it. For more information on paper, see the Special Report *Buying Book Printing* in Appendix 2 or at http://ParaPublishing.com and the book *Pocket Pal:*

A Graphic Arts Production Handbook by Michael Bruno, available on Amazon.com.

INK comes in a lot of colors and types, but both you and your printer will probably want black. If you're doing something special, ask to see the printer's ink color sample books and run some tests. Remember that inks are transparent. If you print a drawing in blue and then overprint part in red, that part will become purple. Similarly, if you print blue ink on yellow paper, the print will be green. Unless you are doing a special art-type book, you should stick to the traditional black ink on white paper. Using more than one color of ink inside your book can increase the printing cost considerably. The job has to be run through the press separately for each color, and there may be additional wash-up (press-cleaning) costs. One different color ink (such as navy blue or dark brown) will also require additional press-cleaning expenses.

HARDCOVER OR SOFTCOVER

Traditionally, publishers printed in *hardcover* at a higher price and waited until sales dropped to come out with a cheaper *softcover* version. They might also publish a *library edition* with a supposedly reinforced hard cover or maybe an extra-fancy *deluxe edition* on special paper with gold-stamped leather covers, with the books numbered and autographed. Then, finally, there would be the inexpensive *mass-market paperback* edition. Today, more and more books are being published in a softcover edition only. Softcover books are printed on the same quality paper as the hardcover version. The differences are that the softcover edition is not normally sewn, has a thinner cover and usually does not have a jacket. Today your choice of covers is usually narrowed to a hardcover or a softcover.

> *Catalog copy [is] designed for the people who will sell the book and the flap copy for those who will buy it.*
>
> **—Hugh Rawson**

HARDCOVER BOOKS are somewhat more expensive to produce and must carry a higher cover (list) price—libraries used to prefer them. Today, however, libraries know how many times books can be lent out (about 18 for softcover) before they fall apart. If the price difference between the two is too great, it becomes less expensive to purchase copies of the softcover edition and replace them more often.

Some people and a few reviewers still don't take soft-cover books seriously; they do not consider a title to be a real book unless it is published in hardcover. Some also assume a softcover book is not new and that the reviewer just missed the hardcover version.

It's usually less expensive to publish all the books in either hardcover or softcover than to split the run. Hardcover will cost about $1 more per book to print than softcover, and you can usually charge an extra $5 or more for the book. Give your customers what they expect. If this is a business book, they expect hardcover with a jacket. Most people still think hardcover books are fresher, newer and more important. If your major mission is to use your book as a "business card," an introduction to your consulting, speaking or other work, consider hardcover. Hardcovers do make a more impressive presentation than a softcover edition, which can be especially important if you're trying to impress a large corporation to hire you as a high-paid consultant.

COATING SOFTCOVER BOOKS: The covers of soft-cover books must be coated. Traditionally, the cover made another pass through the press filled with varnish instead of ink. Today, ultraviolet-set plastics and plastic laminates are more popular. The extra treatment on the cover protects it against scuffing during shipment and provides a shiny *glossy finish* or wet look. An alternative is the same plastic film with a duller *matte finish*. The slight additional cost is easily justified, because fewer books are returned scuffed.

The plastic laminate used to be polyester or polypropylene, which was moisture proof. Since humidity could not enter the plastic-coated (out) side, the cover would curl as the underside expanded. Now there is a *lay-flat laminate* made of nylon film that has very tiny holes for admitting humidity. Always specify lay-flat laminate.

THE BOOK COVER

The cover of your book has two purposes: (1) to protect the contents and (2) to sell the text. And book covers do sell books, just like packaging sells other products. In the U.S., companies spend over $50 billion on design and packaging. That huge sum is not for the products themselves or for the wrapper—but just for the *design* of the wrapper. Good packaging sells soap, breakfast food, computer games—*and books*. A good spine, front cover and title say, "Pick me up." Good back-cover sales copy says, "Buy this book."

> *A book cover should stop browsers cold in their tracks at 10 feet and suck them in like a magnet.*

According to *The Wall Street Journal*, the average bookstore browser who picks up a book spends four seconds looking at the front cover and 14 seconds reading the back. And this assumes the spine stood out enough to catch their attention, enticing them to pick up the book in the first place. Every word on the outside of your book must be used to sell what is inside. In mass-market (small-size, high-volume) fiction paperbacks, this hype consists of about 12 words on the front cover and 75 on the back. The blurbs use words such as "stunning," "dazzling," "moving" and "tumultuous."

STARTING WITH THE OUTSIDE

Alan Gadney commissioned covers for three computer books he planned to write. He had the covers printed in four colors and made into dummy books for display at the ABA Book Fair in Dallas. His books were the talk of the show and he took a number of large orders. Covers must be important—he had not yet written one word on the subject.

FRONT COVER: The front cover should include the title, subtitle (helps identify the subject), name of the author and a related photograph or drawing with impact. The print shouldn't be so fancy that it's hard to read at a glance. It is said that red attracts and sells best, and many cover designers like to use it. Visit a bookstore and check the section where your book will be shelved. Consider what colors are there and pick something contrasting and bright that will stand out. For an action sport, an eye-catching color photo will sell more books than straight lines of type.

Your front cover is the "sales poster" for your book. It must be bold, distinctive and intriguing enough to catch the eye and sell; it must stand out from the thousands of books around it. For later editions, a gold stick-on medallion with black-and-white type announcing that the book won an award has been known to boost sales exponentially. Other important new information, such as a quotation from a prestigious book review, can be printed on a later edition to interest book buyers.

The design and production of a good softbound book cover will cost about $1,800 for the complete mechanical (front, spine and back) ready for the printer. That may sound like a major portion of your book-production budget, but it's worth it, because book packaging affects the sale of the book. A good cover designer will read through the text to get the feeling of the manuscript into the cover. For a list of book cover designers, see Book Designers & Cover Artists in Appendix 2. Also see the Suppliers listing at http://ParaPublishing.com.

The cover outside should reflect the text inside.

SPINE: The spine usually has the title, the name of the author, and an eye-catching symbol. If this is a dog book, for instance, it might include the outline of a dog. The symbol may attract a buyer more readily than the printed word. Traditionally, the name of the publisher is included on the spine. If you're a new publisher and no one has heard of your company yet, you may not want to include this reference to your publishing firm.

Beware of too much spine clutter, such as trying to include a lengthy subtitle. Your book will probably end up on the bookstore shelf with only the spine showing. Make the spine an eye-grabber.

Stacking the title on the spine (see this book) will make it legible on the shelf from a distance.

BACK COVER layout is covered in Chapter 2. Many back covers have a photo and biographical sketch of the author. If you are a well-known person, put your photograph there; if you are not immediately recognizable, do not waste this valuable selling space with your picture. Instead, put your photograph inside in the back matter with your extended About the Author blurb. Sometimes the back cover is used to promote other books by the author, but I recommend that you only list relevant ones in a brief author sketch that shows your expertise. Use only words that will sell the book in that valuable back cover territory. Make every word count on the front cover, spine and back cover.

COVER OVERRUNS: Ask your printer to send you 200 extra covers (trimmed to proper size), plus the *overrun*, which will come off the print line before the covers are scored, folded and installed on the texts. These covers are beautiful and look very nice framed. You might like to send flat covers to those who provided you with a lot of help, such as the cover designer. Commissioned sales representatives carry covers to the bookstores and wholesalers rather than heavy books, so your book trade distributor and library distributor may each need 20 to 30 covers.

THE BINDING

Binding is your book packaging—the final touch. There are many binding choices; here are the most common types.

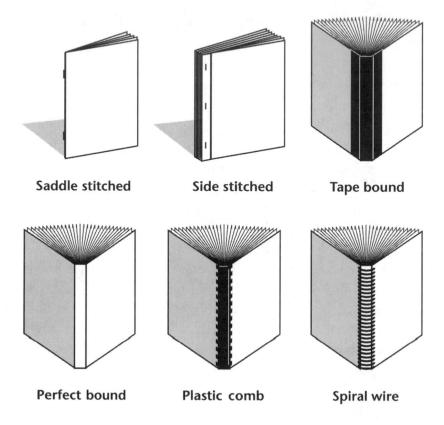

Saddle stitched   Side stitched   Tape bound

Perfect bound   Plastic comb   Spiral wire

•• **Perfect binding** is the standard glued-on cover you see on most softcover books. The pages are folded into signatures, often of 48 pages each, stacked and roughened on the edge, and then the cover is wrapped around and glued on the spine. The greatest advantage, besides cost, is that perfect binding presents a squared-off spine on which the book title and name of the author can be printed. A text of at least 50 pages is required for a square spine; you might have to use a high-bulk paper to achieve a sufficient thickness.

●◆ **Lay-flat binding:** If it's important that your perfect-bound book open to lie flat, such as with a cookbook or exercise manual, specify Otabind or a similar lay-flat binding. This system leaves the cover stock free of the spine as it goes around to the back of the book, so the book flexes better when opened and will easily lie flat. Multiple scoring is another way to help the perfect-bound book to open and lie flat. Lay-flat binding is much better than comb or spiral binding because the title of the book can be printed on the spine. Another benefit is that narrower gutter (inside) margins are possible with lay-flat, which means you can get more type on a page. Lay-flat, however, is not durable enough for thick books—those over 400 pages. Get and test samples from your printer.

●◆ **Cloth binding** (case binding or hard binding) usually consists of *Smyth sewing*, or *side stitching*, individual signatures together. Then they are installed (and glued) between two hard paperboards. Some hardcover books today are manufactured with just an adhesive rather than sewing and hold up quite well. A glue-only hard binding (called *perfect bound case bound*) can also have the glued area of the spine scored with notches (*notch-binding*) so that the glue can run down into the notches for more glue coverage and strength.

●◆ **Wire stitches** are staples and can be used in binding thin paperback booklets. Wire stitches can be *saddle stitched* (the staple is on the fold) or *side stitched* (the staple is driven through from front to back cover). Saddle stitching will handle 80 pages (20 full sheets) or fewer, depending on the thickness of the stock, because of the amount of paper "lost" in wrapping around the spine. On the other hand, side stitching can be used to bind even several hundred pages. Side-stitched books won't open to lie flat, so this method shouldn't be used in manuals. The stitches come from a roll of wire and are adjustable in length. Wire-stitched booklets do not have a spine for printing the title and they have a low perceived value, so I do not recommend this method.

•• **Spiral wire binding** will allow books (such as automotive manuals and cookbooks) to open and lie flat, but spiral looks cheap. Spiral-bound books rarely sell well in bookstores because the spine cannot be printed with the title, and libraries don't care for them because the pages are easy to remove. It's possible to spiral bind pages inside a heavy cover stock that wraps over the spiral (called *concealed spiral binding*) so that the spine can be printed. Some computer manuals are bound this way. But spiral still costs more. A better alternative is lay-flat binding (see above).

•• **Plastic comb binding** allows the book to open and lie flat and is often used for mail-order books directed at professionals, short-run academic texts and industry manuals. This system may be used on books up to 1.5 inches thick. Comb binding is relatively expensive, and the plastic spine can be imprinted. However, it still looks cheap, the pages tear out and comb-bound books don't stack well, making shipping a chore. Again, a better alternative is lay-flat binding.

•• **Velo-Bind** is similar to side wire stitches but uses melted plastic rivets. This method is very strong and can be used to install either special Velo-Bind hardcovers or soft document covers. The books will not lie flat when opened.

•◦ **Notebooks or binders** are sometimes used for very expensive manuals directed toward professionals, especially as a mail-order product. They have the usual advantages of a binder—pages can be removed and added, for instance. However, the binders are expensive, hard to ship and their pages tear out easily. It's better to choose between hardcover and softcover.

PRINTING BOOKS

YOUR CHOICES FOR PRINTED BOOKS (pBooks): Putting a lot of ink on paper with a large print run is now just an option, and it's a good one if there is large prepublication demand such as advanced sales to bookstores and/or a sale to a book club. Today, with digital (toner) printing, there is no longer a requirement to print 3,000 or more copies of your book "on spec." Here are your choices.

A. Print-On-Demand (POD) Publishers

 Print-on-demand is a way of doing business, not a method of printing. POD means receiving an order (and payment), manufacturing the book and then delivering the book. Most POD books are produced with digital printing, but they could be produced with other methods.

Hundreds of years ago, those monks in the abbeys were POD publishers. They received an order, manufactured one book and delivered it. The only difference from today's POD publishers was that the monks hand-lettered the pages.

POD publishers supply some extra services for their relatively low price. They may take care of the cover, editing, ISBN, Library of Congress number, etc. However, the cover may be pedestrian, the editing may be minimal or absent and the customer service may be close to nonexistent. You get what you pay for.

Most POD publishers sell more books to their authors than to the public. If you take the number of books published and divide by the number of titles, you will find that fewer than 100 books for each title are sold.

Deal with a POD publisher when you need just a few copies of a book. For example, if you have written a family history, have a very limited budget and need up to 30 copies for your relatives, the deal offered by most POD publishers is hard to beat.

The cost per copy may be $5 to $10 depending upon the number of pages and the trim size. POD publishers offer an economical service when you want only one to 50 copies of the book.

POD publishers are relatively new, so their businesses are evolving. See their Web sites for information on how they conduct business. For example, some require an exclusive right to use your material and some will not put your ISBN on the back cover.

See the list of POD publishers in Appendix 2.

B. Print-On-Demand (POD) Printers

POD printers, like all printers, are in the book manufacturing business and don't invest in the product.

The cost may be $5 to $10 per book copy depending upon the number of pages and the trim size.

A POD printer is a good option when a book has run its course, your inventory is exhausted and you still receive orders for a couple of copies a month. Rather than invest in inventory, you can have books made one at a time as needed. And you don't lose money on an additional print run.

Some of our books are produced by LightningSource, a POD printer. See *Writing Nonfiction* in LARGE PRINT at http://www.amazon.com/exec/obidos/tg/detail/-/1568601166/ref=lpr_g_ and http://www.amazon.com/exec/obidos/tg/detail/-/1568601158/.

The Large Print Edition is being produced one at a time on-demand for Amazon orders. But the edition is being promoted by sending the regular-print version to writing and publishing magazines, etc. There's no need to send them the Large Print Edition.

POD printers offer an economical service when you only need one copy of the book. POD printers don't own an exclusive on your book or supply the ISBN; they just supply a printing service. The best known are LightningSource (LSI), a division of Ingram (the largest wholesaler), and Replica Books, part of Baker & Taylor.

See the list of POD printers in Appendix 2.

C. Digital Printers—Print Quantity Needed (PQN)

The digital process is cost-effective for quantities from 100 to 2,500 copies. It uses laser printing with toner.

THE QUALITY of the toner-based printing is very good. There are no light and dark pages as in ink-on-paper printing. The softcover or hardcover books look just like traditional books. Excellent, crisp color covers are usually done with the same toner process.

AUTHORS may send printed copies to agents and publishers. If an agent or publisher responds, you can entertain the offer. If not, no matter, the book is launched and you're on your way. If you send a finished book to agents and publishers, they will treat you like an author. If you send a manuscript, you will be treated like a writer.

PUBLISHERS may send copies of the book to major reviewers, distributors, catalogs, specialty stores, associations, book clubs, premium prospects, foreign publishers suggesting translations and various opinion-molders. After two to three months, you will go back to press for more books. At that point, you will be able to make *an educated decision* on the print run based on the sales rate of the book. Therefore, PQN digital printing is a great way to start the publishing of a book.

HARDCOVER: Most books are manufactured with soft covers, called perfect binding. In *offset* (ink) printing, hard or "case" binding runs about $1 extra per book. That includes the hard covers and the dust jackets. However, for *PQN/digital production*, the cost for case binding is $2 to $4 each, depending on the page count (thickness) of the book. Case binding requires a lot of setup time. Therefore, it rarely pays to put hard covers on a short run of books.

TIME: Delivery for PQN digitally printed books is normally five days from press proofs, and reprints take three to four days. With your disk on file, reprints can be initiated with an email message, and the books may be shipped directly to your buyer. The press proof is usually a single softcover book printed on the same paper stock you propose for the finished book.

THE SIGNATURES of a digitally printed book are just two pages because the print engines print cut sheets, two pages (both sides) at a time instead of 32 or 48. Now you don't have to design your book's page count in large signature increments.

MASS CUSTOMIZATION: Since the print engines are computer-driven and your books can be printed two pages at a time, you may customize your book for your customer. If you make a premium sale to a company, it will cost just pennies to bind in a letter from the CEO or to add the company logo to the cover. You can send the insert or logo to your printer as an email attachment to save time and money.

Digital printers offer an economical service when you want a small inventory of books.

See the list of digital printers in Appendix 2.

D. Offset Printers

Deal with an offset printer when you need 2,500 books or more. This process uses ink printing with plates.

For offset printing, the cost is around $1.25 per copy for 3,000 books (this is for a softcover [perfect-bound] 144-page 5.375" x 8.375" book with black text and a four-color cover). Offset printers offer an economical service when you want a larger inventory of books.

See the list of offset printers in Appendix 2.

HOW MANY BOOKS TO PRINT?

You must consider both your purpose for writing the book and how many you can expect to sell. Do you want just a few books for family and friends? Will it be a high-priced, mail-order book with a small target audience? Or will it be a popular book, with a wide audience, that should sell well in bookstores? How many books will be used for review copies, gifts and other freebies? Make a list.

INITIAL PRESS RUNS should normally be limited to no more than the number of books you can reasonably estimate will be sold in the first year. Unless you have a substantial number of prepublication sales (such as to a book club or large corporation), it's a good idea to limit the first printing even further to 500 books. No matter how diligently you proofread, some errors will not surface until they appear in ink. Also, once you see the book in its final state, you will wish you had done some things differently—especially on a first book. By printing a smaller number, you can use several weeks to catch your errors and make some design changes before a larger print run.

So set the first press run conservatively. It's better to sell out and have to go back to press quickly than to find yourself with a garage full of unsold books. You'll be spending a lot of money on promotion, so it's best to hedge your bets by tying up less money in the book—even though you have to pay a premium in printing costs to do so.

PRINTING & ECONOMY OF SCALE: *Printing is a quantity game: the more you print, the lower the per-unit cost.* You've probably heard this statement before. But with printing, economy of scale is only true up to a point, since the price differences become smaller and smaller as the press runs increase. Each run of the next thousand books does become cheaper. Then the price breaks fail to maintain significance after about 9,000 copies. Normally, between 9,000 and 10,000 copies you save so little that printing more isn't worth the storage space or the price of borrowing money. Therefore, you don't want to print more than 9,000 unless you have some books presold and are certain that number will move out within the year.

Depending on the size of the book, number of pages and so on, you could receive comparative printing/binding quotes such as these (using the appropriate method for the size of each print run).

No. of copies:	500	1,000	3,000	5,000	7,000	9,000	10,000
Total cost:	$1,625	2,750	5,400	7,000	7,700	8,100	8,500
Unit cost:	$3.25	2.75	1.80	1.40	1.10	.90	.85

In general, it's to your advantage to order as many books as you can sell in order to get the best unit price. And you want the best price, as long as you are fairly sure you can sell the higher number.

Remember that printers make money on printing. Don't let them talk you into more books than you need. There is some economy in scale, but there are no savings in paying for books you can't turn into cash. Consider the total printing bill as well.

PRINT RUNS ARE NEVER EXACT: Usually a print run is prepped for a certain number of signatures and a cover. The printers always run a few extra pages, expecting some to be spoiled. When all the sheets are gathered, there are some that must be thrown away. Accordingly, it's customary in the trade to have overruns and underruns, and your bill may be adjusted higher or lower—up to 10%. A print run of 3,000 will wind up anywhere between 2,700 and 3,300.

ESTIMATING SALES

Projecting sales that first year will be difficult with your initial book, because you won't have personal sales experience in its category. Still, you may be able to find out how similar books have done by calling their publishers.

Or for *comparative* sales figures, call Ingram's automated stock sales system at 615-213-6803. Just punch in the ISBNs (found on the back covers) to check the rate of sale for the various books you've located on your subject. The automated voice will tell you how many books are stocked in each of the Ingram warehouses, how many copies Ingram sold last year and how many they have sold so far this year. These numbers are not total sales figures; however, since Ingram handles more than half of the books in the U.S., the figures will give you an idea of the rate of sale of that category of book and are good for comparison.

Also, log on to an online store such as Amazon.com. Search for your category of book and chart the books that are close to your project.

Amazon provides the sales ranks, and they also tell you how the books are selling against each other. Write down the numbers. For historical Amazon sales data, go to http://www.titlez.com/welcome.aspx.

In addition, get a copy of *Financial Feasibility in Book Publishing* by Robert Follet. It contains guidelines, worksheets and rules of thumb for estimating sales. Find it listed by title under Para Publishing Special Reports in Appendix 2 or order it from http://ParaPublishing.com.

Do some market research. How many associations, magazines and conventions are there participating in this activity? How many people care about this subject?

With proper promotion, any reasonably good nonfiction book, aimed at all but the tiniest markets, should sell 2,500 copies in its first year (plus require up to 500 promotional copies).

REPRINTS

Reprints should be well timed. If you order a reprint too early, you may tie up more money before the first run is paid for, and many of those books from the earlier run could be sitting on the shelves in the stores—unsold. It's a good idea to make some telephone calls to assess dealer inventories. On the other hand, if you wait too long to reprint, you run the risk of being out of stock and losing the all-important sales momentum the book is enjoying. Reprints from offset printers take two to five weeks. Coordinate with your printer so you can get a fast reprint if necessary. It's much better to be out of books for a few weeks than to have the truck arrive with 5,000 more as bookstores are returning copies.

REVISION VS. REPRINT: A "reprint" means there are no changes; a "revision" means you have made updating content corrections. As the publisher, you decide how many changes are necessary for the book to qualify as a revision. Books may be "revised" or "completely revised."

Always include a new ISBN when you publish a revision so the book industry will treat the book as new. Your distributor will put it back in the front of the catalog ("front list") as a new book. The book trade is new-product driven. Make a legitimate revision, assign a new ISBN and bar code and keep your book *new*.

SIZE OF INVENTORY

The demand for some books continues on and on; others have a definite life. The trick is to know when the sales cycle is over. It's nice to run out of stock just before the demand curve ends in a cliff. Watch your sales and don't reorder until the last minute.

PRINT-ON-DEMAND (POD): If your sales are down to three or four per month, you don't want to invest the money and inventory space in 3,000 copies. With POD, you can print one book at a time, but the cost per unit is much higher.

THE BEST AND SAFEST ANSWER in this situation is to print a small quantity of books. You're more likely to hear a publisher complain he or she printed too many books rather than too few. See http://parapub.com/sites/para/resources/newbook.cfm. And listen at http://www.jackstreet.com/jackstreet/RR.Newbookmodel.cfm. (Wait for the sound to load.)

RUN THE NUMBERS/DO THE MATH: Select the method of printing that best fits your situation. Remember that publishing involves printing, and printing is to a large degree a quantity game. The more you print, the lower the per-unit cost.

SELECTING A BOOK PRINTER

Each printer is set up differently. Some specialize in case binding (hardcover), and some in perfect binding (softcover). Some are equipped for very short runs (under 500), short runs (3,000 to 5,000), long runs (100,000) and on up. Any item in your specifications varying from their system will drive up their costs and your quotation. When they have to take a book off the assembly line to shift it to the other side of the factory or send it out to a binder, costs go up.

As a publisher, you don't have to learn printer capabilities and printing equipment. Just send out a Request for Quotation (RFQ) describing your book to the book printers listed in Appendix 2. Then accept the lowest bid. If your next book has similar specifications, you will probably deal with the same printer. Once you establish a relationship with the printer, your costs will probably go down further because you will require less hand-holding, and the printer may extend you complete credit. But also send out RFQs to other printers from time to time to make sure your printer is still giving you a good price.

Beware of "job printers" soliciting book printing. Many printers are looking for new territory and are attracted to books—a big-ticket item.

For the best quality, lowest price and on-time service, stick with printers who print nothing but books. How can you tell? Just ask what they print. For lists of book printers, see Appendix 2.

REQUEST FOR QUOTATION (RFQ): To calculate book production costs, send an RFQ to all the book digital and/or offset printers. See examples in the following RFQs.

Request for Quotation—Digital Printing

Please quote your best price and delivery in printing and binding the following book:

Identification

Title of book:
Author:

Specifications

Quantity:	500
Number of pages	
including front matter:	144
Trim size:	5.5 x 8.5 - Full
Method of printing:	Digital
Copy:	Customer to provide PDF file
Illustrations:	7 JPG images, no bleeds
Cover:	Print sides 1 and 4 only.
	Customer to supply file.

Paper

Text: 60# white offset book. Printed Right Grain.
Cover: 10 pt. C1S with lay-flat film lamination

Ink/toner

Text: Black throughout
Cover: Four colors

Binding: Perfect

Proofs: Yes

Packaging: Shrink-wrapped in stacks of six. Cartons shall be tightly packed and sealed and shall weigh no more than 40 lbs. each.

Terms: Net 30 days. Credit references available on request.

Your Quote

Price for 500: $

Price for 1,000: $

Delivery charges: $

Discount for prompt payment:

Delivery time:

Other miscellaneous charges:

Remarks:

Signed: _____

For: _____

Date: _____

Quote valid for: _____

Are there any minor specification changes that will result in a lower price? Please explain.

Any item in this RFQ takes precedence over any industry convention.

Request for Quotation—Offset Printing

Please quote your best price and delivery in printing and binding the following book:

Identification

Title of book:
Author:

Specifications

Quantity:	3,000 and 5,000
Number of pages	
including front matter:	144
Trim size:	5.5 x 8.5 - Full
Method of printing:	Offset web press

Copy: Customer to provide PDF file
Illustrations: 7 JPG images, no bleeds
Cover: Print sides 1 and 4 only.
                         Customer to supply file.

Paper

Text: 60# white offset book. Printed Right Grain.
Cover: 10 pt. C1S with lay-flat film lamination

Ink

Text: Black throughout

Cover: Four colors

Binding: Perfect

Proofs: Yes

Packaging: Shrink-wrapped in stacks of six. Cartons shall be tightly packed and sealed and shall weigh no more than 40 lbs. each.

Terms: Net 30 days. Credit references available on request.

Your Quote

Price for 3,000: $
   Overruns: $
   Reprint of 3,000: $

Price for 5,000: $
   Overruns: $
   Reprint of 5,000: $

Delivery charges: $

Discount for prompt payment:

Delivery time:

Other miscellaneous charges:

Remarks:

Signed: _____

For: _____

Date: _____

Quote valid for: _____

Are there any minor specification changes that will result in a lower price? Please explain.

Any item in this RFQ takes precedence over any industry convention.

Sample Requests for Quotation

Hardcover and dust jacket: If you want a hardcover book, 3,000 is a practical minimum because of the time required to set up the case-binding machinery. Alter the RFQ for offset to something similar to:

Binding: Case plus dust jacket. Three-piece cover consisting of four-colored marbleized paper front and back (approx 4.375" wide) and cloth along spine. One-hit imitation gold foil stamping of the title on spine. Customer to furnish file. Printer to furnish dies. 80# colored end sheets. Adhesive, notch bound. .085 pasted boards. Round back and headbands to match.

Jacket: 80# enamel with 3.5" flaps and lay-flat film lamination. Printer to wrap dust jackets.

Simply make up an RFQ similar to one of the examples and send it to all the printers on the list. See Appendix 2 for their email addresses. Send the email to yourself and type all the printers' addresses into the bcc box in your email program.

Don't send your RFQ to just a few printers; the inquiry will not result in enough comparative data. The only way you will know you're getting the best price is if you get quotations from all the listed printers. Don't worry about their reception of an emailed RFQ; printers are used to making competitive quotes.

When the RFQs are returned to you, spread them out for comparison and interpretation. Examine any items that you didn't request, and add up all the miscellaneous prices. Some printers will follow your RFQ, but others will use their own form. Make sure the quotes are "FOB destination"—that is, that trucking to you is figured in. You may find that the distant printers quote much lower prices even with the trucking costs. Asking for estimates for both printing and trucking levels the quotation playing field. Compare the *delivered* prices.

Also send the RFQ to a couple of local print shops for comparison. Don't be concerned about hurting the feelings of your local printers. If their bids are not the lowest, show them the other bids. This is your excuse for not giving them the work. They'll be interested in what the competition is quoting and will appreciate your openness.

SHRINK-WRAPPING: Have the printer shrink-wrap your books in stacks of two or more to a maximum depth of 5"; the cost is about 20¢ per shrink. Shrink-wrapping will protect your book by providing a moisture/dust barrier and will also prevent scuffing. However, if you shrink-wrap the books individually, the stores usually will not break the wrap. Then the customer can't look inside, and that usually results in a lost sale. If you wrap the books in larger increments, you may have to break the wrap for small orders.

PROOF COPIES: Always insist on proofs prior to printing. This is your last chance to check the printer's work prior to the book going on the press. Proofs used to be called "bluelines"; today, they are one-off laser copies of the book with a perfect-bound blank cover.

At the "bluelines" stage, you're checking that all pages are straight and in sequential order, photos and graphs are placed and reproduced correctly and there are no dirt spots or negative scratches on the pages. You should not start extensively editing or rewriting (AA or Author Alteration) your book at bluelines as the printer will charge you for each page you replace that is not a printer mistake (PE or Printer Error).

GET IT IN WRITING: Get *everything* in writing. You're new to publishing, and what *you assume* may not be the same as what your *printer assumes*. Good faith, trust and friendship are fine until the books arrive. Many printers do not read or retain written documents. Cover yourself. Never rely on oral directions.

Ask for samples and show the printer what you like, what you expect. Get estimates explaining exactly what each part of the job will cost. Then if you have two more pages than you planned or want to make minor author–alterations, you and the printer will arrive at the same added figure. Submit detailed printing instructions along with your page and cover files.

Make sure your RFQ includes a clause that states, "Any item in this RFQ takes precedence over any industry convention." You aren't familiar with the printing industry and aren't interested in how business is normally done. You simply want an attractive book and you want to know what it will cost.

KEEP YOUR ARTWORK: Put all the artwork, photos, drawings, etc., into a large envelope. If you need them again (and you do hope for many happy reprintings), you don't want to have to regenerate lost material. You want to be able to find them easily if you contract for a translation or other foreign edition. Keep the disks of all promotional material, such as brochures and order forms.

The art and disk for the book are the publisher's property. Many *job printers* will tell you that the large, thin metal printing plates and even your disk belong to them, because they are the product of the printer's craftsmanship. Printers who argue this point simply want to ensure that you return to them for reprints, whereas in fact the plates are difficult to store and printers usually throw them out.

Fortunately, most *book printers* do not want to keep your flats and will even charge you for storage if they have not been reused or returned within three years.

WHEN THE BOOKS ARRIVE from the printer, count the cartons. Books sometimes disappear in transit. Compare the carton count with the number on the bill of lading. Your cartons should be shipped together to each destination, or, if a large quantity, the boxes should be strapped on wooden pallets and covered with plastic sheeting.

Open random cartons and check for damage. If the books were loose in the carton, the top ones will be scuffed. You may also find your extra covers that were inadvertently packed in a book box.

For more information on printing, see Document 603, *Book Printing at the Best Price* and/or the Special Report *Book Printing* at http://ParaPublishing.com.

OTHER EDITIONS

To serve those people who cannot read your printed book due to disability or lifestyle, you'll produce additional formats. This is wringing more value out of your Work.

LARGE PRINT BOOKS (lpBooks) appeal to the visually impaired and the reading challenged. Once your type is set for a 5.5" x 8.5" book and converted to a PDF file, you will reset the Adobe Acrobat settings to produce a PDF file conforming to 8.5" x 11".

Rather than inventory a large stock, you may send the file to a POD printer who will post the description with Amazon.com and other online booksellers. Books will be manufactured only after being ordered and paid for. Your up-front costs will be minimal.

The Self-Publishing Manual and *Writing Nonfiction* are available in large print from Amazon.com and other online booksellers.

See Document 642, *Large Print Books*, at http://parapub.com/sites/para/resources/allproducts.cfm.

ELECTRONIC BOOKS (eBooks) appeal to travelers who don't have room in their luggage for printed books.

The electronic edition of your book can have even more features and benefits than the print version; it may have color, sound, video and hyperlinks. Your e-edition will take up less shelf space, be even less expensive to produce and will provide a richer experience to your reader.

You'll send your Word (DOC) file for conversion into the four basic eBook formats: LIT (for Microsoft Reader), PDF, MobiPocket (popular in Europe) and Palm. Palm is the largest reseller of eBooks.

Then you'll send the files to LightningSource, Inc. (a division of Ingram, the largest book wholesaler) and your eBook will be offered for sale from Amazon.com and more than a dozen eBook retailers.

The Self-Publishing Manual, Writing Nonfiction and *Successful Nonfiction* are available for electronic download from Amazon.com and other online booksellers. Now you can have a fully searchable edition of these best-sellers. Visit the sites and see how eBooks are sold.

See Document 615, *Electronic Books,* at http://parapub.com/sites/para/resources/allproducts.cfm.

AUDIOBOOKS (aBooks) appeal to people behind the steering wheel—long-haul truckers, sales reps and commuters. Audio allows people to get where they have to go and consume your book at the same time.

> *Spoken-word audio turns your car into a university.*
> **—Judith Kaye Sinclair**

Once your book is printed, it becomes a script for your audiobook. You may read it aloud yourself or hire a voice talent.

Writing Nonfiction is available in audio from Amazon.com and other online booksellers.

See Document 635, *AudioBooks: Turning Books &
Speeches into Spoken-Word Tape & Disc Products* at http://
parapub.com/sites/para/resources/allproducts.cfm.

*Be accurate with facts. You will be repeated. When you
write a book, you are committing history.*

Para Publishing is a unique book business. It doesn't operate like a big traditional publisher, and it doesn't lose money. Here are some tips for making your publishing firm successful:

• Publish your own material. Don't waste your time on, or split the money with, other authors.

• Perform every publishing and business function yourself. After your first book, farm out those tasks you do not wish to perform.

• Operate as a sole proprietorship, not a corporation, and keep your books on a (modified) cash basis.

• Don't mimic the large traditional New York publishers. Many are not making a sufficient return on their investment. Some of their procedures exist for a good reason, while others are just convention (also known as a rut). The trick is to know the difference.

• If you cannot find a need and fill it, then create a need and fill it. Decide on your market before you write the book, and write to that market.

• Market your books like breakfast food—not like a film. Nonfiction is not one-shot entertainment; go after a market share and keep selling that book year after year.

• You'll have to spend more time selling than you will writing. Concentrate on marketing rather than editorial functions.

• Produce valuable information, aimed at a small target audience, and charge a fair price.

• Stay in a single field and produce more information for it.

A book should not be just something to read, it should be something to possess.

—Lee Collins

5

ANNOUNCING YOUR BOOK

TELLING THE BOOK WORLD
YOU'RE A PUBLISHER AND AN AUTHOR

B efore you run off to promote your book to potential readers, you should announce it to the book industry and register it with government offices. Make your book and your company easy to find. Some of these announcements must be made before you go to press. For a clear understanding of when each of the following should be done, see Appendix 1, "Your Book's Calendar."

As you use this chapter, remember that if the people at some registration offices and directories reject your application, you shouldn't give up. Try to figure a way around their objection and file a new form. It's very doubtful that they will remember rejecting your initial application.

Since these people may not have a lot of confidence in publishers with a single title (who may never publish again), it's best to represent yourself as being larger. After all, this will not be your only book. Use different names when you refer to your company, publisher and author, rather than repeating the same name in each. Talking about

Sam Horn Publishing, Sam Horn the publisher and a book by Sam Horn is a sure tip-off that you're a small and new publisher.

Names and phone numbers change as people and offices move. For a free, current list of contacts see Document 112, *Poynter's Secret List*, at http://parapublishing.com/sites/para/resources/allproducts.cfm.

INTERNATIONAL STANDARD BOOK NUMBER (ISBN)

The ISBN is a worldwide identification system that has been in use since the late sixties. There is a different ISBN for each edition and each binding of every book so the number's use avoids errors in identifying the books ordered, shipped, received, etc.

You may purchase ISBN blocks of 10, 100, 1,000 and so on. Since you'll be publishing in print, audio, eBook format, etc., a block of 10 won't last very long. The charge for blocks of ISBNs varies depending on how many numbers you want. For the latest information and prices, see http://www.bowker.com/ and/or http://www.ISBN.org. Once you get your ISBN block, you'll assign an ISBN to each edition of each book you publish.

You don't have to start at the beginning of the numbers. If you use the first number on the logbook sheet, the "0" at the end of the string will tip off those in the industry that this is a first book.

ISBN changes: There was a need to increase the number of ISBNs available around the world. So starting on January 1, 2007, new ISBN numbers were assigned that are 13 digits long to replace the 10-digit numbers previously in use. As of January 1, 2007, the numbers issued by all ISBN agencies now have the new 13-digit structure; but as blocks of ISBN-13s built on existing ISBN-10s are exhausted, new blocks will be prefixed with 979 instead of the current 978. See http://www.isbn-13.info/index.html and http://www.bisg.org/docs/BISG_Special_Session_09-23-04.pdf.

BAR CODES

The bar code on a book identifies the ISBN, which in turn identifies the publisher, title, author and edition (hardcover, etc.). The wholesalers, chains and other bookstores will not accept your book or audiobook without a bar code. If your book arrives at a wholesaler without a bar code, they will sticker one on and charge you for it. Further, since most books have bar codes, your book will look odd in the marketplace without one, and will not be taken seriously.

The bar code you want is the "Bookland EAN/13 with add on,"** and it should be printed on the lower half of "cover 4" (the back cover) on hardcover and softcover books.

**The Bookland EAN bar code
with price extension for bookstores**

The **UPC bar code** is used on smaller mass-market paperbacks (usually sold in drugstores and grocery stores) and other forms of merchandise. The cost of the UPC bar code starts at $300. See http://www.gs1us.org/gs1us.html. However, it's very unlikely you will need a UPC bar code.

See *Machine-Readable Coding Guidelines for the U.S. Book Industry* from The Book Industry Study Group, http://www.bisg.org/isbn-13/barcoding.html.

Bar code/ISBN files cost $10 to $30. For a current list of bar code suppliers, see http://parapublishing.com/sites/para/resources/allproducts.cfm.

Assign an ISBN to your book, order a bar code file and give the file to your cover artist for incorporation into your back-cover design. If the book is already printed, order bar codes on self-adhesive labels.

OTHER IMPORTANT FILINGS

Standard Address Number (SAN): The SAN identifies each separate address of every firm in the book publishing industry—from publishers, to wholesalers, to libraries, to bookstores. SANs sort out the billing and shipping addresses and help to determine which "Book Nook" will receive an order.

Since you probably have just one address for editorial, shipping and returns, and because Bowker is now charging for SANs, you can forget about this number. See http://www.bowkerlink.com if you want more info.

Advance Book Information (ABI) is another Bowker service. By adding your new titles to the database, your book will be listed in *Books in Print* and several other specialized directories. *Books in Print* is published in October of each year and is a most important directory.

See http://www.bowkerlink.com/corrections/Common/ LearnMore.asp#vautitles.

Use BowkerLink.com to submit forthcoming title information to *Books in Print* 180 days before publication and inform them of updates as soon as they occur. Once enrolled in the ISBN system, you can go online and update or change your listings.

Library of Congress Control Numbers (LCCN or PCN): The LCCN or Library of Congress Control Number is known as the PCN or Preassigned Control Number when it is assigned prior to publication of a book. The PCN appears on the copyright page of each book, and it is also included in lists and reviews appearing in the leading journals of the book trade. The PCN differs from the ISBN in that one ISBN is assigned to each different *edition* of a work (hardcover, softcover, etc.); the PCN number is assigned to the work itself, no matter how many different editions of the books are printed or bound. Use of the number enables subscribers to the Library of Congress's Catalog Card Service to order bibliographic data by number and thus eliminate the searching fee. PCN numbers have been important for selling to libraries. The PCN must be requested prior to the publication of the book so that the number may be printed on the copyright page.

Control numbers are preassigned only to books that the Library of Congress assumes will be added to library collections or for which they anticipate substantial demand for PCN bibliographic data. The types of material that the Library collects only in a very limited way and for which PCN numbers are generally not available include: calendars, laboratory manuals, booklets of fewer than 50 pages, brochures, advertisements, bank publications designed for customers, blueprints, certain kinds of light fiction, privately printed books of poems, religious materials for students in Bible schools, catechisms, instructions in devotions, individual sermons and prayers, question-and-answer books, most elementary and secondary school textbooks, tests except for standard examinations, teachers' manuals, correspondence school lessons, translations from English into foreign languages, picture books, comic strip and coloring books, diaries, log and appointment books, prospectuses and preliminary editions, workbooks and vanity press publications. Since the people at the Library of Congress sometimes confuse self-publishing with vanity publishing, it is best to fill out the forms using different names for the author, the publisher, etc.

New publishers should contact the Copyright Office via http://www.LOC.gov or http://www.Copyright.gov.

You must complete the Application to Participate and obtain an account number and password. Then you can apply for a PCN. The Library of Congress will send you your number. See http://pcn.loc.gov/pcn/pcn007.html and http://ecip.loc.gov/pls/ecip/pub_signon?system=pcn.

The first two digits of the PCN do not indicate the year of publication, but the year in which the card number is preassigned. If you register after January 1, your book will appear to be a year newer.

The PCN Office must be advised of all subsequent changes in titles, authors, etc., and cancellations. This notification is important as it prevents duplication of numbers. A new number is not necessary when changes are made. Changes will not be acknowledged unless requested by the publisher.

There's no charge for the preassignment of a card number. An advance complimentary copy of each publication must be sent to the CIP Office, Library of Congress, Washington, DC 20540. This copy is used for final cataloging before the book is released. The CIP Office provides postage-free mailing labels for use in sending these advance publications.

Cataloging in Publication (CIP) is a separate Library of Congress service that supplies additional cataloging numbers that may be printed on the copyright page of the book. These numbers help libraries to shelve your book in the correct category. Having the data block also makes the smaller and newer publisher appear to be established. During 1990 and 1996, the CIP office ran out of funds and stopped accepting new publishers into the program for several months. This may happen again.

---

❶ Library of Congress Cataloging-in-Publication Data
❷ Poynter, Dan.
❸ Dan Poynter's self-publishing manual : how to write, print, and sell your own book / by Dan Poynter. -- 15th ed., completely rev.
   p. cm.
   Rev. ed. of: Self-publishing manual. c2003.
   Includes bibliographical references and index.
❹ ISBN-13: 978-1-56860-134-2 (trade pbk. : alk. paper)
❺ 1. Self-publishing--United States. I. Poynter, Dan. Self-publishing manual. II. Title. III. Title: Self-publishing manual.
❻ Z285.5.P69 2006
   070.5'93--dc22

   2006010649

Typical CIP data block

Once you have published three books, you're eligible to participate in the CIP program and receive library-cataloging data for printing on your copyright page. The Cataloging in Publication Office supplies postpaid mailing labels once you have been admitted to the CIP program. See http://www.loc.gov; http://cip.loc.gov/cip/.

Publisher's Cataloging in Publication (PCIP): Now Quality Books, the library supplier, is filling in for the Library of Congress with *Publisher's Cataloging in Publication* (PCIP) data blocks. A staff librarian will catalog your forthcoming title and will send you a data block ready to be inserted into your copyright page.

Contact Quality Books for an application: http://www. Quality-Books.com.

The Copyright Office is operationally separate from the CIP Office. But the CIP and LCCN/PCN offices are the same. Control numbers (PCNs) may be applied for per the above or when applying for Cataloging in Publication Data.

A Copyright may be registered before your manuscript is published, but most publishers wait for books to come off the press. Your work is automatically *copyright protected* under Common Law because you created it; it just isn't *copyright registered* yet.

To register your copyright, follow these three steps:

1. **Print the copyright notice on the copyright page.** The notice takes the following form: "© 2006 by Dan Poynter." You may use the word "copyright," but the "©" says the same thing and it's necessary for international protection. Also add "all rights reserved" and expand on this if you like. Check the wording in this and

other books. The copyright notice must appear in *all* copies of the book to protect you, so double-check it and all the numbers on the copyright page every time you proof copy.

The copyright should be in the name of the owner. The owner may be the author, the publishing company or whoever created or paid for the work.

2. **Publish the book.** Check for the copyright notice before any of the books are distributed.

3. **Register your claim with the Copyright Office within three months of the book coming off the press.** To do this, send a completed Form TX, two copies of the "best edition" of the book and a fee of $30. The "best edition" would be the hardcover if both the hardbound and softcover came from the printer at the same time. However, since the hardbound edition often takes longer to produce, the softcover may be the "best edition at the time of initial publication." If you enclose softcover copies with the Form TX, be sure to note that they were produced first. For forms, see http://www.loc.gov/copyright/forms/.

The Copyright Office will add a registration number and date to the form and will send you a photocopy containing a seal and the Registrar's signature.

The time it takes the Copyright Office to process your application varies. Nine months is not unusual. Sending your application by UPS or FedEx will be much faster than via the Postal Service. Due to the anthrax scare, all Postal mail is diverted to Florida for (slow) decontamination. The office receives more than 600,000 applications each year!

DIRECTORIES TO LIST YOUR BOOK IN

You have many opportunities to list your book in directories and with associations that are referred to by thousands of people. The following pages include the most important of the directories and associations. I suggest you list your book in as many of them as possible.

The *ABA Book Buyer's Handbook* is used by bookstores to find your shipping, discount, STOP and returns policies. To be listed, your company must be at least a year old and you must have published at least three titles. Contact the American Booksellers Association for an application. See http://handbook.bookweb.org/.

NACS: The Book Buyer's Manual is published by the National Association of College Stores.

The manual is a listing of publishers, distributors and wholesalers who serve the college and university bookstore industry. This listing will include each firm's ordering policies, discounts and returns schedules and is a critical resource for buyers to utilize in their ordering of both faculty-requested course materials and general books.

For an application, see http://www.nacscorp.com, http://www.NACS.org and http://www.NACS.org/forms/bookbuyers/.

The *Book Dealers Dropship Directory* will list your book for individual drop-ship sales. Contact Al Galasso at marketbooks@juno.com.

Book Trade in Canada is the *Literary Market Place* of the Canadian book publishing industry. If you are located in Canada, contact *Quill & Quire* magazine, http://www.quillandquire.com.

Canadian Books in Print is the *Books in Print* of the Canadian book publishing industry. If your book is being printed in Canada, contact Marian Butler, University of Toronto Press, 10 St. Mary's St. #700, Toronto, ON M4Y 2W8, Canada; Tel: 416-978-2239.

The *Canadian Publishers Directory*: If you're located in Canada, request an application from *Quill and Quire*, http://www.quillandquire.com.

Directories in Print will accept your book listing if it has an extensive Appendix. Request a form from the Gale Group, http://www.galegroup.com.

The *Directory of Mail Order Catalogs* and the *Directory of Business-to-Business Catalogs*: If you have several books and offer them in your own brochure or catalog, see http://www.greyhouse.com.

The *International Directory of Little Magazines and Small Presses* is another place you'll want to list your new firm. For an application, see http://www.dustbooks.com/.

The *Small Press Record of Books in Print* is a special *Books in Print* for smaller publishers. For an application, see http://www.dustbooks.com/.

Law Books in Print: If you're publishing books for the legal profession, get a listing in *Law Books in Print*. See http://www.oceanalaw.com.

Literary Market Place (LMP) is one of the most important reference books in the publishing industry. It lists every major publisher, publicity outlet and supplier. An inclusion here will help your customers and suppliers find you. See http://www.literarymarketplace.com/lmp/us/index_us.asp.

The *National Directory of Catalogs*: If you have several books and offer them in your own brochure or catalog, send for an application form for this directory. See http://www. mediafinder.com/.

Online bookstores: Some of the following online bookstores allow you to register your book. Contact them online regarding information for publishers. Annotate your listings by sending cover art, the table of contents, back-cover copy, etc.

http://www.amazon.com
Go to the bottom of the page and click "Sell Items."

http://www.bn.com
Go to the bottom of the page and click "Publisher and Author Guidelines." And see http://www.barnesandnoble.com/ help/pub_confirmation_form.asp.

http://www.borders.com
Go to the bottom of the page and click "Sell Items."

http://www.booksamillion.com/ncom/books/
Go to the bottom of the page and click "For Publishers."

The Para Publishing Web site: My site offers a free listing. Once your book is published, you may list it on the Para Publishing Web site at no charge. Just click *Success Stories* and fill in the form. Include your email address and URL so that interested surfers can click directly back to you. See http://parapublishing.com/sites/para/resources/ success_list.cfm.

Publishers Directory is another publication in which you may have a free listing. See http://www.galegroup.com.

The Publishers Marketing Association (PMA) is an international association of more than 3,000 publishers who band together to promote their books in a cooperative manner. PMA holds educational seminars, does cooperative mailings and operates booths at major book fairs. Local affiliates of PMA are located all over North America. Their annual directory lists member publishers. Contact PMA for a sample newsletter and a membership application: http://www.pma-online.org.

Quill & Quire Spring and Fall Announcements: If your books are being produced in Canada, request an application from *Quill & Quire*, http://www.quillandquire.com.

The *Small Press Record of Books in Print* is a special *Books in Print* for smaller publishers. For an application, see http://www.dustbooks.com/.

Writer's Market: A listing here means you want manuscript submissions from authors. For an application, write *Writer's Market*, Writer's Digest Books, 1507 Dana Ave., Cincinnati, OH 45207. (Phone 800-289-0963 or 513-531-2222; Fax: 513-531-4744) See http://www.writersdigest.com.

Ulrich's International Periodicals Directory: If you have a magazine or newsletter, see http://www.ulrichsweb.com/ulrichsweb/default.asp#.

The *Oxbridge Directory of Newsletters*: If you publish a newsletter, see http://www.mediafinder.com/.

An important way to become noticed as a publisher is by getting reviews for your books. For details on sending review copies and making galleys, read our Special Report, **Book Reviews**. See http://parapublishing.com/sites/para/information/promote.cfm#bkrev.

For information on book promotion, see Chapter 7.

If you want a response, you have to ask for it.
—John Huenefeld

Writing a book is an adventure. To begin with, it is a toy and an amusement. Then it becomes a mistress, then it becomes a master, then it becomes a tyrant. The last phase is that just as you are about to be reconciled to your servitude, you kill the monster and fling him to the public.

—Winston Churchill

6

WHAT IS YOUR BOOK WORTH?

PRICES, DISCOUNTS, TERMS, COLLECTIONS AND RETURNS

Book pricing is a complicated affair that strikes a compromise between a price high enough for the publisher to stay in business and low enough to overcome customer price-resistance. The first book is often for recognition and, once that is out of your system, the second is for money. Consequently, the author is likely to underprice the first book, but work with a very sharp pencil on the price of the next.

The higher your price, the more mistakes you can afford.

THE LIST PRICE

Many first-time author–publishers ask themselves whether they want maximum financial return or maximum distribution, feeling they can't have both. Usually they wind up with a price on the cover that's too low. As a result, many small publishers have a garage full of books that they cannot afford to market effectively. Without a high enough price, there will not be enough money for promotion, and without letting people know about the book, it will not sell.

In addition, the price printed on the cover is not what you will receive for the book. Dealers require a percentage for their selling efforts. Everyone in the book-selling process takes a cut—distributors, wholesalers, bookstores and other sales outlets.

Your promotion costs—expenditures related to letting people know the book exists—are likely to be much higher than you originally anticipated—around 25% of the list price. Some 10% to 20% of the books may be shipped out as review copies, as only one factor. Advertising might be another cost. Some books may come back from bookstores damaged and unsalable. Returns take a big chunk out of the list price.

Depending upon the subject matter and the size of the potential audience, I often send out more than 500 review copies to appropriate magazines, newsletters, newspaper columns, news syndicates and opinion-molders. Reviews are the most effective and least expensive promotion you can do for your book.

In a how-to book, you're selling exclusive information. Your book is unique—like you, it's one of a kind. It's true that customers will not pay more than what they figure is a fair price. However, if your book is a good one and they want it badly enough, they will pay what you ask. The selling price is not nearly so frightening to the buyer as it is to the author.

Books are becoming increasingly more expensive to buy. Visit a bookstore and compare prices.

Underpricing a book to increase sales is a big mistake. In fact, it may even undermine the credibility of the book. And remember, price can have a reverse impact when a book is purchased as a gift.

Also, keep in mind the gender factor, which can be a reason to keep prices reasonable. According to *Publishers Weekly*, women are more resistant to book prices than men. Women buy most of the books on cooking, health, diet and gardening, as well as fiction. In fact, women buy 68% of all trade books.

ALWAYS CHARGE $_.95: It may seem old and silly, but $19.95 still seems a lot cheaper to the subconscious mind than $20, and there is no good argument for a mid-price like $19.50.

THE PRICING FORMULA

Here's a procedure for pricing your book. *You must look at price from both the bottom up and from the top down.*

BOTTOM UP: Books you intend to sell through bookstores and mail order should be priced at a minimum of eight times production cost, textbooks at five times. Production costs include printing and trucking in. I am not counting typesetting and other prepress costs as I assume the book will go through several revisions—spreading out those costs over many books.

> *BOTTOM-UP PRICING – If it costs you $2 to print and truck, and you have to mark it up times 8, the result would be... $15.95.*

The "eight times formula" does not fit every case; there may be a few exceptions. Consider your audience and the cost of reaching them. If you write a pictorial history of your town, and the chamber of commerce is buying all the books to give to tourists, your promotion and distribution costs will be much lower. For nonfiction aimed at a small target audience that continuously sells, you may be able to justify seven times. If eight times seems like a lot, you should know that audiovisual materials are often marked up 11 times.

Direct Mail: If you plan to sell your book through direct mail advertising, you will get the full price of the book by avoiding book trade discounts. However, your list price will have to be higher, not lower, because direct mail is so expensive. A direct mail offer will cost more than 50¢ each for bulk rate postage, envelope, cover letter, mailing house stuffing, etc. Your expected response may be 2% or less. Conventional direct-mail industry wisdom says you can't profitably sell a book through direct-mail advertising unless it is priced over $35. Savvy publishers avoid direct mail and use their Web site to market to buyers.

Pricing the book any lower than 8X is courting financial disaster. If the projected list price seems too high, consider cutting out some of the copy or photographs, or selecting a smaller type size and narrower leading (space between the lines) to get more text on each page and reduce the total number of pages. If your book has a huge number of pages, you might consider dividing it into two volumes. Check with your printer for other ways to reduce costs. Now, if the customer still won't pay that much, you picked the wrong subject to write about.

There's really no formula for pricing books...
You must go to the bookstore or marketplace, and
study the prices of the competing titles.

TOP DOWN: The price you put on your back cover, embed in your bar code, put on the order blank on the last page of your book and list in all your promotion should be *as much as the traffic will bear.* Visit a bookstore, look on the shelf where your book will be and check other books like yours. Look for other books on the same subject that would be purchased by the same type of person.

WHO'S YOUR REAL TARGET CUSTOMER?

Yes, I know, you think your book is for everyone. Look, I publish books on skydiving. I want everyone to jump—to have fun, to skydive safely and to come back, make more jumps, join the club, buy equipment and (hopefully) buy more books. But I'm realistic. I know skydiving is not for everyone.

Just because you spent the last year pouring your heart, soul and credit limit into your tome does not mean everyone is interested enough to buy and read it. Now, that said, what is the profile of the typical potential purchaser for your book?

You want to find out what your potential buyer is willing to spend. If you're selling to teenagers, your price will have to be low and the book printed in softcover. If yours is a business book, a price of $34.95 and a hardcover with a dust jacket might be right. If this is a professional book aimed at doctors or lawyers, a hardcover book without a jacket at $90 would not be out of line.

> *Before you can sell a person anything, you have to make him or her want it more than the money it costs.*

Look at the range of prices in your category on a bookstore shelf; the price for your book must be right in the middle. Also, look at the formats of other books like yours—hardcover, softcover, size, shape, color printing and so on. And remember, books with old copyright dates will many times have inordinately low prices, as their prices have not increased along with normal inflation.

> *Retail price should depend more upon the value the buyer places on the product than the cost to the producer.*
> **—Leonard Shatzkin, In Cold Type**

If you poll bookstore managers on pricing, remember their perspective is that lower prices will sell more books. As a result, they will often advise a price that may be too low.

> *Book buyers are less influenced by price differentials than almost any category of customer.*
> **—John Huenefeld, Huenefeld's Guide to Book Publishing**

COMPARE UP AND DOWN: Now, *hopefully, your bottom-up price (8X) is lower than your top-down price. If there is an overlap, you'll have to reformulate your book, because there's no room to make a profit.* If so, see how you could cut back on your production costs—trimming the number of pages, for example.

> *If the cover price is too high, you will price your book out of the market.*

If it is too low, the book will not be credible; potential buyers will think there is something wrong with it.

REVISED EDITIONS: You can price revised editions a bit higher. When updating a book and going back to press, there is an advantage: your book has been out there working for you. A revised edition is a new book—with a track record. It has a reputation and can command more attention and more money. Price the revision toward the top of the range of the books on its shelf.

OTHER PRICING CONSIDERATIONS

RAISING THE PRICE: If you do raise the price with a revision, remember to change your ads, brochures, Web site, etc., and send off a news release about the reprint to *Publishers Weekly*. (Every little mention helps.)

To ease the blow to your better dealers, those who have listed your book in their catalogs, consider offering them a one-time buy on the new edition at the old price to protect their catalog listing. This offer will also generate quick cash to help you pay your printing bill.

The book How to Beat Inflation *has just gone from $14.95 to $19.95.*

REVISE THE ABI FORM: If you have already filled out Bowker's ABI (Advance Book Information) form, don't worry. Just go to the Bowker *Books in Print* Web site at http://www.bowkerlink.com. Once you have your username and password, you can update your listing (and submit new-title ABI forms online) anytime.

PRICE GOES ON THE BOOK: Your book *must* have a price on it—and it should for three reasons.

1. If you don't print your price on the back cover of a softcover book or on the jacket front flap of a hard-cover book, the distributor or the bookstores will sticker it. If the book comes back, you won't be able to remove the sticker, so you have to destroy the book or replace the jacket.

2. The price is reflected in the price extension of the bar code on the back cover, and savvy buyers can deci-pher the code.

3. Your book should have an order blank on the last page—facing out. To use the form, customers will need to refer to a price. We sell more books each week on these order blanks than on any other promotion we do.

So, if you are pricing your book on the order blank and/or on the back cover in the bar code, why not also print the price on the back cover in Arabic numerals?

The price should be printed at the bottom of the back cover on a softcover book. Don't place the price at the top of the back cover where it may turn off potential buyers before they read down through the sales copy.

DISCOUNTS

Discounts must be set down in a definite policy right from the beginning. Discount structures have to be clear to both you and your customers to avoid any misunderstanding.

END-USER CONSUMERS placing individual orders usually pay the full retail price (they don't get a discount), and they send cash with their order (CWO). When an order is received without a check, it's best to return the order with a short note requesting payment in advance. Direct the customer to your Web site for details. Some people order asking to be billed, because they don't know what the full price will be. By asking for payment in advance you'll lose a few orders, but it will stop credit losses and cut billing costs. Also, avoid COD shipments. They require too much paperwork for a small sale, and the collection charges often upset the customer.

Retail your books for full list price. Don't compete with your dealers or cheapen your product.

BOOK-TRADE DISCOUNTS: The terms publishers extend to booksellers vary so much from firm to firm that the American Booksellers Association publishes a loose-leaf handbook that tries to list them all. Discounts are supposed to be based on the theory that there's a savings in bulk shipments. However, book-selling tradition bases the discount rate on the *category of the wholesale customer,* arguing that certain intermediaries need a greater discount because they're buying in quantity, providing a service and passing on part of the discount.

•• **National Distributors** usually take 25% to 30% of the net (what they collect from the stores and wholesalers). That may work out to be around 67% off the list (cover) price. That 67% may sound like a lot, and it is. But distributors have sales reps who visit the stores and chain buyers to take orders. It's virtually impossible to get books into stores without a personal visit to the appropriate buyer.

Distributors want an exclusive, but most just serve the book trade (wholesalers and bookstores). You can turn that portion of the business over to them, forget about the stores and go on to the nontraditional markets, which are easier, more lucrative and more fun. You'll pay the freight to your distributor (FOB destination), but you'll usually ship to them directly from your printer. See the distributor discussion in Chapter 8.

•• **Wholesalers** get 50% to 60% off the list (cover) price on the theory that they purchase large quantities for resale to retailers and libraries. Often they are regional suppliers providing stores with both one-stop shopping and a short supply line for quick and easy restocking. Wholesalers, in turn, usually allow bookstores 40% to 45% off the list price, depending on the size of the order. Stores are allowed to mix titles in an order to get a larger discount. Wholesalers usually extend discounts of 20% to 33% to libraries. Wholesalers sometimes pay the shipping (FOB origin) when purchasing from the publisher.

The largest wholesaler in the country is the Ingram Book Company. Based in Nashville, Ingram works through regional warehouses. They have a warehouse within one-day UPS service of 92% of the bookstores in the U.S.

•• **Retail bookstores:** Discounts to individual bookstores start at 40% for single-title orders. This comes as a shock to many new publishers, but one has to consider the high overhead of retail outlets for rent, taxes, salaries, utilities, insurance, etc. They need at least 40% to stay in business. Incidentally, bookstores enjoy a smaller markup than gift, sporting goods and many other stores, which often get a 50% discount or more. The publishing industry has been able to justify the lower discount by making the books returnable if they aren't sold. Fortunately, books are uniform in size, easy to store, simple to ship and unbreakable. Shipping charges are paid by the bookstore (FOB origin).

•◦ **College bookstores** get 20% to 25% off list price on (text)books to be sold to students. The quantity is often large, and any books not sold after the school term begins are returned. There is very little risk to the store, because it's only acting as an order taker. The "short discount" results in a lower price to the consuming student.

•◦ **Online bookstores:** Contact each of the online bookstores (see the listing in Appendix 2) for their information for publishers. Some have special programs requiring a higher discount such as the Amazon Advantage at 55%.

•◦ **Libraries:** Some publishers give libraries a 20% discount, but most libraries don't expect a discount and many orders will arrive with a check made out for the full list price. Libraries are only ordering one book for an end-user, so there is no justification for a discount. Most small publishers charge libraries full list price.

Most publishers publish a universal discount schedule; however, they extend 40% to bookstores, 55% to wholesalers and 67% to distributors regardless of the number ordered.

Your distributor will order by the carton, usually 1,000 to 4,000 books. The wholesaler will in turn order 10 to 50 books from the distributor, and the bookstores will usually take one to three books from the wholesaler.

Resale Prices for Books & Tapes on
Book Writing and Book Publishing

Dealer Bulletin   **January 1, 2006**

Featuring new and better discounts as well as a greater selection. See our Web site for descriptions and list prices. Please order using full title and/or ISBN for identification.

Terms are 30 days from date of invoice. A finance charge of 1.5% per month will be added to all balances over 30 days.

Discounts:

1	book	No discount
2-4	books	20% off
5-9	books	30% off
10-24	books	40% off
25-49	books	42% off
50-74	books	44% off
100-199	books	48% off
200 or more	books	50% off

Credit: Orders over $50 must be prepaid or send bank and three trade references.

Shipping: Books are best shipped via UPS or USPS Priority Mail. We can ship via truck or Federal Express, but do not recommend them for long distances because the rates are considerably higher. Shipping is FOB Santa Barbara.

We dislike **drop-shipping** individual books but will do it at list, less 40% plus $4.

STOP Orders are accepted for individual books at list, less 40% plus $4.

Shortages or nonreceipt must be reported to us within 15 days of the ship date.

Resale Numbers: California dealers must mention their resale number with their order.

Promotional Materials: We can supply photographic files of all our publications for your catalog work. See the press room on our Web site.

Book trade: Our books are available from major wholesalers such as Baker & Taylor, Ingram and others. Our distributor to the book trade is National Book Network.

Orders may be sent to the address below. Telephone orders may be made to 800-PARAPUB, 9:00 AM to 5:00 PM, Monday through Friday, Pacific Time (or to the answering machine after hours). Purchase orders may be faxed to 805-968-1379 or emailed to orders@ParaPublishing.com at any time.

A universal discount schedule for the Book Trade

FEDERAL TRADE COMMISSION RULES: The FTC requires that the discounts you offer one dealer be offered to all dealers who are purchasing the same quantity on the same terms. You are not required to extend credit, but if dealers are paying cash and want the same quantity, you must sell at the same discount. Search for "price discrimination" and the "Robinson-Patman Act" at http://www.ftc.gov/.

DISCOUNTS OUTSIDE THE BOOK TRADE are dictated by that individual industry. Sporting goods dealers, baby shops and auto-supply stores may expect larger discounts and may purchase in specific increments. They are not served by the book trade distributors; they have their own system.

Your discounts and terms should be printed in your dealer bulletins, on your Web site, in the *ABA's Book Buyer's Handbook* (http://www.bookweb.org) and where requested in other listing forms.

By the way, don't confuse "discount" with "markup." A discount of 50% from $2 to $1 is the same as a 100% markup from $1 to $2.

When figuring your discounts, total the order and then subtract the discount. You will come out with a slightly higher figure than if you figure the discount per book and then extend it out. For example, 200 $5.95 books at 50% off = $595.00 but $5.95 - 50% = $2.97 x 200 = $594.00, a $1 difference.

Once you have published your prices and terms, stick to them. Besides the need to obey the FTC rules, it just is not profitable to deviate from those figures that took you so long to calculate. Some dealers will be asking for a better deal, and some publishers feel that any sale above their cost is a good one. But it's not fair to give one customer a better deal than another. You have to draw the line somewhere.

CONSIGNMENTS are when the dealer takes delivery of the books but doesn't pay the publisher until they are sold. Most distributors operate on consignment inventory and pay 90 to 120 days after they sell the books to the bookstore or wholesaler. While publishers should avoid selling to small accounts on consignment, there are good arguments for these terms with major distributors. Part of your inventory might just as well sit in another warehouse as well as your own.

SHIPPING CHARGES are usually charged in addition to the price of the book for wholesale accounts as well as retail sales to individual customers (FOB origin). FOB means Free on Board. The receiver pays the shipping if it's FOB origin.

HANDLING CHARGES upset many customers because they feel that *handling* is a cost of business. If you charge for *postage* and it's not the same as the amount on the package, you will also hear about it—especially from bookstores. So if you do plan to tack on a little extra to pay for the invoice and shipping supplies, call the "postage and handling" charge "shipping."

Those dealers who object to any figures higher than the actual postage on the carton usually just scratch it off the invoice when paying the bill. Invoice altering becomes more frequent after each postal-rate hike.

STOP (Single Title Order Plan): Like the SCOP (Single Copy Order Plan), "Stop" is an easy method for bookstores to order single books for their customers. A "stop order" consists of a special multipart order form that arrives with a check. Because the store is paying in advance, they assume a discount of 20% to 40%. The check may be filled in or blank and restricted to a certain maximum amount. Sometimes the order asks that the book be shipped directly to the customer and other times to the store. Part of the order form may be used as a shipping label.

Many publishers agree to accept STOP orders based on the list price less a 40% discount, plus $4 for shipping. Terms of sale for individual publishers are listed in the *ABA's Book Buyer's Handbook*. See the American Booksellers Association for details: http://www.bookweb.org.

TERMS OF SALE

Terms and credit are different in the book trade. Most wholesalers and bookstores routinely take 60 days to pay, many take 90 and some get around to mailing out checks in six or eight months. This forces the publisher into a frustrating banking situation. There are very few small publishers who can afford to finance the inventories of their dealers.

> *The publisher is financing the author on one end and the bookstore's inventory at the other. We are in a consignment business that pretends it is not.*
>
> **—Sol Stein, president, Stein and Day**

The customary terms for the book industry are that invoices should be paid within 30 days of an end-of-the-month statement (30 EOM). This is up to 30 days longer than "net 30-day" terms. Some publishers, eyeing other industries, offer "2% 10-day" terms, but the dealer usually pays late and still takes the 2%. Many of the newer small publishers don't subscribe to the 30 EOM terms or discounts for fast pay; they quote strictly "net 30 days."

"Advance dating" of invoices is sometimes done for seasonal businesses and catalog houses. The invoice is dated a couple of months after the books are shipped. This provides the dealer with the opportunity to get the books into stock in advance before the rush—important where timing is critical and sales are not immediate.

Ship your invoices separately via first-class mail or email them; don't just enclose them in the carton with the books, as invoices can be misplaced at the receiving dock. The longer it takes the invoice to reach the accounting department, the longer accounting will take to pay it!

CREDIT: It's only practical to extend credit and ship quickly to new accounts. You will receive all sorts of small orders from distant stores, and it is not worth the time and effort to run a credit check on each one. It may cost $50 or more to run a credit check, even if you do it all yourself by telephone, and it will take a lot of time. On one- and two-book orders, credit checks are not worth the effort for the occasional bad pay or bankruptcy.

If a large order out of nowhere (such as Nigeria) seems too good to be true, it probably is. A few people have ordered large quantities of books (200 of a title) from small publishers without ever intending to pay for them. They turn around and sell the books to stores and remainder houses at a great discount.

RIP-OFF ARTIST

In 1982, I suffered a serious accident just prior to the ABA book fair. I was in the hospital for five weeks and could not work for almost six months. While in the hospital, I received a very large order from someone who pretended to be a big wholesaler in Michigan. The buyer even had the nerve to write across the bottom of the purchase order: "Missed you at the ABA. Get well soon." It took several years to put him out of business, and at last report even his bankruptcy trustee couldn't collect from him.

Set a limit of, say, $50 for any dealer order coming in on a letterhead or purchase order. Enclose your brochure, statement of terms and return policy with the invoice. You could even slip in a form letter welcoming their account, explaining that you are happy to extend credit, and that prompt payment of this invoice will raise their limit to $100. Beyond that, you will require trade and bank references. Those who do not stand your test, or who are awaiting a credit check for a large purchase, can be urged to pay in advance via a *pro forma invoice* (you make out a complete invoice to include shipping charges, but you don't ship the books until the invoice is paid). Another clever trick is to ask for 50% of a large invoice in advance—then ship just 50% of the order.

Schools, libraries and state and federal governments are good pay but often pay slowly. Just make sure their request comes on their purchase order. Too often someone in the parks department will write to you on city letterhead asking for a book, with no mention of money. This may well be an unauthorized order.

Sometimes schools or government agencies will telephone or fax an order and then follow this with a written purchase order. If you're lucky, they will mark the second message "Confirming order—do not duplicate." Otherwise, you might wind up shipping twice.

Join publishing electronic mailing lists and meet some of the people in other book firms. If you question an account, often one of your contemporaries will provide the credit information you seek. See the list of mailing list servers in Appendix 2.

"SURE-FIRE" CREDIT GIMMICK BACKFIRES

Recently a business publisher used a "sure-fire" credit gimmick to increase his mail-order sales. He offered an expensive business materials kit to large businesses on a "free trial" basis. They could use the materials for 14 days at "no risk," then either pay for them and receive a free bonus disk, or return them. He figured most large businesses would buy the materials once they started using them. The orders came in and he shipped hundreds of kits... (you finish the story)...

Hint: Since the businesses had already received the kits, hardly any were paid for or sent back.

Foreign orders can be treated in the same way as domestic ones. There will be a difference in shipping charges, sometimes higher and sometimes lower. Unless they pay in dollars drawn on a U.S. bank, there may be a check-cashing (currency-conversion) charge. Foreigners have about the same payment history as U.S. customers. The simplest way to avoid extra bank charges is to specify that all orders are payable in U.S. funds drawn on a U.S. bank.

Some publishers place a surcharge on foreign orders, and it might be appropriate to add a small paperwork fee to very large orders requiring customs forms. However, since most foreign orders do not require much more work than domestic shipments, a surcharge can simply discourage foreign sales and insult foreign customers.

STATEMENTS: Wholesalers and bookstores are accustomed to receiving end-of-the-month statements of their accounts; they want a recapitulation of the many small orders they have placed. Statements are not a requirement, but they may speed payment. Your accounting program can generate statements or you can photocopy the invoices and mail them.

COLLECTIONS

When the money does not come in on time, you have to exercise your collection process.

When addressing these and other invoices, always include the name of the person signing the book order. This focuses your claim on a specific individual, where it will have more impact than if you simply send invoices and statements to the company. Now pen a nice personal note to this particular person on the bottom of the statement.

Your collection message might include:

•◆ Is there any reason why this past due bill has not been paid?

•◆ If you are unable to pay the whole bill, won't you evidence your good faith by sending us a partial payment?

•◆ We subscribe to Dun & Bradstreet's Commercial Collection service.

•◆ If payment is not received within 10 days, we will be forced to turn this matter over to our attorney for collection.

Enclose brochures on new books with the statements. You might as well fill up the envelope to its full postage limit.

If the account goes another month without a response, pen a stronger note on the bottom of the statement. Then wait two weeks and make a telephone call. If they don't pay in 90 days, cut them off. You don't need customers like them. In most other industries, 30 days would be the limit; the book industry is much slower in paying.

After this, there are a couple of options. You can arrange with your attorney to send a standard collection letter. The charge might be $20 each for a quantity of collections. You might also consider a collection agency. Your local agency (see the *Yellow Pages* under "Collection Agencies") will have affiliates all over North America, or you might contact a large firm with many offices, such as Dun & Bradstreet.

Collection agencies usually take one-third as their collection fee, and they prefer the easy cases. They have little power and usually get their money through a personal visit, which embarrasses the bookseller. They will threaten legal action and will turn the case over to a local attorney if they fail to collect. Generally, the older the debt, the harder it is to collect.

SKO-Brenner-American is a collection agency that specializes in the book trade. They publish a monthly confidential list of delinquent bookstores and wholesalers. They will also handle collections. For information on their services and a subscription to their newsletter, see http://www.skobrenner.com/.

The telephone is a powerful collection instrument and a good supplement to dunning notices. Many callers use scripts to make sure they get their complete message across quickly.

Also, remember, it's better to have the books returned unsold than to have the books sold and not get paid.

If a customer has been bouncing large checks, put the next one in "for collection." Your bank will send it to the customer's bank with instructions to hold the check until there is enough money in the account to pay it.

To collect a large bill from a foreign customer, try calling the cultural attaché at the nearest embassy or consulate. Often the attaché will relay your message, and this puts pressure on the foreign debtor.

Whatever collection system you select, make it automatic, so that you can be objective and will not allow deadbeats to negotiate delays. Let customers know you mean business. See *Business Letters for Publishers* in the Para Publishing Special Reports in Appendix 2 or at http://parapub.com/sites/para/resources/allproducts.cfm for some suggested collection letters.

ACCOUNTS RECEIVABLE

This is one of the most pleasant operations, because it's fun to count your money. As the checks arrive, match them with the invoices.

Checks will be made out to the publishing company, the author or the name of the book. List them all on your check deposit rubber-stamp. Pay a little extra for a self-inking stamp; it will save you a lot of time.

Bank deposits can be made up every few days. If you don't use a computerized bookkeeping system, add the checks up and submit your adding machine tape with your deposit slip. If your bank wants you to list each check individually on the deposit slip, threaten to go to another bank. Big corporations do not have to do this, and you won't either if you are assertive. Keep it simple!

RETURNS

Returned books are one of the biggest controversies in the publishing business, amounting to more than $7 billion annually. Distributors, wholesalers and bookstores expect to be able to return all books they do not sell. Bookstores return more than 18% of the books they order to the distributor, but the distributor returns just 2% to the publisher and they are shelf-worn. If this still sounds like a lot, then consider that the returns are so high for mass-market paperbacks that the dealers save shipping costs by "stripping" the books and sending back only the covers for credit! That's why mass-market paperbacks have their ISBN printed on the inside front cover.

The returns system almost amounts to *consignment*, and you are caught in a bind. Unfortunately, if the booksellers did not have the return privilege, they would be far less likely to carry your books. You want your books displayed and so you have to take the chance of having several of them come back. Returns result in zero profit transactions (ZPTs). The books went out with costly paperwork and came back with paperwork; everyone was busy, but nothing was sold.

From time to time, people in the book industry suggest changes to the system of returns. One popular recommendation is to eliminate the returns and pass the savings on to the bookstore in the form of higher discounts. Because we operate in a free-market economy with a lot of competition, none of these suggestions have ever caught on.

Make up a return policy and post it on your Web site. Baker & Taylor and some of the other wholesalers will probably ask for your return policy when they first open an account with you. Also call attention to the policy when a bookstore or wholesaler requests permission to return some books.

Most publishers will allow returns between 90 days and one year of the invoice date. They specify 90 days because they want to make sure the books were given a fair trial on the shelves, but one year because they don't want the books sitting around too long—the title may go into a revised printing.

Many publishers require the bookseller to request permission for returns and specific shipping instructions first, but few stores do this. They just ship the books back.

The paperwork that comes with the return should identify the original invoice number under which the books were purchased. You want to credit or reimburse the bookseller with the correct amount. You also want to make sure the books came directly from you. If the books were purchased from a wholesaler, they should be returned to the wholesaler.

Books must arrive back at the publisher in good, unblemished, resalable condition so that they may be returned to stock. This is the biggest failing of the bookstores. They almost never pack the books properly. They just throw them in a carton, often without cushioning material, and send them back. During the long trip, the books chafe against each other and the carton and consequently arrive in a scuffed, unsalable condition.

If the return is from a yet-to-be-paid-for order, the bookstore should be credited against their original invoice. If it is against a paid-for order and you are a small publisher with a limited number of titles, you could issue a refund check. Most bookstores buy on a net 30-day basis, but that doesn't mean you'll see your money in 30 days. Usually they pay within three to four months. Large publishing firms with many titles usually don't send refunds on returns from bookstores. They issue *credits* because they're dealing with the bookstore on a continuing basis.

> *Long-term planning does not deal with future decisions, but with the future of present decisions.*
> **—Peter F. Drucker, management consultant**

BOOK RETURN AUTHORIZATION

1. OUR BOOKS ARE RETURNABLE. If a title isn't moving in your market, we want to get it back before a new edition makes it obsolete. Thank you for giving it a chance on your valuable shelf space. Our return period is normally between 90 DAYS AND ONE YEAR of the publisher's invoice date; however, we will accept the book for return after one year as long as the edition is still in print. To keep our products current, we update our titles every one and a half to two years.

2. RETURN PERMISSION MUST BE REQUESTED so that we can issue detailed packing and shipping instructions. This is your authorization and the instructions are below.

3. NOTICE OF SHORTAGE OR NONRECEIPT must be made within 15 days of the shipping/invoice date for domestic shipments, 60 days for foreign.

4. BOOKS DAMAGED IN TRANSIT are not the responsibility of the publisher. Please make claim to the carrier.

5. Returns must be accompanied by your packing slip listing QUANTITY, TITLE, AUTHOR, ORIGINAL INVOICE NUMBER and INVOICE DATE. Books returned with this information will be credited with 100% of the invoice price minus shipping. Otherwise, it will be assumed that the original discount was 60%. Some books have been returned to us when they should have been directed to one of our wholesalers; books should be returned to their source.

6. ROUTING: Ship books via parcel post (book rate) prepaid or UPS prepaid to Para Publishing, Attn: D. Poynter, 530 Ellwood Ridge, Santa Barbara, CA 93117-1047. Note: This is not the same as our order address.

7. To qualify for a refund, returned books must arrive here in good RESALABLE CONDITION. If they are not now resalable, please don't bother to return them. If you are not willing to package them properly for the return trip, please don't waste your time and postage.

To package the books so that they will survive the trip, we suggest you wrap them the same way they were sent to you. There are two important steps in successful book packaging: Keep them clean and immobilize them. Place the stacked books in a plastic bag. This will separate the dirty newsprint and greasy "peanuts" from the book edges and will prevent grit from creeping between the covers. To keep the books from shifting (which causes scuffing), cut a shipping carton to the right size and stuff it tightly with padding.

Since it has been our experience that books shipped loose in oversize Jiffy bags always arrive scuffed, it is now our policy to simply REFUSE them at the post office so that they will be returned to the bookstore. DO NOT USE JIFFY BAGS!

8. A credit memo will be issued toward future purchases.

9. The industry tells us that it now costs more than $8 to write a letter. Correspondence, packaging and postage cost us all a great deal in money and time (and time *is* money). Years ago, when postage was cheap, it made sense to return slow-moving books. Today, however, many bookstores are finding it is far more cost-effective to simply mark down the books and move them out.

Sample returns policy statement

Dan Poynter preaches what he practices.
—Don Paulin, author and speaker

7

PROMOTING YOUR BOOK

MAKING THE PUBLIC AWARE OF YOUR BOOK WITHOUT SPENDING FOR ADVERTISING

A major way authors measure their success is with money. And to make a profit, you'll need good promotion. This chapter covers those promotional methods that require some time and effort—but no big advertising dollars. Of course, there will be a certain amount of overlap with these areas.

> *It doesn't matter if you go with a publisher or publish yourself; the author must do the promotion.*

Your most important reference book will be the *Literary Market Place (LMP)*. Although you can use the copy in your local library, this book will be used so often that you should buy one for use at your desk or get an online subscription to it. Visit http://www.literarymarketplace.com/lmp/us/index_us.asp.

The two basic secrets to book sales are: (1) to produce a good product that has a market and (2) to let people know about it. Many small publishers receive very little publicity for their books. This lack of attention is not because of any great conspiracy between the big (New York) publishers and the media; it's simply because the neophytes do not ask for coverage. Many small publishers are good at publishing, but haven't any experience in promoting. They seem to have little interest in their books beyond the editorial work and production. They don't want to promote; they just want to create. Some beginning publishers feel the marketing end of publishing is too "commercial," and this becomes their excuse for neglecting the most important part of any business—informing the buying public of their wares. However, if you don't sell your product, eventually you won't be able to afford to produce more of it.

> *Being an author is 5% writing and 95% promotion.*
> —*Russ Marano*, **Hi-Tek Newsletter**

Twenty-five percent of the population consists of introverts, and many writers fall into this category. It's hard for them to promote their books on radio, on TV or in stores. The good news for this type of writer is that most of the things I suggest for promoting books can be done from home—almost anonymously.

THE COST OF ADVERTISING

Selling books through space advertising is expensive, because books are a "low ticket" (low selling-price) item. If you were selling airplanes, one sale would pay for a lot of ad space, and if you were selling something less expensive such as candy, you would sell so much to so many people that the ads might pay. It's tougher to break even when advertising a low-priced product to a small and scattered group of people. For example, a half-page ad in a national book-oriented magazine might cost $1,850. Using round numbers and assuming you printed the book for $2 and are selling it for $20, you would have to sell 102 books at retail, or 308 books at wholesale, just to break even on the ad. Experience tells us you'd be lucky to get five orders.

Do not spend money on advertising until you have exhausted all the free publicity.

ADVERTISING VS. PUBLICITY

The major differences between advertising and publicity are cost and control. Publicity is free, but advertising is not. On the other hand, you can control your advertising, but your news release (publicity) might be rewritten by an editor, drastically changed or not run at all.

Just as a parent's responsibilities do not end with giving birth, an author's do not end with publication. The child must be raised and the book must be promoted.

EDITORIAL COPY VS. ADVERTISING COPY

Generally, book promotion is less expensive and more successful when you use book reviews, articles and news releases.

Book reviews are "editorial copy" that is far less expensive and far more credible than space advertising. For many nonfiction books, there are hundreds of appropriate magazines and newspaper columns that receive and review books, and the number of review sources is growing with the proliferation of online reviewers. For a list of more than 90 categories of magazines, see http://parapub.com/sites/para/resources/maillist.cfm.

On the average, people spend seven minutes with each of their magazines. Obviously, they see very few of the ads. Of those ads they do see, they read very few. Of those ads they read, they believe very few. Of those ads they believe, they act on very few. People are skeptical of advertisements. On the other hand, readers tend to believe editorial copy. Now ask yourself: How much advertising space can I buy for $1,500? Not much—and it won't sell many books anyway. For the same amount, you can send out 500 review copies, many of which will result in editorial copy (articles and reviews) that people will believe. The public is usually more receptive to publicity because editorial copy is viewed as news and advertising is perceived as self-serving. An industry rule of thumb is that editorial coverage is seven times as valuable as paid coverage.

However, competition for free space is a tough proposition. More than 500 new titles are published each day, and with the growth of purely electronic books the daily output may be considerably higher. More books are published in the fall than the spring. You have to compete for attention in a crowded field and against much larger, more knowledgeable firms. But you will be surprised at how successful you can be when you jump into the fray, exploiting the media through news releases, review copies, radio and TV appearances, feature stories, interviews and presentations—especially when you target specific audiences.

Large publishers are lucky if 40% of their titles make money, and remember that they have whole departments of experts to launch their promotions. They also have built up thousands of key media contacts during their many years in the business. You have only one book, your first, and therefore you have only one chance to make it. But look at the brighter side. The big firms often work by routine and without imagination, spending only a short time promoting a book before moving on to the next one in line. You'll probably know more about the subject matter of your book and the groups of people who care about this particular subject.

And your overhead is much lower. You cut out the intermediaries by publishing yourself. You will do a more effective job of promotion because you have a greater interest in your book than a publisher who is looking after several titles (or several hundred titles) at one time. There's a lot of room for the very small independent publisher with imagination, initiative and a well-defined target market.

By doing the promotion yourself, you avoid the most common problem in author–publisher relationships—differing on the amount of effort that should be invested in each area of promotion and advertising. The author cannot be objective about his or her product and is convinced that the book would sell better if only the publisher would spend money to promote it. The publisher, on the other hand, needs more sales to convince him or her that it is worth investing more dollars in promotion. As both author and publisher, you see both perspectives and make the final decisions.

> *Many, many times, I have said, "This is too hard. I am getting out of this business," but then something good will happen and my enthusiasm is replenished.*
> **—Patricia Gallagher, For All the Write Reasons**

BOOK PROMOTION TAKES TIME: Writing the book is the easy part—the tip of the iceberg. The real work begins when you switch hats to expend time and money on promoting the book.

Book reviews can take three months or longer to appear, because magazines and sometimes even daily newspapers have long lead times. Don't get discouraged. The easiest mistake is to send out books for review, email news releases on your book or post an email offer, and then sit back and wait for the results. The secret of savvy book promotion is to keep up the pressure—keep sending out the packets and continue making the telephone calls.

BEGINNING THE PROMOTION

FIRST ANALYZE THE MARKET by determining who might purchase your book, and then figure out the best way to reach them. Your buyers must be *identifiable* and *locatable*. Ask yourself what stores they frequent, what magazines they read, what associations they join, what conventions or events they attend, what channels they watch, what emailing lists they join and so on. Where can you find a high concentration of people interested in your book's subject matter?

> *Analyze carefully the type of person who is a prospective purchaser of your book. This is perhaps the single most important thing to consider.*

If your book is on auto repair for the car owner, one prospect is car enthusiasts. What do they read? You'll want to send news releases, review copies and articles to auto magazines. Where do car enthusiasts congregate? Auto supply stores, car rallies, auto shows? Think about how you can get exposure in these places. If this repair manual covers one type of car, you may be able to find a highly targeted mailing list of owners of that type of car. Also, check the Internet for emailing lists and chat groups for auto repair. The trick is to think about who the buyer might be and then think about where this type of person can be found. Rarely is the answer bookstores or libraries.

Show me a publisher who says you can never tell which book will make it and I will show you a publisher who evaluates manuscripts without considering the market.

One reason the demand for books is constant is that the book-buying public is not static. It's constantly changing. New readers are entering the bookshops all the time, while old readers are going to that big library in the sky.

—Max Alth

As you read through the next few chapters, think about your book and its market. Make a list of, or underline, those ideas mentioned that best fit your book. Then go back and work out a promotional schedule, by the week, for several months. Set a schedule so you won't lose sight of it later when you are busy keyboarding orders and stuffing cartons.

If your book fails to sell, you don't know your market.

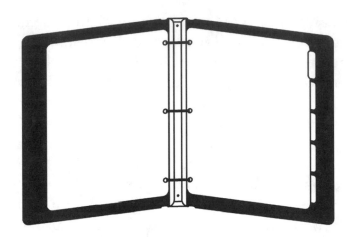

Set up a promotion binder for each book.

ASSEMBLE A BINDER: Organize your promotion thoughts and record your work by setting up a binder for your book. Use a 2" or 3" three-ring binder with dividers for five sections. Slant-ring binders with inside pockets are best. Now set up each section as follows:

•❖ **Section 1** is where you record your **promotional plan.** Type up your initial plan and check off the items when completed. Whenever you have a new idea, turn to another page of Section 1 and make a note. Use the balance of this section to store every news release you write, every emailing you make and every brochure you design. Date each promotional piece and record the results. In the back of Section 1, store copies of the publishing forms you file. You may have to subdivide Section 1 as the amount of your promotion increases so that you can easily file and locate your materials in each marketing category.

•❖ **Section 2** is for all your **costing information.** Store copies of all printing, artist, trucking, etc., bills as well as all the printing quotations. With this information all in one place, even after six printings you'll know exactly how many books have been printed and what each edition cost.

•◆ **Section 3** is where you store the **reviews, testimonials** and **other publicity** you have generated. All the good things that have been said about your book will be kept in one place; that way, when you want to make a list of testimonials and quotes from reviews, they will be easy to find.

•◆ **Section 4** is for any **important correspondence**. Here you will store some of the more interesting letters that don't fit in the other sections.

•◆ **Section 5** is the **revision section**. As you come across new material or think of something that should be included in the next edition, make a note and store it here.

You'll appreciate the promotion binders even more after you publish several books. All your costing, promotion, review and revision information will be easy to find.

KEEP TRACK OF CORRECTIONS

Also take one copy of the book, mark it "Correction Copy" and keep it near your desk. Cut off a corner of the front cover so that it won't walk out of your office or find its way back into stock. As you find small errors or want to make changes, mark this book. Then when it comes time to return to press, all your revision information will be in the correction copy and the fifth section of your binder.

PATTERN OF SALES

You can expect your sales to take on an airfoil shape if your promotion is well-organized. For most books, sales will climb rapidly, level out, taper off and become steady. Thereafter, you will notice bumps in response to seasonal changes or when your promotional work is successful. The big initial jump is due to your prepublication publicity.

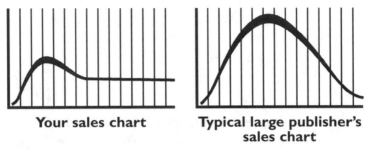

Your sales chart **Typical large publisher's sales chart**

The large New York publishers promote books in the same way Hollywood publicizes a motion picture: they throw it out on the market with some publicity to see if anyone likes it. If it gets a response, they dump in more promotional money. Then they may push it for a couple of months. When the interest cools, they bring out another product and start the process all over. As a small publisher, it makes more sense to market your book like breakfast food or soap. Develop your product, pour on the promotion, establish a niche in the market and then continue to sell at the same level for years. This can be done with a nonfiction book that is revised and kept fresh at each printing.

BEST-SELLERS

"Best-sellers" for books are only a name, a myth. This is not like a gold record in the music industry or another service to the trade run by Bowker. National best-seller lists (there are several, and they don't often agree) are assembled from certain bookstore and other sales reports. Even if you move a million books via mail-order distribution you won't make a best-seller list, because the list may only track bookstore sales. On the other hand, you may calculate that your book is the best-selling book in its field, and there is no reason you can't mention this in your promotion. For example, *Parachuting Manual with Log* is the best-selling skydiving book of all time. For more information on the various best-seller lists, advice on how to make them and scores of great promotional ideas, see Document 612, *Best-Sellers*, at http://parapub.com/sites/para/resources/allproducts.cfm.

PROMOTION IS UP TO THE AUTHOR

Large publishers do not effectively promote books. One of the biggest misconceptions in traditional publishing is that the publisher will take care of all the promotion. Publishers actually do little promoting, and by the time the author figures this out the book is not new, making any further promotional efforts too late. The media is geared toward reporting about the latest current releases (front list titles), they rarely pay attention to older books.

PROMISES, PROMISES

A self-publisher had his book acquired by a major publisher at a recent BEA convention. He was promised a 20-city author tour and much specialized promotion. The reality?—the book had a limited print run, was dumped into the bookstores, there was no special promotion to his target market and he was allowed one day of promotion in three cities. On top of all this, he had to share expenses for the mini author tour.

Bookstores make your book available, but do minimal if any promotion for it. These outlets provide availability, but you must encourage people to go into the stores to buy your title. Authors create the demand. If your book becomes a hot seller, many bookstores will want to carry it.

Authors need to be assertive and take control of their book's promotion. Start by gathering media contact lists and drafting news releases. There's a lot to learn from this chapter even if you aren't self-publishing.

KEY MEDIA CONTACTS

Key media contacts are those people who can help you move the greatest volume of books with the least expenditure of time and money. These contacts must be developed if you're going to promote your book properly. The only difference between you and a professional book publicist is that the professional already has media contacts. There are many wholesalers, TV people and subsidiary rights buyers who are just waiting to discover you and your book. Even though most are very busy, they want you; that is what their job is all about. You'll meet a great number of nice, helpful people, but only a few key contacts will do you a great amount of good. What you have to do is locate them and then carefully cultivate them. Some of the people will be listed in *Literary Market Place* and other directories available at your library. (See "Selecting Review Periodicals" later in this chapter.) Online sources of media outlets include www.mediapost.com, www.gebbieinc.com and www.bacons.com. Keep in mind that often a smart promotional strategy is to start locally.

For contacts of particular people who are current, you may have to call selected companies and ask for the name of the buyer or acquisitions person, for example. Tell the company operator (or even better, someone in the special division you are targeting) who you are and ask who you should properly correspond with. Email or call this contact and field your sales pitch; establish a rapport, but also be brief, as these people are usually very busy. Maintain credibility, and remember that they are everyone else's key contact too. Do not expect them to return calls. Send review copies of your book and follow up in a few days with a telephone call asking, "Have you received it?"

Start files on these key contacts and fill the folders with letters and notes of your telephone conversations. Track them with a contact-management software program such as ACT!, Goldmine, TELEMagic or Maximizer. Note the personal likes and dislikes of your contacts so you can bring them up in future conversations. Treat contacts well and with intelligence, and they will be there to help you with your next book too.

PROMOTIONAL MATERIALS

Spend most of your time and money on your Web site; it replaces brochures and mailings. Your business card and email signature should drive eyeballs to your site. Make your company Websitecentric; all your promotional materials should start there.

BUSINESS CARDS are less expensive than brochures and are more likely to be kept by the recipient. The mission of your card should be to send people to your Web site; the Web site is your brochure. Let the card do the telling and the site do the selling.

Include a photo of you as well as the front cover of the book on your business card. Show people who you are and remind them of the book.

Some author–publishers use a folded business card to include more information. They list the benefits of the book or what can be found on their Web site.

Business card printing is relatively inexpensive. Most of the cost is in the setup; when you purchase over 500 cards, they are nearly free. Print lots of cards and distribute them everywhere.

EMAIL SIGNATURES are the lines of type at the end of an email message. If you have a business card, you need a signature. If you're in business, you must let people know. You want people to know who you are, what you do and where to find you.

Para Publishing. Dan Poynter: Author (100+ books), Publisher (since 1969), Speaker (CSP).
Information Products on Book Writing/Publishing/Promoting, Parachutes/ Skydiving, Expert Witness & Aging Cats. PO Box 8206, Santa Barbara, CA 93118   USA. Tel: +1-805-968-7277; Fax: +1-805-968-1379; Cell: +1-805-448-9009. DanPoynter@ParaPublishing.com. More than 500 pages of helpful information: http://ParaPublishing.com. Showing people how to write, publish and promote their books—one presentation at a time. http://parapub.com/speaking. F-R-E-E Writing-Publishing-Promoting InfoKits: http://parapub.com/ getpage.cfm?file=/infokit.html

A .sig or email signature

Setting up your .sig takes just a few minutes and is free. Go to your email program (Outlook, AOL, etc.), click Help and type in *signature*. Follow the instructions. Your .sig does not have to be perfect. In a week or two, you will improve it.

Each time you send an email, your .sig will be automatically appended to it. You don't have to retype it and you don't have to proof it. It's always inserted and it's always the same.

PROFESSIONAL BOOK PUBLICITY/MARKETING SERVICES are available if you don't have the time or desire to organize your own promotion.

More and more frequently, authors who are published by large New York publishers are hiring their own PR firms to promote their books. Why? Because they know that the publishers will do little to promote their titles.

> *Hiring a publicist isn't a vanity; it's a realistic commercial decision.*
> **—Paul Cowan, Mixed Blessings**

Book publicists primarily write and place news releases, organize autograph parties and place authors on TV and radio. They usually work on a retainer basis, some on a per-placement basis, and rarely do they work by the hour. The average monthly retainer is between $2,000 and $4,000. Publicity takes time; you must hire the publicist for several months. Many ask for a six-month contract.

Marketing services, on the other hand, specialize in securing distribution; promoting to libraries and special-sales sources; sending out galleys and review books; organizing co-op marketing, Internet promotion, exhibits and advertising; and creating promotional materials and sales brochures. A few target new sales outlets, including specialty stores, and sell foreign and sub-rights.

Some publicists/marketers will have an expertise in specific markets—cookbooks, computer books, fiction, Christian, Spanish-language, etc.

If you decide to hire a professional publicist or marketing service, start early. Don't wait until your publication date.

> *Books do not sell themselves. People sell books.*

Publishers Weekly estimates that there are close to 200 independent book publicists. Some are listed in Appendix 2 under Publicists/Marketing, and more may be found in *Literary Market Place* under Public Relations Services.

Publicists are very expensive. Most self-publishers are better advised to follow this book and promote the book themselves.

TESTIMONIALS AND ENDORSEMENTS: Testimonials sell books because many people feel that there is no greater credibility than a recommendation from a satisfied customer. Testimonials and endorsements will be used in three places— on the back cover of the book, on the pages before the title page and on your Web site.

Endorsements for your **Back Cover** may be gathered from "peer reviewers" who read and comment on your completed manuscript or individual chapters. Initially, you want their comments as peer reviewers to double-check your work, and then you want to quote their praise. Therefore, they must be "opinion-molders." This means that you want people known in the book's field or known to the general public. They should be people with recognizable names or recognizable titles, who are connected to well-known companies or organizations, or who have professional credentials (doctor, lawyer, professor, author, politician, etc.).

RELEVANT ENDORSEMENTS

You might ask me to endorse your book if it's on writing, publishing or skydiving. My endorsement on other subjects would not be appropriate or valuable since I'm not known outside these fields.

You'll want to add testimonials, along with excerpts from your reviews, to all your sales literature and to your Web site, as well as to your "Review & Testimonial sheet." The Review & Testimonial Sheet is an important part of your publicity package, because it indicates that other people like your book. This sheet should be assembled from incoming reviews and sent to later reviewers, prospective dealers and anyone else you're trying to convince that the book is liked and respected in the marketplace.

You may need endorsements on a particular point, or you may need a variety of endorsements. You don't want all the blurbs to say the same thing or to be very general, such as "It is a great book." After someone has peer-reviewed your manuscript, approach him or her again. Write out an endorsement making a particular point (relating your book to *his or her* audience), and ask the peer-reviewer to look it over and edit it. Say that you need a quotation in this area. Editing is much easier than creating, and most people will accept the prompting quickly or just go with your version of the endorsement.

The best way to collect testimonials is to ask for them. It's easier than you think, because people like to see their name in print. As long as your book is good, experts in the field will jump at the chance to be mentioned. If they sell products or consulting, the exposure is valuable to them. Whether due to vanity or possible financial gain, high-profile people want to have their names in print. Stephen King seems to endorse (and get his name on) every book he can. Don't pay for endorsements; quotations cannot be considered valid if payments are involved.

Shoot high. Solicit testimonials from the most important and most recognizable people in your industry or activity. You can find just about anyone with an online search.

Unsolicited testimonials will arrive after the book is published. They should be acknowledged, added to your Review & Testimonial Sheet and filed for future use. For more detailed information, see Document 609, *Blurbs for Your Books: Testimonials, Endorsements and Quotations*, at http://parapub.com/sites/para/resources/allproducts.cfm.

PUBLICATION DATE

The publication date is a place in the future, well after your books are off the press, when your books will be available in the stores and your promotion will be working. The publication date is a means of focusing attention. The idea is to have the product accessible when public attention peaks in response to your promotion. You want to time book reviews, TV appearances, autograph parties, etc., to hit after your book is in the bookstores and readily obtainable.

The publication date has nothing to do with the date your book is published (the day it comes off the press and you have finished books in hand). It's the date you list on the ABI (Advance Book Information) form, but it is not the *day of publication* you list on the copyright form. The publication date is a *fiction* for the benefit of a few big important prepublication review magazines such as *Publishers Weekly*. There is nothing to stop you from selling or shipping books before the "pub date." Sometimes entire print runs are sold-out prior to the publication date.

After your publication date has passed, remove mention of it from your review slip, news releases, etc. There's no need to remind the media that your book is no longer new. Let them focus on the content of the book.

The big, important prepublication reviewers need three to four months of lead time. *Publishers Weekly* and the other wholesale trade review magazines need this time to select your book, assign it to a reviewer, write the review and get it into print for the benefit of the stores. Monthly and bimonthly magazines such as *Kirkus Reviews* need even more lead time (five months). The stores, in turn, need time to order the book and receive it into stock so it will be available to the public on or before your publication date (known in the bookstore as your "in-store" date). When planning your publication date, remember that Media Mail shipping can take three weeks from coast to coast.

Production is always subject to delay, so it's recommended that for your first book, and until you learn the challenges exacted by the printing trade, you wait until the book is off the press before you set your publication date.

If you have achieved sufficient prepublication momentum, you should make a significant amount of sales before the printing bill arrives. It is a matter of planning, scheduling, timing and work. The big publishers expend 90% of their promotional effort before the publication date. You, of course, will keep up the pressure.

The best publication dates are probably in the first quarter of the year. Most of the big publishers aim for October and November to take advantage of the Christmas gift-buying season. Avoiding the last quarter of the year will decrease your competition for publicity. But get your book to market; never hold it back for a better release date. Sell fresh information.

Some publishers tie their publication date to a significant date to hitch onto publicity naturally occurring on that date. For example, if you have a book on an aspect of World War II, you might tie in to D-Day. People will be thinking about the war on this date, so your book will benefit from the memorial publicity. For tie-in dates, see Chase's *Annual Events*, Kremer's *Celebrate Today* and Beam's *Directory of International Tourist Events*.

It's always smart to take advantage of a prime selling season. A book on a summer sport should come out in early spring, when people are making plans for the summer—not in the summer, when they are outside and not reading. A book on skiing should come out in the fall.

For a fuller explanation and a chart, see Document 608, *Your Publication Date*, at http://parapub.com/sites/para/resources/allproducts.cfm.

The **ship date** is the month your book arrives from the printer and will be available to your distributor and dealers. It's preferably four to five months prior to the publication date.

BOOK REVIEWS

Reviews sell books. They're the least expensive and most effective promotion you can possibly do for your book. Considering the cost of producing the book, promotional materials, mailing packaging and postage, each promotional package usually costs less than $4.50 as it goes out the door. That means you can send review copies to over 300 magazines for around $1,350. If you're writing on a subject of interest to businesspeople, your book should be of interest to 820 business-oriented magazines, newsletters and newspaper columns around the world. Most large New York publishers are very cheap with review copies—sending out less than 50. Reviews cost you very little in time and money.

Because nonfiction books are news, we get our products reviewed free.

There are two major types of book review media: (1) "prepublication date" or wholesale reviews and (2) "postpublication date" or retail reviews. They cater to separate markets, and the approach to each is different. In addition, there are early reviews and continuing reviews. The book review order and breakdown look like this:

- **Prepublication date reviews** aimed at the wholesale book market (stores)
- **Early reviews,** copyright and directory listings
- **Postpublication date reviews** aimed at the retail market. These include:
  - **sure bets:** those periodicals that *will probably* review the book
  - **the rest:** those periodicals that *might possibly* review the book
- **Continuing review program**

PREPUBLICATION REVIEWS are directed toward the book industry. Certain magazines will review your book prior to publication so that the bookstores and libraries will have the opportunity to stock it before patrons start asking for it. Since more than 500 new titles are published each day, there is no way a store can stock every book. In fact, booksellers can't even spend time to evaluate them all. Consequently, many book dealers and librarians depend on the summaries in industry review magazines when making their purchasing choices. Prepublication reviews are directed at the trade and should not be confused with the regular book reviews aimed at the consumer/reader. Good reviews in the prepublication review magazines will bring you more good reviews in other publications later, because many reviewers want to review books that arc already starting to get recognition and have been pre-selected by others.

> *There is no way anything you send to PW can be too early.*
> —*John Baker, editorial director,* **Publishers Weekly**

Prepublication reviewers expect to receive **bound galleys.** Galleys can be the same as the laser output you sent to your book printer (each book page centered in the middle of an 8.5" x 11" sheet of paper), but you stand a much better chance of review if the pages are trimmed to the final size and perfect bound with a plain typeset cover.

On the other hand, if you send a completed book with a finished cover to a prepublication reviewer it will not be reviewed, because it is obviously not "prepublication." For instructions on preparing galleys or Cranes, see *Book Reviews in Para Publishing Special Reports* in Appendix 2 or at http://ParaPublishing.com.

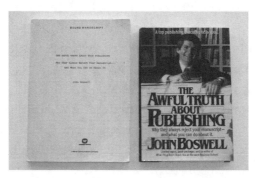

Bound galley and finished book

F&Gs are the Folded and Gathered signatures of the printed book ready for binding. F&Gs formerly were sent to the publisher for final approval prior to binding the print run. Bound galleys are F&Gs with a generic perfect-bound cover added.

Four to five months prior to your publication date, send bound galleys with a cover letter and a news release to the following prepublication reviewers. You never know what might happen. Then send a follow-up copy of the finished book one to two months after sending the galley. But you *must* send the galley first.

Publishers Weekly, Forecasts, 360 Park Avenue South, 13th Floor, New York, NY 10010-1710. Tel: 646-746-6758; Fax: 646-746-6631. *PW* is directed at the book trade (bookstores, wholesalers, libraries and publishers). A good review here will result in many bookstore orders; most will come through wholesalers. *PW* gives priority to books with broad general appeal. They review new books only, no reprints, reissues or new editions. Send two galleys between 12 and 16 weeks before your publication date. Circulation: 38,000. Contact *PW* for their "Forecast Submission Guidelines" and see the first page of the Forecasts section for recent submission details. See http://publishersweekly.reviewsnews.com/ index.asp?layout=submissions.

Library Journal, Book Review Editor, *Library Journal*, 360 Park Avenue South, New York, New York 10010. Tel: 888-800-5473 or 212-463-6818; Fax: 212-463-6734; Email: bkrev@lj.cahners.com. *LJ* is a magazine directed to general public librarians. They review 4,500 books each year, from the 30,000 received, specifically to assess their value to the library market. For many nonfiction books, a good review in *LJ* will sell over 1,000 copies. A rave review on a high-demand topic may move 5,000. Most of these library orders will come through a library wholesaler, and some 80% of these through Baker & Taylor. Therefore, it's important to let the wholesalers know about your book too. *LJ* will review from galleys or the finished book. Circulation: 28,000. See http://libraryjournal.reviewsnews.com/index.asp?layout=for ReviewersLJ.

Foreword Magazine, Alex Moore, 129½ East Front Street, Traverse City, MI 49684. Tel: 231-933-3699; Email: Reviews@ForewordMagazine.com; Fax: 231-933-3899. *Foreword* receives more than 400 galleys and audiobooks each month, and can review about 10 percent of them. The controlled-circulation magazine is sent to 15,000 booksellers and librarians as well as other trade professionals. See http://www.forewordmagazine.com/reviews/revguidelines.aspx.

Kirkus Reviews, Library Advance Information Service, 770 Broadway, NYC, NY 10003-9595. Tel: 646-654-4602; Fax: 646-654-4706; Email: kirkusrev@kirkusreviews.com. *KR* is a book review magazine directed toward libraries and bookstores. They review most any fiction and nonfiction except poetry, mass-market paperbacks and children's books for toddlers. *KR* likes to see galleys three to four months prior to publication of the book. Circulation: about 5,400. See http://kirkusreviews.com/kirkusreviews/about_us/submission.jsp.

ALA Booklist, Up Front, Advance Reviews, 50 E. Huron Street, Chicago, IL 60611. Tel: 800-545-2433 or 312-944-6780; Fax: 312-337-6787. *Booklist* reviews books for small and medium-sized public libraries. They review fiction, nonfiction, reference, young adult and children's books. This does not include textbooks, workbooks, pamphlets or coloring materials. Send galleys or finished books. Circulation: 31,500. See http://www.ala.org/booklist/submit.html.

The New York Times Book Review, Nancy Martinez, 229 W. 43rd Street, New York, NY 10036. Tel: 212-556-1234; Fax: 212-556-7088. *The New York Times* is one of the most prestigious of review publications. *Times* reviews are also syndicated, so a review there may appear in papers throughout the country. The *Times* does not review very technical, specialized titles or juvenile books. Send galleys and then send books when printed. Circulation: 1,600,000. See http://www.nytimes.com/books.

> *The primary review medium in the United States for popular trade books is* The New York Times.
>
> —**Nat Bodian**, **The Joy of Publishing**

The Los Angeles Times Magazine, Times Mirror Square, Los Angeles, CA 90053. Tel: 213-237-7811; Fax: 213-237-4712; Email: LATMag@latimes.com. *Times* editors look for books that are of general interest to their newspaper readers. Circulation: 1,100,000 daily, 1,300,000 Sunday. See http://www.latimes.com.

School Library Journal (two copies), Attn: Trevelyn Jones, 360 Park Avenue South, New York, NY 10010. Tel: 212-463-6759; Fax: 212-463-6689; Email: tjones@cahners.com. *SLJ* prints 2,500 reviews annually by school and public librarians of new books for children and young adults. They will consider for review any book appropriate for school library use. This monthly (except June and July) has a circulation of 43,000. See http://www.slj.com.

BookPage reviews almost every category of new books, including literary and popular fiction, nonfiction, children's books, audiobooks and gift books. They rarely review poetry or scholarly books, and they don't give review consideration to self-published books, print-on-demand titles or books from presses that lack major distribution (so make yourself look mainstream).

To have your book considered for review in *BookPage*, send an advance review copy at least three months prior to a title's publication date. Early receipt of a galley or bound manuscript gives them adequate time to assess the quality of a book and assign it to an appropriate reviewer. If no galleys are available, send a finished book as soon as possible. They cannot consider a book for review if they receive it after the publication date.

Along with your galley, include a letter with the name, phone number and email address of a publicity contact for the book. The letter should also include the book's publication date, price, number of pages and ISBN number.

Send adult titles to: Lynn Green; send children's titles to: Julie Hale. Address: 2143 Belcourt Avenue, Nashville, TN 37212. See http://www.bookpage.com/.

Quality Books, Inc., New Title Acquisitions, 1003 W. Pines Road, Oregon, IL 61061. Tel: 800-323-4241 or 815-732-4450; Fax: 815-732-4499. Quality is not a reviewer, but a distributor of small-press titles to libraries. They want to know about your nonfiction books and tapes early, in order to get a jump on distribution. See http://www.quality-books.com.

Major and matching book clubs. Send bound galleys to the major clubs, such as Book-of-the-Month and Literary Guild and those specializing in the book's field. See *Literary Market Place* for a list of book clubs. See http://reference. infotoday.com/lmp/us/servicesOrgList.asp?ID=27.

Giving presentation copies to opinion-molders. The best way to get sales moving is to get the book talked about by the right people. This group may amount to just a very few people to hundreds. Sometimes the publisher uses special bound galleys to get the public talking about the book. Many people feel that receiving an advance bound galley is more impressive than receiving the actual book. Some opinion-molders should get bound galleys, but others should receive the finished product.

EARLY REVIEWS, COPYRIGHT, LISTINGS, ETC.: In anticipation of your new book coming off the press, address shipping bags to selected places from the list below and stuff the bags, as appropriate, with review slips (see sample later in this chapter), a news release, your Review & Testimonial Sheet, etc. Add brochures, copies of early reviews and other materials to convince reviewers the book has been accepted by others. Do not skimp here. Then when the truck arrives from the printer, stuff the books into the bags and ship them off.

Note what is said about each of the addressees below, because some may not be appropriate for your book. If yours is an adult scientific text, do not bother sending it to the *Horn Book* magazine, which reviews children's books, etc. But do get your review packages out; you want the world to know about your new book.

American Book Review, Rebecca Kaiser, Illinois State University, Campus Box 4241, Normal, IL 61790. Tel:

309-438-3026; Fax: 309-438-3523. This bimonthly, with a circulation of 15,000, reviews 240 books each year.

Baker & Taylor. B&T is a wholesaler, not a reviewer. To establish a business relationship with book wholesaler Baker & Taylor, contact Robin Bright, Publishers Services, PO Box 6885, Bridgewater, NJ 08807. Tel: 908-541-7000; Email: brightr@btol.com. See http://www.btol.com.

Baker & Taylor, Academic Library Services Selection Department, PO Box 6885, Bridgewater, NJ 08807. Tel: 908-704-1366. Would your book be appropriate for Academic Libraries? Again, B&T is a wholesaler, not a reviewer. Enclose a photocopy of the Advance Book Information (ABI) form. See http://www.btol.com.

Booklist, American Library Association, 50 E. Huron Street, Chicago, IL 60611. Tel: 800-545-2433 or 312-944-6780; Fax: 312-440-9374. You should have sent bound galleys to ALA's *Booklist* some months earlier. This is a confirmation copy to show that the book has been published. See http://www.ala.org/booklist.

Chicago Tribune Books, Carolyn Alessio, 435 N. Michigan Avenue, Chicago, IL 60611. Tel: 312-222-3232. See http://www.chicagotribune.com/features/booksmags/.

Choice, Editorial Dept., 100 Riverview Center, Middletown, CT 06457. Tel: 860-347-6933; Fax: 860-704-0465; Email: choicemag@ala-choice.org. *Choice* is a publication of the Association of College and Research Libraries, a division of the American Library Association. *Choice* reviews 6,600 books annually for the $300-million academic library market: high school, college and special libraries. Monthly except August. Circulation: 4,800. See http://www.ala.org/acrl/choice/index.html.

Gale Group, Attn: *Contemporary Authors*, 27500 Drake Road, Farmington Hills, MI 48331. Tel: 800-877-GALE or 248-699-4253; Fax: 248-699-8070; Email: alan.hedblad@galegroup.com. *Contemporary Authors* will not list you in their directory if they think your books are self-published. See http://www.galegroup.com.

Heartland Reviews is a venture by book veteran Bob Spear. See http://www.heartlandreviews.com and contact him before sending books. Email: bobspear@lvnworth.com.

Horn Book magazine, Roger Sutton, 56 Roland Street #200, Boston, MA 02129. Tel: 800-325-1170 or 617-628-0225; Fax: 617-628-0882. *Horn Book* reviews about 420 books each year for children and young adults. It's published bimonthly and has a circulation of 24,000. See http://www.hbook.com.

> *There are only two phases to the promotion of your book: the first 90 days and everything else.*
> **—Joel Roberts, broadcast media coach**

Independent Publisher magazine, Jenkins Group, 121 E. Front Street #401, Traverse City, MI 49684. Tel: 800-706-4636 or 231-933-0445; Fax: 231-933-0448; Email: jenkinsgroup@publishing.com. Bimonthly, *Independent Publisher* reviews 75 to 100 titles every issue. Circulation: 7,000. See http://www.independentpublisher.com/.

Ingram Book Company, Express Program, PO Box 3006, La Vergne, TN 37086. The book must not be marked or identified as a promotional copy. Enclose your brochure and discount schedule (a higher discount on single orders will allow them to give stores a discount that will increase sales). If you have a distributor, let Ingram know that your books will be available from that source. See http://www. ingrambook.com/new/publishers.asp.

Kirkus Reviews, 770 Broadway, New York, NY 10003-9595. Tel: 646-654-4602; Fax: 646-654-4706; Email: kirkusrev @kirkusreviews.com. You should have sent bound galleys to *Kirkus* some months earlier. This is a confirmation copy to show the book has been published.

KLIATT Young Adult Paperback Book Guide, Paula Rohrlick, 33 Bay State Road, Wellesley, MA 02481. Tel: 781-237-7577; Email: kliatt@aol.com. *KLIATT* annually reviews some 1,600 softcover books for young adults. The magazine is bimonthly and has a circulation of 2,300. See http://hometown.aol.com/kliatt.

Library Journal, Barbara Hoffert, 360 Park Avenue South, New York, NY 10010. Tel: 888-800-5473 or 212-463-6818; Fax: 212-463-6734. Again, you should have sent bound galleys some months earlier. This is a confirmation copy to show the book has been published.

Library of Congress Acquisitions and Processing Division, Washington, DC 20540, along with your brochure and dealer discount schedule. See http://www.loc.gov.

Library of Congress Cataloging, CIP Office, Library of Congress, Washington, DC 20540, if you are in the CIP program. Once you have published three books, you are eligible to participate in the CIP program and receive library-cataloging data for printing on your copyright page. See Chapter 5. The Cataloging in Publication Office supplies postpaid mailing labels (once you have been admitted to the CIP program) for sending your books in. See http://www. loc.gov and http://cip.loc.gov/cip/.

Library of Congress Copyright Division (two copies), Library of Congress, Washington, DC 20559, for copyright registration, along with your check for $30 and copyright Form TX. See Chapter 5 and http://www.loc.gov.

The Los Angeles Times Book Review, Times Mirror Square, Los Angeles, CA 90053. Tel: 800-LATIMES or 213-237-5000; Fax: 213-237-4712. See http://www.latimes.com.

Midwest Book Review, James A. Cox, 278 Orchard Drive, Oregon, WI 53575. Tel: 608-835-7937; Email: mwbookrevw@aol.com. Jim favors the small press and will review your book sooner than most reviewers. His reviews are also posted at Amazon.com, Barnes&Noble.com, Borders.com and other sites. See http://www.midwestbookreview.com/.

Newsday, Estelle Miller, Two Park Avenue, New York, NY 10016. Tel: 212-251-6623; Fax: 212-696-0590; Email: muchnick@newsday.com. *Newsday* reviews general-interest books such as fiction, history, politics, biographies and poetry. They don't review how-to books. Send books to the appropriate departmental editor. Circulation: 800,000 daily, 950,000 Sunday. See http://www.newsday.com/features/books/.

New York Review of Books, 1755 Broadway, Floor 5, New York, NY 10019. Tel: 212-757-8070; Fax: 212-333-5374; Email: nyrev@nybooks.com. This biweekly (except January, July, August and September, when it is monthly) magazine publishes reviews, prints excerpts and buys serial rights. They review 400 books each year, and the circulation is 130,000. See http://www.nybooks.com.

The New York Times, Daily Book Review Section, 229 W. 43rd Street, New York, NY 10036. Tel: 212-556-1234; Fax: 212-556-7088. See http://www.nytimes.com/books.

Dan Poynter, PO Box 8206-380, Santa Barbara, CA 93118-8206, autographed. Yes, I receive 15 to 20 books each week. That's why *The Self-Publishing Manual* has been called "the book that has launched thousands of books." All books are acknowledged. See http://ParaPublishing.com.

Publishers Weekly, Attn: Weekly Record, 360 Park Avenue South, 13th Floor, New York, NY 10010-1710. Tel: 646-746-6758; Fax: 646-746-6631. You should have sent bound galleys to *PW* some months earlier. This is a confirmation copy to show the book has been published.

Rainbo Electronic Reviews, Maggie Ramirez, Senior Editor, 8 Duran Court, Pacifica, CA 94044-4231. Tel: 650-359-0221 (9 to 5 Pacific time); Email: maggie@rainboreviews.com. Reviews 300 books a year and posts them online on a monthly basis. See http://www.rainboreviews.com for submission guidelines.

Reader's Digest Condensed Books, John Bohane, Editor in Chief, Pleasantville, NY 10570. Tel: 914-244-1000; Fax: 914-238-4559; Email: john.bohane@readersdigest.com. See http://www.rd.com/.

Rebecca's Reads, Rebecca Brown, Editor, Big River Productions, PO Box 371 Clallam Bay, WA 98326. Email: big.riv.prod@rebeccasreads.com. Books submitted for review must be available for purchase on Amazon.com. They do not review poetry, true crime, pulp romance or textbooks. Web site provides a link to Amazon for purchasing. Initial inquiries should be made via www.rebeccasreads.com.

Reference and Research Book News, Jane Erskine, 5739 NE Sumner Street, Portland, OR 97218. Tel: 503-281-9230; Fax: 503-287-4485; Email: booknews@booknews.com.

This quarterly, with a circulation of 1,700, reviews some 1,200 books per issue. See http://www.booknews.com.

Romantic Times, Nancy Collazo, 55 Bergen Street, Brooklyn, NY 11201. Tel: 718-237-1097; Fax: 718-624-2526; Email: info@romantictimes.com. *Rave Reviews* folded into *Romantic Times*. This monthly is aimed at consumers, and it focuses on romance, historicals, mysteries with romance elements and occasionally science fiction. They don't review techno thrillers, horror and men's westerns. More than 150 reviews are printed in each edition. See http://www.romantictimes.com.

Ruminator Review, Bart Schneider, 1648 Grand Avenue, St. Paul, MN 55105. Tel: 651-699-2610; Fax: 651-699-0970. *Ruminator Review*, formerly *Hungry Mind Review*, is a quarterly book review magazine founded in 1986 and distributed free in more than 600 independent bookstores around the country. Each print issue is built around a particular theme and includes reviews and essays by some of America's finest writers. See http://www.Ruminator.com.

San Francisco Chronicle, Attn: David Kipen, Book Editor, 901 Mission, San Francisco, CA 94103. Tel: 415-777-6232; Fax: 415-957-8737. Circulation: 570,000 daily, 715,000 Sunday. See http://www.sfgate.com/eguide/books/.

School Library Journal, Attn: Trevelyn Jones, 360 Park Avenue South, New York, NY 10010. Tel: 212-463-6759; Fax: 212-463-6689; Email: tjones@cahners.com. You should have sent bound galleys to *SLJ* some months earlier. This is a confirmation copy to show the book has been published. See http://www.slj.com.

Small Press Review, Attn: Len Fulton, PO Box 100, Paradise, CA 95967. Tel: 800-477-6110 or 530-877-6110;

Fax: 530-877-0222; Email: dustbooks@dcsi.net. This monthly publication has a circulation of 3,500 and specializes in fiction and poetry. See http://www.dustbooks.com.

USA Today, Deirdre Donahue, Book Editor, 1000 Wilson Boulevard, Arlington, VA 22229. Tel: 703-276-3400 or 202-276-6580; Email: ddonahue@usatoday.com. This daily national newspaper prints reviews every Friday and other times under special subject areas such as sports, money, lifestyle or art and entertainment. Circulation: 1.9 million. See http://www.usatoday.com/life/enter/books/leb.htm.

Voice Literary Supplement, *Village Voice*, Joy Press, 36 Cooper Square, New York, NY 10003. Tel: 212-475-3300; Fax: 212-475-8944; Email: editor@villagevoice.com. They review 500 books each year in 10 issues. Circulation: 180,000. See http://www.villagevoice.com/vls.

Washington Post, Marie Arana, Book World, 1150 15th Street NW, Washington, DC 20071. Tel: 202-334-6000; Fax: 202-334-5059; Email: aranam@washpost.com. Circulation: 780,000 daily, 1,100,000 Sunday. The *Post* reviews about 2,000 general fiction and nonfiction books each year. A favorable review in *The New York Times* or the *Washington Post* tends to stimulate good reviews in the book sections of smaller newspapers. See http://www.washingtonpost.com/wp-srv/style/.

You should send one copy to each of the 8 to 10 **major wholesalers**. See Chapter 8 and Wholesalers in Appendix 2.

Again, one copy goes to each of the 6 to 10 most important **opinion-molders** in your field. If these people talk up your book, you'll be off to a good start. Personally autograph the books.

Time is of the essence. These early review copies must be sent out as soon as the truck arrives from the printer. Reviewers like *new* books. Books are copyright dated so it's easy to tell when they are not new. Equally important, most of your initial sales will come from these reviews. So if you don't get moving with your review copy program, that inventory will not move out. Meanwhile, the dated books are getting older every day.

By the way, while most reviews are free, they can take three months or more to appear. Just send the books out and then go on to other promotion projects.

REVIEWS TO THE ULTIMATE CONSUMER: Now that the prepublication and early review packages have been sent, it's time to get to the *retail* reviewers. These are the rest of the book review magazines, newspapers with book review columns, general interest magazines that review all types of books, freelance book reviewers, radio and TV stations with talk shows and book programs, other online reviewers and—last but not least—special-interest periodicals that cater to the book's field(s).

It would be very expensive and terribly inefficient to send review copies to every reviewer, yet some publishers do this. Many of the larger publishers automate their review-book process. The result of taking the human touch out of the loop is that some reviewers get more than one package, while others receive large numbers of books they do not review. Big publishers often even ignore reviewers who request a specific title, because the promotion people are by now concentrating on a new line of books. Smaller publishers tend to be smart enough to always send out a "requested title," knowing there's a very good chance of its being reviewed.

Since book reviews are very effective and review copies are very inexpensive, it makes sense to spend more time and effort on reviews than on most other forms of promotion or paid advertising. For most books, it's not unusual to send out 300 to 500 review copies. This may seem like a lot, because many large publishers circulate less than 50; however, they are a sound investment. Several inches of review space in magazines, major and minor, is extremely valuable. And this is editorial copy, far more credible than advertising puffery. For example, 94% of the librarians rely on reviews they read in *Library Journal*, but only 35% believe the ads. The more reviews you receive, the more likely librarians will see the reviews and buy your book. And, of course, you will repeat the best reviews on all of your library flyers.

If only 30% of the magazines you target review your book, you are way ahead on your investment. Considering that reviews return so much, it is wise to follow these two simple rules:

1. Don't be stingy with review copies, but do not waste your money either.

2. When in doubt, ship it out.

UNDERSTANDING THE REVIEWER: There are two basic types of reviews. A *summary* review relates the contents of the work without issuing an opinion on its value. These reviews help potential readers select books for their particular needs. An *evaluative* review decides whether the author has covered the topic and compares the book with similar works. It usually ends with a favorable or unfavorable recommendation, and may be brief or long.

Your book is a product of you. You poured your time, heart and soul into it. But just because you were interested enough to take the time to write it doesn't mean a reviewer will be interested enough to take the time to read it all. A book critic will read your entire book, but a book reviewer will probably only check the front matter. Some reviewers write reviews on 10 to 15 books a week. Most of the reviewer's comments will come from your news release and other enclosures. Make them good. Also consider this: if a reviewer elects to use large portions of your superbly written news release in the review, then to some degree you are actually controlling the content of the review.

It helps to understand the lot of the editors and/or reviewers. Whether they are full-time or freelance, they have one thing in common—they are extremely busy. Neither time nor room is available to review all the books that come in. Even the prestigious and prolific Sunday supplement of *The New York Times* can only cover about 10% of the books received. All books are not assigned, and most reviewers select the ones they want to review. You can't change the situation, so you might as well understand and take advantage of it.

ON OVERLOAD

A few years ago, I was dropping off a batch of books at the loading dock in back of the post office in Santa Barbara. I saw a young man (not in a postal uniform) with a cart full of packages near the dumpster, and my curiosity mounted. As I watched, the man ripped open the cartons, took out what appeared to be books, and placed them in a large carton. Then he threw the wrappers in the trash. Unable to stand it any longer, I approached the man and asked if these were *lost-in-the-mail* books. Turns out the packages were for Los Angeles book critic Robert Kirsch. This gigantic load of books was being received at his home address (imagine what showed up at work), and he not only didn't have time to pick up the books himself, he didn't have room for the wrappers. There is a second lesson here too. Much of the material you ship with review copies is likely to become separated from the books.

Ruth Coughlin of the *Detroit News* says, "I arrive at my office each Monday morning to find 200 books in unopened mailing envelopes stacked outside my door." Alice Digilio of the *Washington Post* says, "We have somebody here 20 hours a week whose only job is to tear open book packages."

If your book has special-area appeal, you can greatly increase your chances for review by submitting your book to the special publications reaching that particular group. For example, if my book were on skydiving, I might send review copies to all 68 parachute magazines and newsletters worldwide. Then I could also consider every aviation, outdoor, sport, recreation, do-it-yourself, teen, men's, etc., magazines I could find. There are some 60,000 magazines being printed in the U.S. today (and a lot more foreign). There must be some reaching the groups you want to target.

Be prepared for delays with publications from the smaller associations. They may want to review your book, but they have staff and budget limitations. Usually they rely on outside free help for book reviews. Typically, the editor will only scan a book before sending it off to an appropriate expert requesting him or her to review it. Often, the reviewer is very busy too.

SELECTING REVIEW PERIODICALS

One way to expand your list of appropriate media is to visit the reference desk of a large public library and ask to see the periodical directories. There are at least two for magazines, two for newsletters and several for newspaper columns. (Stop by the bank first for a roll of coins for the copy machine.) Copy just the pages you need and bring them home to enter the addresses of the periodicals into your computer; you'll use these addresses over and over again.

A main public library in a large city will have a larger budget for directories, and their books are more likely to be newer. *You can find many of the directories online, but there is usually an expensive charge to access the listings.* Some of the directories you will consult follow. You will also find directories of associations.

Standard Periodicals Directory: Thousands of magazines. More than 56,000 magazines, newsletters, etc.
http://www.oxbridge.com/

Oxbridge Directory of Newsletters
http://www.oxbridge.com/

The National Directory of Magazines
http://www.oxbridge.com/

Ulrich's International Periodicals Directory: Many U.S. and foreign periodicals.
http://www.ulrichsweb.com/ulrichsweb/

Hudson's *Subscription Newsletter Directory*
http://www.newsletter-clearinghse.com/

Gale's *Newsletters in Print*
http://www.galegroup.com/

Literary Market Place (LMP): Many good lists such as book review syndicates, book review periodicals, book

columnists, cable networks, radio and TV stations with book programs, book clubs, news services and newspapers with book sections. This resource is so valuable, you may want to buy a copy of your own.
http://www.literarymarketplace.com/lmp/us/index_us.asp

Bacon's Directories
http://www.Bacons.com

Gebbie's All-in-One Media Directory
http://www.gebbieinc.com/

Editor and Publisher International Yearbook: The key radio and TV personnel.
http://www.editorandpublisher.com/eandp/index.jsp

Directory of Literary Magazines by the Council of Literary Magazines & Presses.
http://www.clmp.org/about/dir.html

Writer's Market: Directed at writers in search of magazine publishers.
http://www.writersmarket.com

Encyclopedia of Associations directory: Lists 18,000 special-interest trade and professional organizations.
http://www.galegroup.com

National Trade and Professional Associations: 7,600 associations, unions and societies.
http://www.columbiabooks.com/

A handy resource is *The Pocket Media Guide.* It lists major trade, business and general-interest magazines and newspapers in its 33 pages. Free from Media Distribution Service (MDS).
http://www.prplace.com/mds_guide/

Address review books to a *specific person* or your book may get ripped off by someone else on the staff. When this happens, you not only waste a book, you lose out on a potential review. Also address review books to the *position*, not just the name, of the editor or reporter in case he or she has moved on.

Depending on your subject, you may find 300 to 500 potential reviewers for your book. Don't be surprised if you come up with more. On the other hand, if the topic is very specialized, you may find there are only a few dozen interested and qualified potential reviewers. The best rule is to contact everyone who might possibly review the book. Divide the periodicals into two groups:

•◦ **The good bets:** Those magazines you have heard of; good matches that are published regularly and have a large circulation. These periodicals *probably* will review the book.

•◦ **The rest:** Those you have not heard of, the title does not sound as though the periodical matches your book, it is published quarterly and/or the publication has a circulation of 600. These periodicals might *possibly* review the book.

Some magazines will be perfect matches for your subject, and some, although more general, will have such a large circulation that they cannot be ignored. Send books to the group of good bets, but email the rest asking if they're interested in seeing the book. You are fishing at this point; you won't hook a fish with every cast, but you have narrowed your odds by asking first.

Go through the directories and make up lists of newspapers, weekly magazines, review journals and specialized periodicals. Many smaller newspapers do not have reviewers on their staffs; they use syndicated columns. Be sure to send review copies to all syndicated reviewers.

ParaLists maintains lists of more than 90 categories of magazines. If you don't have time to go through the exercise of compiling your own, they can be downloaded in an Excel spreadsheet and maintained on your computer for repeated use. You can update the lists yourself and print out mailing labels at any time. Your mailing lists become a valuable company asset. See http://parapub.com/sites/para/resources/maillist.cfm.

ONLINE BOOKSTORE REVIEWS: Online booksellers such as Amazon.com and BarnesAndNoble.com have grown to be major forces in the industry. A good review at Amazon can move books; a bad review can hurt sales. Encourage those who like your books to post reviews on those sites.

REQUEST REVIEWS VIA *PPM*

Once your book is listed at Amazon, B&N and other online booksellers, you may request reviews via my spin-off newsletter *Publishing Poynters Marketplace*. See http://parapub.com/sites/para/resources/newsletter.cfm. People with an interest or expertise in your book's category will read and post a review on the Amazon and B&N Web sites. These comments can be used elsewhere in your promotion as well, and you could also request stories to use in the books you're developing.

REVIEW PACKAGE

The package sent to reviewers should include a book, review slip (see sample later in this chapter), a sample review, news releases, reprints of other reviews and your business card. Here are the details:

1. BOOK: Don't send a damaged book or *selected second* as some publishers do. You want to put your best foot forward, hoping to get the attention of the reviewer. Make sure the book looks new. Pack the book as you normally do so that it will arrive in good condition.

Some reviewers still assume that in real publishing the hardcover edition comes out several months prior to the softcover. If they receive a paperback, they take for granted the title is old. Today, with the increasing dominance of the *quality* or *trade paperback*, this barrier is beginning to be breached, and many books are being selected for review on their own merits, rather than being sorted by their cover. If you're publishing in softcover only, make sure the point is clear in your review package.

Use a rubber stamp to mark the review copies. Rubber-stamp the *edges* of the pages (side of the book) so that the marking is visible without lifting the cover. It is embarrassing when a marked review copy finds its way back into your for-sale stock.

WOW! A review copy

Review book rubber stamp

The rubber stamping will not stop the sale of a review book, but it will ensure the book will not be returned to you by a bookstore for credit.

DON'T GO THERE!

In mid-1979, the newspaper and book industries were scandalized when 10 newspaper book reviewers were accused of selling review books to the Strand bookstore in New York. Apparently, several bookstores sent form letters to reviewers soliciting books. The stores typically buy the books at 25% of list price and resell them at 50% of list. One reviewer estimated that he had received 30,000 review copies in seven years! Today, we're hearing a lot of complaints about the resale of review and promotional copies on Amazon. Fortunately, many periodicals have a policy of donating review copies philanthropically—to hospitals, charitable book fairs, etc.

Certainly the ability to easily sell review copies may promote more requesting of books without a real intention of considering them for review. There's nothing wrong with a reviewer requesting a book if he or she plans to review it. But it is wrong if he or she plans to sell the book without first considering it for review. It has recently been noted that along with the burgeoning growth of Web-based book reviewers, more and more brand-new books are being offered for sale as "slightly used books" on the Web—many times before their publication dates and at inflated prices. So the practice of requesting review copies, primarily to be sold, may be with us. Stay savvy when responding to requests for review copies.

Review copies are the least expensive and most effective way to promote your book.

▀▟ ▆▆ Para Publishing Presents for Review

Title: *The Self-Publishing Manual*

Author: Dan Poynter

Edition: 15th, completely revised. (A new book with a track record)

Number in print: More than 205,000

CIP/LCCN: 2006057841

ISBN: 1-56860-134-2

Pages: 472

Cover photo in ParaPub.com Pressroom

Price: $24.95

Season: Spring 2006

Publication date: May 2006

Rights:

a. Book clubs: Writer's Digest Book Club, Independent Book Club, Small Press Book Club.

b. Condensations: Publishing Trade, Income Opportunities.

A copy of your review to the address below will be appreciated.

Para Publishing
Reviewer Relations Department
PO Box 8206
Santa Barbara, CA 93118-8206 USA
Tel: 805-968-7277; Fax: 805-968-1379
info@ParaPublishing.com
http://ParaPublishing.com

Book review slip

2. REVIEW SLIPS contain the basic bibliographic data on the book. Most publishers slip the loose sheets between the pages. However, pasting the book review slip inside the cover with a spot of rubber cement or double-sided tape will make sure it stays with the book. Alternatively, review slips may also be made by computer-generating the information on mailing labels and pasting them on the inside front cover or flyleaf of each book.

3. SAMPLE REVIEW in the form of a news release. This could be generated by you or by a copywriter you hire. It highlights the features and strengths of a book, saving the reviewer time. It's an honest assessment, but by a knowledgeable source that knows the book in and out. Many reviewers find these sample reviews very helpful, and some publications will run them verbatim. In fact, it won't hurt to write up two samples, a short one and a long one.

Book review for *Choices: A Teen Woman's Journal for Self-awareness and Personal Planning*
    by Mindy Bingham, Judy Edmondson and Sandy Stryker.

For Immediate Release:

"As a little girl, did you ever wonder what became of Snow White, Cinderella, and Sleeping Beauty after they married their princes and retired to their respective castles?"
    And so begins a revolutionary new book, *Choices: A Teen Woman's Journal of Self-awareness and Personal Planning* by Mindy Bingham, Judy Edmondson and Sandy Stryker (Advocacy Press). This refreshing book is a welcome change from the traditional offerings for teenage girls. While the publishing industry continues to produce more and more romance novels for adolescent girls that reinforce the "they-lived-happily-ever-after" Cinderella syndrome, *Choices* gives the message, at a critical time, that the teenage girl has to take charge of her life—that she can't just drift and hope for some Prince Charming who will take all her burdens away.

Sample review

4. OTHER REVIEWS: Reviewers are more apt to review your book if big-name reviewers have treated it favorably in prepublication reviews. One way to convince them your book is worthy of their attention is to include copies of other reviews. Cut out or scan each review, and paste it on a piece of plain paper. Then cut out or scan the masthead or title of the magazine and paste it in for source and date identification. Underline the best parts of the review to draw attention to them. Make photocopies for your review kit.

Pasted-up prepublication and early reviews

Take advantage of a good review: Besides being very good for the ego, it can be used to further stimulate your promotion and sales program. You want your distributors and wholesalers to know you are promoting the book, so send them a copy. If a review appears in a local newspaper, send copies to the local bookstores. Keep these pasted-up reviews on file in your promotion binder and send them out with future review copies, letters to foreign-rights buyers or for use anytime you need more promotion. When you set up a booth at a bookfair, enlarge the reviews as part of your booth dressing and counter display.

5. **A COVER LETTER** is not necessary as long as the book is clearly marked as being a review copy. Stamp the book and assemble the usual package.

STAY SINCERE

Some public relations people like to get very personal in review copy mailings. They jot a little personal note to the reviewer, hoping to snow them into thinking they have met before, or that the reviewer may have made some long-forgotten promise at a cocktail party. This technique should only be used with great caution, as it can easily backfire and destroy the relationship.

---

6. **COVER PHOTOGRAPH:** Artwork will command much more space and make the review more attractive, resulting in a higher degree of readership. Provide the URL where a 300 dpi TIF file can be retrieved. Mention it on the review slip, the news release, etc.

7. **THE REVIEW & TESTIMONIAL SHEET:** The "rev/test" sheet lists excerpts from previous reviews and testimonials along with pertinent number-in-print and rights information.

MORE ON REVIEWS

CONTINUING REVIEW PROGRAM: Your review-copy program will not end at the publication date. Requests will come in as other reviewers hear of your book, and you should be on the lookout for new reviewers.

Read what others are saying about

Parachuting,
The Skydiver's Handbook

This is only up-to-date basic sport parachuting handbook and it is highly recommended. —The Next Whole Earth Catalog.

For a lesson or just some vicarious thrills, read Parachuting, The Skydiver's Handbook. —New York Post.

A valuable collection of information and a good first look at the sport.— Library Journal.

Dan's strength as a writer lies in his technical descriptions of equipment; these are faultless. —British Sport Parachutist magazine.

This handy volume falls into the "Everything you need to know about..." category and is required reading for everyone who wants to jump out of an aeroplane. —Flight International.

All aspects are covered in a clear and authoritative fashion. —Air International.

Poynter's latest fills the bill of educating while entertaining. He says it well. —Parachutist magazine.

Chapters cover an overview of the sport, detailed discussion of each facet of the first jump, the history of parachuting, and an in-depth study of parachuting emergencies. Other sections discuss specialized jumping and equipment. Appendix contains a glossary and a list of drop zones, books, magazines and films. —Sporting Goods Business.

Well-written, this volume is profusely illustrated with photos and drawings. A useful addition to the public library collection. —Choice magazine.

Dan Poynter has done it again. —Spotter NewsMagazine.

Dan Poynter has generously guided thousands to authorship. Their books make this a better world.
          —Dr. Robert Müller, Past Assistant Secretary General of the United Nations
                    and author of 2000 Ideas & Dreams for a Better World.
After eight revised editions, **over 70,000 copies are in print.**

- ➤ **Honored** with an Award of Excellence by the Aviation/Space Writers Association. Named the best technical/training book of the year.
- ➤ **Selected** by the U.S. Parachute Association, the Canadian Sport Parachuting Association, and other national organizations for sale to their members.
- ➤ **Serialized** in Parachutist (USA), Free Fall Kiwi (New Zealand), Fritt Fall (Norway), and CanPara (Canada).
- ➤ **Mentioned** in Joint effort, Aviation/Space, SAFE Journal, Flyv (Danmark), Soldier of Fortune, Thrill Sports Catalog, Alaska Flying, Skydiver Magazin (Germany) and many more.
- ➤ **Selected** for transcription for the blind by the Milwaukee Public Library and the Florida Department of Education.
- ➤ **Translated** and published in Spanish by Editorial Paraninfo of Madrid.

Parachuting, The Skydiver's Handbook by Dan Poynter & Mike Turoff. All new, completely revised, eighth edition. 5.5 x 8.5, 400 pages, 260 illustrations. ISBN 1-56860-062-3, LC 97-22061. $19.95. Publication: Winter 1999-2000.

Para Publishing, PO Box 8206, Santa Barbara, CA 93118-8206 USA. Tel: (805) 968-7277, Fax: (805) 968-1379.
Email: DanPoynter@ParaPublishing.com; Web site: http://www.ParaPublishing.com

Review/Testimonial sheet

THOSE UNSOLICITED REQUESTS: From time to time, you'll receive unsolicited requests for review copies. You could look up the periodical for its frequency, circulation and audience match, as well as whether this person is really on the staff or a bona fide stringer. However, since the review package costs you so little, you may decide to just respond cordially. Certainly the free publicity a review can provide is worth many times the cost of the book. When in doubt go with your gut feeling, or explore it further if you're truly suspicious.

PRESS CLIPPING SERVICES employ people who regularly read all major publications and clip out mentions of their clients. You can subscribe to one of these services (see listings in *Literary Market Place*), but it probably is not worth the expense. The clipping services cannot read every periodical; they often send clippings that mention your key word but not you, and you do not need all these clippings anyway.

Google and other online services provide a faster and cheaper service.

Many smaller periodicals will send you copies of their magazine containing the review. Plus, some customers enclose a clipping with their order. There will be very few reviews you do not hear about.

TRADING ADVERTISING FOR REVIEW: Never suggest to an editor that you might be willing to advertise in the magazine as a way of gaining a review. Most editors do not sell advertising—that is the job of the advertising department. Petty bribery will repel most review editors, who view themselves as independent. On the other hand, when the ad sales representative calls, it's OK to say that you are "waiting for the review to appear to test the match between your book and the magazine's audience." You want to see how the review pulls before investing in an ad. Let the review test the medium.

BAD REVIEWS: Some of your reviews may be negative, and one reason (but not the only reason) is that some reviewers are negative. Some of these critics are frustrated writers who try to bring all other published authors down to their level. They take cheap shots or use the book as a springboard for lofting their own views.

> *Many book reviews are mean-spirited. Even if a reviewer likes a book, he or she must find fault and write snide and/or patronizing little asides about the author's character or motives that demonstrate the reviewer's intellectual and moral superiority.*
> **—Andrew Greeley in Publishers Weekly**

Reviewers tend to be very cautious people. Even a very favorable review will probably contain one negative sentence or paragraph. This is a cover to save the reputation of the reviewer in case the book turns out to be a loser.

In smaller publications aimed at a select target audience, an author may know every qualified reviewer! This could work for or against you. Books are sometimes unknowingly assigned to a reviewer who has an axe to grind with the author. (Some reviewers write negative reviews on purpose.)

> *There is nothing like a good negative review to sell a book.*
> **—Hugh R. Barbour, bookseller**

Don't worry about a negative review. Any review is better than no review, because people tend to remember the subject more than the details of the critique. Even a bad review will arouse reader curiosity. Libraries must cover every subject, and acquisition librarians are always searching for something new.

> *Ellipses are often the enemy of truth.*
> **—Brigitte Weeks, editor, Washington Post Book World**

When you quote the negative review, just use the good parts. If there are no good parts, just say "as reviewed in the *Washington Post*" or "find out why *Consumer Reports* hated this book." Do not edit out the bad words so that the review appears to be favorable.

It's flagrant misrepresentation to edit out less desirable phrases if they change the meaning and intention of the review. Reviewers and editors are writers too, and most have excellent memories. If you misquote them, they'll probably catch you and certainly remember you when your next book arrives for review.

> *Someone once remarked that we have the power of life and death over a book. Life perhaps, but not death. We could devote our entire section to loathing the latest Sidney Sheldon, and it would make no difference.*
> **—Stefan Kanfer in Time**

Learn from negative reviews. Perhaps your promotional approach is misleading. Think about changing your news release. Help the reviewers understand the book. Try to direct their thinking. The same goes for good reviews. Focus on the praise—the parts of the book reviewers like. Emphasize these parts in your updated news release.

WHY REVIEWERS REVIEW BOOKS: Many reviewers will spend some 10 hours reading a book, a couple of days thinking about it and perhaps 6 hours writing up the review. Some reviewers are paid a small amount and often get a short description at the end of the review (which may be helpful in promoting their own book or agenda); however, many do not get paid at all. They get the book and the satisfaction of being on the inside of publishing and/or their area of expertise. To add insult to injury, the IRS has attempted to tax some reviewers for the value of the books they receive.

> *Book reviewing is one of the few activities in the world that could be said to depend largely on love.*
> **—Jack Beatty, literary editor, New Republic**

Your local newspapers, magazines and radio and television stations almost *have to* cover you, because you and your book are local news. Get out the *Yellow Pages* and make up a list of local media. You'll probably find more contacts than you expected. Send a review package to each periodical, addressed to a particular features editor. They may not have a book review section, but you would rather have a half-page feature on *you* and your book anyway. Follow up in a few days with a telephone call to the most important ones. Next, do the same for local radio and television stations.

If you know a freelance or staff reviewer personally, send him or her a review copy. Use every possible connection you might have. Hit all your hometowns—where you live now, where you grew up, where you went to school—*all of them*. You may get not only a nice review, but a special feature story as well.

FOLLOW-UP CALLS increase your chances for a review. Don't be a pest, but it's acceptable to call to see if your book *has been received*. You may find that your package has not arrived on the reviewer's desk or that your book or news release should have gone to another editor. Make your calls brief and to the point.

ACKNOWLEDGE ALL REVIEWS with an emailed personal note; praise and thank the reviewer. They will remember you when you send your next book. A small amount of time spent on letters here is an investment in the future. Annotate your computerized list of reviewers to indicate that this reviewer has performed for you.

HOW TO SHIP: Review copies can be sent to most reviewers via USPS Media Mail. If you live near any of the reviewers on your list, hand-delivery never hurts.

MAKING THE ROUNDS

When the *Frisbee Player's Handbook* rolled off the press, I made up a list of reviewers in street-address order. New York co-author Mark Danna made the systematic rounds of reviewers in Manhattan and threw the book at them. The unique circular book was brought to their attention, made an impression and was very well reviewed.

If the reviewer requested the book, make a copy of the request and place it on top of the book. Everyone recognizes and takes an interest in his or her own message. Seeing their message reminds reviewers the book was requested.

CREDIT THE REVIEWER: Reviewers like credit for their work, so mention their name as well as that of the publication. For example: "Kevin Gibson, *Parachutist Magazine.*" In fact, if the reviewer really likes the book, he or she will try to provide a few quotable lines, hoping for a mention.

PERMISSION TO QUOTE: Reviews are written to be quoted. Normally, you don't have to contact the reviewer or periodical for permission. However, in the last few years, a few isolated review publications have begun requesting payment for reprinting their reviews. This is a new development.

PAID-FOR REVIEWS are not as credible or valuable as free reviews.

Put a lot of effort into reviews. Far less expensive than display advertising, they're the best promotional investment you can make. For more details on setting up your review program, see *Book Reviews* in Para Publishing Special Reports in Appendix 2 or at http://parapub.com/sites/para/resources/allproducts.cfm.

NEWS RELEASES

Releases are used to announce products, promotions and events. They accompany galleys and review copies of books, are included in promotional kits to radio, television and print media and are posted in the pressroom on your Web site. Sometimes a release accompanies other promotional or informational material, and sometimes a release is sent alone.

> *"News release" is the modern term for "press release."*
> *Your message will be sent to all forms of media such*
> *as radio, television and other opinion-molders—*
> *not just the print media.*

The media are in the news-gathering and publishing business; they want to hear from you. Publicity is not like *expensive* advertising; instead it involves the use of *inexpensive* news releases. News items receive a much higher degree of readership than advertising, and greater readership leads to more response (sales). News releases generate publicity and invite book reviews. Releases may be used to announce publication of your new book to newspapers, magazines, libraries, radio and TV. In fact, they should be sent to anyone who will read them.

Editors might use only one news release in 10, but news releases are responsible for 20% to 25% of the editorial space in many newspapers and magazines. Some of the smaller, more highly targeted publications use an even higher percentage of news release input.

> *If you make life easy for editors, they will*
> *give you coverage.*
> **—Terri Lonier, Working Solo**

Editors would use even more news release material if the news releases they received were more interesting. Your challenge is to draft copy that is irresistible to the editor— to come up with interesting information the editor will want to pass on to his or her readers. You want the editor to open your monthly mailings first while thinking, "I wonder what good material Drew is sending me today?"

Remember, you're providing a service to busy editors. As an author–publisher, you are an expert in your field and a great information source. You're providing important, timely and interesting information to the editor and his or her readers.

The four steps to placing your news releases are:

1. **Develop an interesting "angle"** that shows how your book will benefit the reader. You need a "hook," an issue.

2. **Locate and cultivate the appropriate media contacts.**

3. **Deliver the information in the proper form.**

4. **Be persistent and follow up.**

Give the editors what they want and need; deliver the information in such a way that it is useful and newsworthy. The less rewriting your release requires, the more chance it will be used.

TAILORING NEWS RELEASES: You'll draft some releases specifically for distribution to a particular publication. Study the publication, imitate the writing style and follow the same article length and layout. The secrets are to know what the editor considers good news value and to know how to write in good press style.

Computers make news release tailoring easy. Most of your release will remain the same, but you will tailor the headline and lead paragraph to the target audience. For a book on publishing, I would have different pitches for releases sent to magazines for publishers, writers or printers. Just change the headline and lead paragraph and let the machine copy the rest of the previous release.

FORMAT AND LAYOUT: The format of the release is standardized. The easiest way to design it is simply to type "NEWS RELEASE" on your own letterhead stationery. Then just type in the date the release is to be used ("For Use the Week of September 17th" or "For Immediate Release").

Place a contact name with telephone number in the upper right-hand corner. If your name is Greg Godek, the book is authored by Greg Godek and/or the book is published by Greg Godek Publishing, make your company look like a larger publisher by selecting another (pen or PR) name for the contact person.

Use 8.5" x 11" paper. Some publicists use legal-size paper, which has the advantage of sticking out of a pile of papers and is more easily noticed. Begin a bit of the way down from the top and leave 1" margins on the sides and bottom. The traditional approach is to double-space the release. Today, with the option of electronic distribution, you may wish to single-space it as shown in the news release sample.

The release can be any length, but one page or two is the norm. Some people prefer one-page releases. If the release runs more than one page, identify the story with a header in the upper left-hand corner of the second page. If you want to keep it to one page, excerpt a portion and place it in a separate release featuring background on the book's subject or an author biography. Another way to condense a release to a single page is to use the computer's ability to change from double-space to 1.8- or 1.5-line spacing or

NEWS RELEASE

For Immediate Release

Contact: Joyce Ready 805-968-7277
JoyceReady@ParaPub.com

Headline
Type a descriptive, clever and catchy headline in capital letters and center it. Lure the editor to read more. Then space down and get into the body of the release.

Issue or challenge
The lead paragraph is designed to invite the largest number of people to read the article. It must have broad appeal; make it interesting. The release should be *issue-oriented*; write about the *problem*, not the book. The release should begin by stating the problem and telling why this is an important subject. Make it provocative.

Development
Spend time on a second paragraph developing the message. Put the most interesting information first to keep the reader reading. Recite the most important items in descending order so that if some are cut from the end, the most important will remain. Provide interesting facts and statistics.

How the book solves the problem
Now move from the *what* to the *how* orientation. It's not necessary to dwell on the book. Anyone who finishes the article will be interested in the book. Then describe the contents of the book; mention it as a resource. Continue with some background on the topic and show why your book is unique, useful and timely. Recite the benefits.

Author
Write a short paragraph about the author and tell why the author is an expert on the subject.

Ordering information
List the price and say that the book is available from the publisher and the stores. List your address so the reader will know where to send the money. Code your address.

End the release with the newspaper termination sign: ### or -30-

News release layout

For immediate release

Contact: Joyce Ready, tel: 805-968-7277

"This book is so reduced, so concise, so easy to grasp—if you're really serious about writing, grab it." —Barnaby Conrad, Founder and Director, Santa Barbara Writers Conference

Bet You Can't Read Just One

Writers love writing and they love reading—especially when it's about writing. This is a book about writing for writers and it is in sound bites. Dan Poynter has taken the whole business of writing nonfiction books and distilled it down to the most important tips or rules. *Successful Nonfiction: Tips & Inspiration for Getting Published* could well be described as *Life's Little Instruction Book* meets *Chicken Soup for the Writer's Soul.*

Each page contains a writing tip, a pertinent illustration, an explanation, a relevant story and a quotation on the point from someone in history. This book could be much longer but Poynter has distilled the 109 inspirational tips into memorable and thought-provoking bite-sized pieces.

Sound-bite books seem to be all the rage now. Maybe it's because people are so short of time. Some books are just groupings of quotations. This book goes much further.

This 144-page gift book is beautifully designed with French flaps, gold stamping, embossed letters, contrasting end sheets and matte lamination. It is a treasure both inside and out.

Dan Poynter is the author of more than 100 previous books, many of them on writing and publishing. He's best known for *The Self-Publishing Manual: How to Write, Print & Sell Your Own Book,* now in its 15th revised edition.

Successful Nonfiction is available for $14.95 in most bookstores or by calling Para Publishing at 800-PARAPUB.

###

Successful Nonfiction: Tips & Inspiration for Getting Published by Dan Poynter. Original edition. 5¹/₂ x 8¹/₂, 144 pages, 110 illustrations. ISBN 1-56860-061-5. $14.95. See our pressroom for a 300 dpi TIF of the cover.

Para Publishing, PO Box 8206, Santa Barbara, CA 93118-8206 USA
Tel: (805) 968-7277, Fax: (805) 968-1379.
info@ParaPublishing.com   http://ParaPublishing.com

News release sample

single-spacing. Never type on the back of the sheet. If it's more than one page in length, put "more" at the bottom of page one so the reader will know to go to the next page.

You can send news releases via email. Editors are more likely to use a news release that's convenient. Include it as part of the email message—not as an attachment. And post it on your Web site.

JOURNALISTIC STYLE: Observe basic journalistic style.

1. Keep your sentences to 23 words or less.
2. Use 3 p.m., not 3:00 P.M.
3. Commas and periods go inside closing quotation marks.
4. No capital letters should be used for anything in the text but initials, first letters of proper names and first characters of sentences (exception: TV, not tv).
5. The first mention of the author should include first name, middle initial and last name (subsequent mentions should include first or last name only).
6. Use a journalistic tone, not an advertising tone.
7. Italicize book titles.

> *Releases should, like all writing, be accurate, consistent, clear, concise, persuasive, interesting and, above all, correct in spelling, punctuation and grammar. (I did not say this would be easy!)*
>
> **—Rose Adkins, past assistant editor, Writer's Digest**

Use the fewest number of words to communicate any thought. Cut unnecessary words. Circle all repeated words in a paragraph and select alternates. Never use a less common word when a familiar one will convey your meaning. Use simple sentences; complex sentences can be hard to read. Do not make judgments. If you say the book is "the most important contribution to literature since the Bible," the editor will cut it out or just trash your release. On the other hand, it doesn't hurt to quote someone else who says something nice about your book. Proofread and re-proofread!

Take your time and compose a good release. Not all news gatherers do their own work all the time, so your release may appear verbatim in print. It may even be reprinted word for word as a book review or wind up syndicated in several magazines.

A release that starts out, "Festival Publications is happy to announce..." sounds self-serving. There's a much better chance your release will be used if an issue-oriented headline begins "Breakthrough found in..." The release is being written for the readers of the periodical; it isn't an announcement for your company picnic. When drafting a news release for a specific section, such as *Publishers Weekly*'s "Back to Press" column, write it in the same format and style as the column you're targeting. Don't make the editors rewrite the release; they may round-file (trash) it instead. Provide a URL where the editor can retrieve a 300 dpi TIF of the cover.

Remember, you want the release to push your *issue*; the book is a secondary message, almost subliminal.

EMAILING THE RELEASE: Send the releases to all appropriate magazines, newsletters, book clubs (see "Book Club Rights" in Chapter 8), subsidiary rights contacts (see "Subsidiary Rights" in Chapter 8), wholesalers, libraries, sales representatives, hometown papers, etc. Don't forget your connections with alumni, fraternal, trade or church publications.

Spread the releases around. Follow up with a telephone call to the most important periodicals.

News releases to local periodicals may be hand-delivered. Personal delivery not only receives more attention, but meeting editors will be a great education for you.

Use news releases liberally. Every time you go back to press or revise the book, issue a release to herald it. Magazines such as the prestigious *Publishers Weekly* may give you a few lines if you just let them know. Releases can also be issued to announce speaking engagements, TV appearances, autograph parties, awards won and any other newsworthy event. If business slows down, think up a newsworthy item and write a release about it.

Always respond to *Publishers Weekly*'s requests for information for their spring and fall announcements issues. Once you register for an ISBN, you will be on R.R. Bowker's mailing list and should receive these requests automatically. You must follow the *PW* submission guidelines in order to be listed. If you're going on tour, send a short release, listing the places and dates, to *PW*'s "Author Publicity" column. Also be on the lookout for special editions of *PW* and other magazines. Some of the special editions are on cookbooks, travel books, sports books, etc. Listings are usually free.

Foreword Magazine has four announcement issues per year for independent and university publishers. See their Web site for submission guidelines: http://forewordmagazine.com/. Tel: 231-933-3699; Fax: 231-933-3899.

Remember that media people work in a pressure-cooker world. Be polite; they won't expect it. You might get a lot of mileage out of one kind word.

For more information on news releases and paint-by-the-number instructions for drafting and using them, see *News Releases and Book Publicity* in Para Publishing Special Reports in Appendix 2 or at http://parapub.com/sites/para/resources/allproducts.cfm.

PRESS KITS

Press kits, folders with information on your book, are being used less as publishers move these materials to their Web sites. It can be more efficient to place all the kit materials on your site on a pressroom page. Then direct the media to your promotional materials with email and business cards.

> *While publicity misused can be nothing but an ego trip for the author, well used it can be a powerful sales tool.*
>
> **—Al Lind**

USE COVER OVERRUNS for book promotion. Print your promotion copy on the other side and mail them out. If your book is 8.5" x 11", fold and trim the extra covers into file folders and hand them out at appropriate conventions. Delegates will carry your folder around, using it to collect other papers, for days. If you have a hardcover book, get extra jackets—not just for promotion but for replacements on the books. Jackets become shelf-worn quickly in the stores. A new jacket will make the book look crisp again. Also, distributors and sales reps need extra covers for their presentations to book buyers. Always ask your printer for the overruns and order a few hundred extra. Run-on printing is very inexpensive, whereas reprinting the cover/jacket later or using color copying can be quite costly.

NOTIFY YOUR FRIENDS of your new book via email. Copy and paste your back-cover sales copy to use in your announcement. Then ask everyone in your address book to forward the announcement to anyone in their address book who might have an interest in the subject matter of the book.

Also email influential people in the field covered by the book. They are prime prospects and will help to promote your book by just talking about it. Influential people in the field should also receive an autographed, complimentary copy; you want these opinion-molders on your side.

RADIO AND TELEVISION TALK SHOWS

Every day, more than 10,200 guests appear on 988 television stations that broadcast 4,250 local interview and talk shows across the U.S. Roughly 94% of the author–guests don't even have recognizable names.

Many people love to go on radio and television. In fact, I think some people write books just to get on the air.

Authors are interesting people. Most people feel that authors are experts and celebrities. Radio and television talk shows constantly need interesting guests to attract listeners and viewers. The fact that you wrote a book will get you on; then you must have something interesting to say that is unique, controversial or fascinating.

Most of the guests booked by the shows are authors, so your book is your entrée to the airwaves and cable. However, you're appearing on the show as interesting, entertaining "talent," not to overtly promote your book. The host will promote your book (or may allow you to plug it), but your function is to impart exciting information about your subject. If you come across as dull or unprepared, the host can always reduce your segment or edit you out later.

Do talk shows sell books? Sometimes, oftentimes, but not all the time. We hear when a show works, but we usually don't hear the rest of the stories. If you enjoy talk shows, do them; if you don't like talk shows, do not feel obligated to go on the air.

FOR-PAY INTERVIEWS: Never pay a station for an interview. If a radio station is charging you, it must be because they don't have advertisers and listeners. Conversely, stations do not pay you for an interview. They are giving you exposure.

START WITH PHONERS on "talk radio." They are fast, easy, inexpensive, and you don't have to get dressed up or travel. You just talk from your own telephone to the radio host, who is probably miles away. Begin with local radio shows and work your way up. Then graduate to local television shows and work your way to national shows. Don't try to start out with *Oprah*. You have only one shot at the top shows, and if you blow one you will not only not be invited back—you won't be invited to any of the others. They monitor each other. On the other hand, if you're a dynamic guest, others will notice and want to book you.

HOW TO GET ON: There are several ways to get on the shows. You can book yourself, advertise your subject and expertise in the publications the producers read or hire a public relations agency to contact the producers for you. For a complete explanation and the very latest in contact names and addresses, see Instant Report 602, *Interviews:*

How Authors Get on Radio and TV, at http://parapub.com/ sites/para/resources/allproducts.cfm. You can also take out a listing in the *Radio-TV Interview Report*. For a sample copy, advertising rates and an application, contact http://www.rtir.com/.

A media flyer

MEDIA FLYER: Another way to let the talk shows know you're available is by sending them a catchy media flyer. The media flyer stresses an interesting issue and offers you as an expert to explain the subject. The back of the flyer can describe the book. The book is not the subject of the pitch; it simply gives credibility to the expert.

TELEVISION: The big television shows are best, of course, because they reach more people. *Today, The Tonight Show, Oprah* and *60 Minutes* are the most influential in book-selling. The best plug for a book is when Oprah Winfrey takes a personal interest. According to *TV Guide*, an appearance on *Today* can sell 3,000 copies of a book, but a few minutes on *Oprah* have moved 50,000.

Don't overlook the smaller and local shows and cable stations. They're much easier to get on, and you can use them to work your way up. Many stations have special shows for interviewing authors, and most have at least one talk show. Your local station may want you on a community-affairs program, for instance. Depending on your subject, the station might even produce a short clip for their news broadcast. Once you have appeared on one local station, do not give up on the others. Use another interesting angle.

To get on a show, find out who the producer is. Simply call the station and ask the switchboard operator.

Once you appear on television, you may want a "clipping" of the show. Some services tape everything on the air and will sell you a copy. Contact Video Monitoring Services of America at http://www.vmsinfo.com/. Or if you ask, the TV station may record the show for you if you supply the tape or disc.

There are two major reasons the Chicken Soup *books are successful. One is Jack and the other is Mark. They spend every waking moment creatively promoting the books.*

YOU'RE ON THE AIR: The show's producer will call you to set up an appointment and then call again at the appointed time. Always clarify the time zone; will he or she be calling at 7:00 a.m. your time or his or her time? Respond by sending a copy of the book, your news release, an author bio and photocopies of any reviews you have received. If you send a list of questions and/or interesting facts about your topic that can trigger questions, most hosts will use them.

When you go on the air, be prepared. Disable call-waiting if you have it on your telephone. (The clicking is annoying.) Several months have passed since you wrote the book, so review it. Practice public speaking. Think about the best answers to the questions most likely to be asked. Rehearse your stock answers and use high-impact words or brief "grabber" comments that are suitable for a sound bite. Make a list of the main points you want to make, and slip them in no matter what the questions are. The talk show host may frustrate you by bouncing from subject to subject, so don't be caught with nothing to say. Push the subject, not your book. Don't mention the book at every opportunity—it only turns off listeners and wears out your welcome.

Before you start the interview, make sure that the show host, producer and switchboard operator all have a card with your complete ordering information—phone, URL and email address and the fact that your book is available in bookstores.

When you start doing a heavy schedule of radio and TV, your book must be in as many bookstores as possible. This is because people are creatures of habit, and they will buy books where they always buy books—regardless of your prompting.

On the big morning shows, you'll be lucky to have three minutes on the air. Later in the day, you might have four to eight minutes. Evening shows may run an hour.

READY WHEN YOU ARE!

A few years ago, I was listening to a local radio station while running errands. I heard a disc jockey talking about making his first parachute jump. Since I had written several books on skydiving, I called the disc jockey, who spoke to me during record plays. An invitation was extended, and I dropped by the radio station for an impromptu interview that lasted all afternoon.

Media people are busy and under a lot of deadline pressures. Even though your book is the most important thing that has happened to you lately, it's just another news item to them. They are not easily impressed; they deal with news-making personalities all the time. Be polite; they won't expect it. Everyone around them is tough and short. A thank-you note afterward will leave a nice memory, and you'll be more likely to get good treatment for your second book.

The biggest challenge all authors face with media interviews is that their books are not in all the stores. Listeners may make one attempt to buy the book and then forget about it. One way to handle this potential disaster is to tell the host you'll send a free information kit to any listener who will drop you a card. Talk show hosts love to give things to their audience and most will repeat your message and URL again and again. Automate your InfoKit with an autoresponder. Let your Web site send out the information and collect the addresses.

AUTHOR PROMOTION

AUTHOR TOURS are the way you promote your book at events and on television out of town, and they are very hard work. There was a time when all authors had to do was deliver their manuscript to the publisher and then go home to await the royalty checks. However, with the advent of TV and more hype in the book business, the toughest promotion effort for the writer now is in criss-crossing the country speaking and selling the book.

For the publisher, it is publicity at low cost.
For the author, it is an endurance test.
—**The Wall Street Journal**

Author tours are often a grueling experience from sunup to sundown, and they are no longer inexpensive (air travel, food, lodging, clothing, car and driver, etc.). However, there is no more effective way of reaching huge masses of the book-buying public.

When you're on a television tour, try to book print media too. Make the most of your time by granting interviews to the newspapers and magazines in the same city. Don't forget college newspapers, if appropriate. Also try to schedule author signings at bookstores and appearances at clubs, organizations and writers' groups. The fact that you're appearing on radio or television will tell them you are important, and they can promote your in-store signings in conjunction with your other appearances and events.

> *When promoting your book, speak proudly about it.*
> *You worked hard on it and should be proud. False*
> *modesty will get you nowhere.*
>
> *—Mark Danna, co–author,* **Frisbee Player's Handbook**

When you know you are going to be on a show, try doing a postcard mailing to all the bookstores in the broadcast area (often your distributor will aid you in this by giving you the lists of important stores). Let the stores know who your distributor or wholesalers are so they can easily order in anticipation of your appearance.

Before appearing at a bookstore for a reading or a signing, send an email message to all your friends, relatives and associates within driving distance of the store. Ask them to alert their friends. The store will drum up a few attendees, but if you want a crowd the turnout is up to you.

FEATURE ARTICLES: Local papers, company magazines, alumni and association publications, etc., are always looking for interesting news about their people. Let them do a story on you and they will mention your greatest accomplishment—your book. You are now an expert, an interesting person and a celebrity just because you're a published author. It's the "magic" of being an author.

You are news to every publication you're connected with—from national associations to local newspapers. Take advantage of having these contacts. Remember, book reviews sell books, but feature stories sell more books.

MAGAZINE ARTICLES are a way to gain publicity for your book while furthering your writing career. It's easy to spin off articles from the pages of your book.

You'll be pleased to find that you will have less difficulty selling articles to magazines now that you're a published author. You are an expert, and magazines want authoritative material. Of course, you will want to end the article with: "Editor's note: Ed Rigsbee is the author of... that is available from..." and type the notice just as you want it to appear. Don't leave this up to the editor. Those who read your article are interested in the subject or they wouldn't be reading about it. Many will want to know more and will seek out your book.

Most national magazines don't pay a great deal for articles—usually just a few hundred dollars. However, the exposure is more important to you than the money. And if you offer the article for free, you have a better chance of its seeing print.

SPEAKING ENGAGEMENTS: As an expert on your subject, you are in demand by service organizations, adult education programs, church groups, PTAs, businesses, conventions, the chamber of commerce and others. Many of these groups feature a guest speaker at every meeting. Sometimes they rotate the responsibility among the membership to find a speaker. Your call to them might actually get someone off the hook.

The possibilities will become obvious once you begin to think of your topic from the marketing standpoint. If yours is a carpentry how-to book, a hardware store or lumberyard might like to build a seminar around you. Your presentation might turn into an annual affair. Think of other possibilities. You'll make good contacts and develop new ideas; it's stimulating.

When you make your speaking appearance, always mention your book. Have one on display, and make several copies available for sale and for autographs in the back of the room. Authors often make more from "back-of-the-room" book sales than they do from the presentation itself. Prepare a short, powerful speech on one small, very interesting related item, and leave plenty of time for questions and answers. Always write out your personal introduction so the host won't stumble around trying to explain who you are.

Speaking engagements will do three things for you— (1) they promote and sell your book, (2) you might receive a fee for speaking and (3) they add to your professional port-folio. Now, in addition to being an author and a publisher, you are a presenter too. You must be an expert!

You may find that you like speaking even more than writing. Both are great ways to get out your message. For information on professional speaking, see http://www.NSAspeaker.org.

PUBLIC SEMINARS are speaking engagements you organize yourself. You set up the program and collect the admissions. A General Motors study found that approximately 40,000 seminars are given in North America each year, and they generate revenues of $100 million to $160 million.

Use your book as a text for the seminar and include it in the admission fee. Display related books in the back of the room and sell CDs of your lecture.

AUTOGRAPH PARTIES may be staged in bookstores or in a backyard around a pool. Sell and sign books.

When my parents taught me not to write in books, they didn't know they were raising an author who would autograph them.

The store will provide the place, but you must get the people in. Do not rely on the regular customers to buy your book. Mail announcements of your appearance to every friend, relative, acquaintance and prospect within driving distance. Make the event sound big and important. Make everyone in town think that everyone else is going, and that if they don't go they'll be the only one not there.

> *Do seminars, not signings. Attract buyers to your autograph parties.*
>
> —*Terri Lonier*, **Working Solo**

Once you know that a local paper is going to review your book or do a feature article on you, visit the bookstores. Suggest to the manager that he or she might like to place an ad to draw readers into the store. Offer to stage an autograph party—another fine tie-in.

Don't overlook fund-raising event autograph parties. Here you do the selling and donate part to the club or organization.

When traveling, drop in on bookstores, and when you find your books on display, offer to autograph them. An autograph makes the book more valuable, and this will provide an opportunity for the staff to become familiar with you and your book. Bookstores will often feature "signed books" in a special sales area. Sometimes you will wind up doing an impromptu presentation.

For more information on author tours, see Document 639, *Autograph Parties & Signing Books*, at http://parapub.com/sites/para/resources/allproducts.cfm.

BOOK AWARDS

There's probably no greater satisfaction for a writer than having his or her book selected for an award. Some book awards are important and well known, and some are obscure. There are those that are general, while others are quite specialized. However, all are awards, and just being nominated for one looks good in your promotion.

THE REWARDS OF AWARDS

After Alan Gadney and Carolyn Porter's book won "Outstanding Reference Book of the Year" in their category from the American Library Association, they reaped the following benefits. Because of the ALA publicity and their award promotion, library sales went through the roof. They managed to place a "Revised Award Edition" with seven national book clubs. With an award sticker on the cover, they took a booth at the ABA/BEA convention, landed national distribution and regional wholesalers, and came out with 22 major publishers interested in publishing a new edition.

Then they went to the convention in New York, where the book was on special display. While there, they negotiated a co-publishing contract—not just for one book, but for a series of 16 books. So awards do count; if you win one, then promote it as much as possible.

Awards can be announced on stickers and applied to the books. These stickers are a bit of extra work, but they get attention. If the organization making the award does not sell the stickers, have them made by a label printer, a quick-print shop or make them yourself with a laser printer. In later editions, the "sticker" can be printed right on the book.

WHEN SMALLER IS BETTER

According to *Publishers Weekly*, the larger publishers say that awards do not sell books. By the time the award is received, the book has been pulled from the stores and the publishers are promoting newer books. So what is the effect of an award? "It prompts the author to ask for more when contracting for his or her next book," said one large publisher.

Fortunately, smaller publishers benefit from awards, because they keep their books alive longer.

Book awards, contests and grants are listed in *Literary Market Place* and *Writer's Market* (available at your library) and in a book titled *Grants and Awards Available to American Writers*, published by PEN American Center. See http://www.pen.org/.

EXCHANGES BETWEEN PUBLISHERS: When two or more publishers of like material handle each other's books, their customers get a wider range of choices and the publishers get an improved response rate to their advertising because they are selling multiple titles. This cross-distribution partnering, formerly available only in other sales channels, is now becoming more common in mail-order book marketing.

Approach publishers with books that complement yours. Trade cartons of books based on their list price, and add them to your brochure. If you don't wish to take on products from other publishers, at least make an agreement to stuff each other's brochures into outgoing packages (called "flyer-swapping").

BOOK LISTS can be used to plug your other books. Each of your books should carry a list of all your books, and these lists should be updated at each reprinting. The list can also be in the Appendix of the book. This is a way to get your sales message to potential buyers in the same field at little cost.

KEEP ACTIVE: Be prepared to move into action when your book takes off. Have your promotional plan organized so you'll be able to gain maximum mileage from your publicity. Capitalize on each piece of promotion. Have your releases, ads and letters drafted.

Take advantage of every possible market. Pursue the most lucrative, but don't overlook the marginal ones—move in as many directions as possible. It costs very little to serve more markets once you have done the initial organization.

See *Book Promotion Made Easy: Event Planning, Presentation Skills & Product Marketing* by Eric Gelb. http://www. SmallBusinessAdvice.com

> *No matter what else you do, do at least five things to market each and every one of your important books each and every day.*
> *—John Kremer*

8

WHO WILL BUY YOUR BOOK?

MARKETS
DISTRIBUTION CHANNELS

Which retailers will carry your book; where will your book be sold? Most people think first of bookstores, but there are many additional places to sell books. More nonfiction titles are sold through the nontraditional (nonbookstore) outlets (e.g., parachute books in parachute stores; other special-interest books in health food, office supply, computer, auto, garden and toy stores), in catalogs, as premiums, etc. These nontraditional sales are usually easier to make, very large and much more lucrative. Of course, you want your book displayed and sold in as many places as possible.

The chain superstores have grown and stabilized somewhat (they build new stores and close others), the chain mall-stores (with smaller selections) are shrinking and many independent bookstores are being killed off by the chains. More and more specialty stores are carrying books, as are grocery stores and drugstores, newsstands, hotels and airports. College chain and franchise bookstores are growing, taking the place of independent college stores. The largest growth has been among Internet book sites such as Amazon.com and BarnesAndNoble.com. Amazon alone sells more than 10% of the books.

Who's buying books, where do they buy them and what are the most popular categories? For the latest numbers on the book industry, see Book Statistics on my site: http://parapub.com/sites/para/resources/statistics.cfm.

First let's explore the book trade, then the nontraditional markets and finally some of the other opportunities.

WHOLESALE VS. RETAIL SALES

Since it's only a bit more work to ship a carton of books than a single book, you want to pursue *quantity* orders. If you're selling more, you can print more and achieve a lower per-unit cost. You'll use distributors and wholesalers and sell to stores, catalogs, etc. You'll give them a percentage of the retail price but sell books in greater numbers.

On the other hand, the advantage of selling directly to the ultimate consumer (the reader) is the elimination of the distributor/wholesaler intermediaries; you keep the entire list price for yourself. But approaching the reader requires greater effort, and the books are sold *one* at a time. Books have been sold door to door, at street fairs, at flea markets and hawked on street corners. Individual sales are not normally efficient.

Using the Internet, publishers and authors are dealing directly with their consumers—the end-user readers. The Web allows the party seeking information to find the party creating the information—quickly, easily, accurately and inexpensively.

The Internet allows us to substitute inexpensive direct email for expensive traditional direct (postal) mail advertising.

It has become less expensive and less time-consuming to alert potential customers to new information products.

MULTIPLE DATABASES: The traditional bibliographic database is *Books in Print*, a multivolume reference book available in print, on CD and online. See http://www.bowker.com/catalog/000005.htm. *Books in Print* lists the nearly 3 million books that are currently available, or *in print*, in the U.S.

Today, many people find the databases maintained by Amazon.com and other online bookstores easier and less expensive to use, and these sellers provide more information about the books.

While you cannot physically place your book in every bookstore, you can make it available through every store by listing in these databases.

DISTRIBUTORS AND WHOLESALERS

Both distributors and wholesalers have warehouses for storing and shipping books. The difference is that distributors have sales reps that visit the chain-store buyers and independent stores; reps show off the new books and bring back the orders. Wholesalers just wait for orders to arrive. Distributors move a lot more product and need a greater discount for their efforts.

There are some 90 distributors across North America. Your *Plan A* is to strike a deal with one of them. Let that distributor sell books to the bookstores and wholesalers so you can concentrate on specialty stores, catalogs, individual mail-order sales and other markets.

Bookstores prefer to deal with larger publishers, several distributors and a few wholesalers. They would rather write 50 checks at the end of the month, not 50,000. And stores prefer to deal with a limited number of suppliers they know and with whom they have established accounts. Meanwhile, bar codes make instant inventory control and just-in-time delivery possible.

THE DISTRIBUTION PROCESS: To help you understand the book-supply pipeline, the following is a listing of the various intermediaries between the publisher and the bookstore. Several of the companies are evolving and growing. Some started off in one category and later changed.

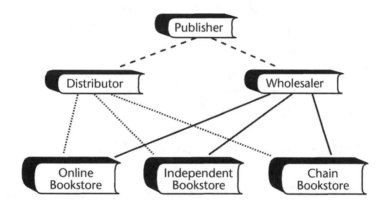

The book-trade sales process

National distributors act as the exclusive sales and fulfillment department for their publisher clients. They are publisher-driven (in other words, they "push" the product into the stores), and their mission is to create store-demand for orders. They usually represent each publisher's entire line of books. Most have a catalog and sales reps who visit buyers at the chains and independent stores. They also supply the wholesalers. Your distributors will launch your books each season in a catalog. Typically, distributors pay you 90 to 120 days after they ship the books.

Your distributor serves the wholesalers (especially Ingram and Baker & Taylor), sends their sales reps to the independent bookstores and other sales outlets and sells your books to the chains. The primary difference between national distributors and the various wholesalers listed below is that only one distributor will sell your books on an *exclusive* basis to the book trade through sales reps who sell to bookstore and wholesaler buyers, usually through a face-to-face meeting.

> *A distributor is a surrogate sales department for a group of independent publishers.*
> **—Julie Bennett, publisher**

Remember, while distributors replace part of your shipping department, they don't replace your marketing department. You must always do the promoting yourself.

The distributor's services to you include warehousing, cataloging, sales representation (to the independent bookstores and chains), shipping, billing, collections, marketing and editorial consultation. Many distributors provide other services at additional cost. Some of those services include an exhibit at the BEA book fair, filling individual (retail) orders, co-op advertising in book trade publications, postcard mailings to bookstores in areas where you are appearing on radio or TV, etc.

The only successful way to get both independent and chain stores to buy is through a face-to-face visit. Publishers have tried less expensive methods such as mailings and telephone calls, but none have worked as well as in-person sales calls. Large publishers have their own group of sales reps. Small publishers use distributors that also have sales reps. You need a distributor both to effectively sell to book-stores and then to make books available through as many wholesalers as possible.

More and more of the chains and larger independent stores are requiring electronic ordering systems (EDI). Few publishers can afford them, so here is another reason to use a distributor. Book reviewers are more likely to review books that have national bookstore distribution and are readily available to their readers (always mention your distributor in your review kit and promo materials). Having a distributor means that a professional book-trade organization has selected *your book* for sale out of all the thousands of books available. Distribution legitimizes your book, separates it from the pack and gives it credibility in the marketplace.

Wholesalers are demand-driven or bookstore-driven. They wait for the orders (they wait for someone to "pull" the product from them); they do not generate orders. But they respond quickly. They carry just those books that are in demand and fill orders when received; some do not even stock the books. They carry books from most publishers nonexclusively, because their main service is delivering books quickly. While many wholesalers may call themselves "distributors," they are actually wholesalers because they do not have sales reps.

Wholesalers perform a valuable order-consolidation and distribution service, but they don't market individual titles.

—Mark Sexton

More than 30% of the bookstores buy from wholesalers regularly and most depend on wholesalers for some of their stock. These wholesalers ask for a 50% to 60% discount from you or your distributor and then sell to their stores at 40% to 45% off, depending upon quantity (titles can be mixed to get a higher discount). Even the big chains make use of wholesalers when they run out and are desperate for a book.

Wholesalers can be subdivided as follows:

•• **National Wholesalers:** There are two national wholesalers that have multiple warehouses in various parts of the country so that they can quickly ship books to libraries and bookstores in the United States. Baker & Taylor has four regional service centers (warehouses) and does about 80% of its business serving the "institutional" market (public libraries, schools, colleges, universities, specialized libraries, etc.) and about 20% serving the "retail" market (bookstores and other retail outlets). Ingram Book Co. has four regional warehouses and focuses its business in exactly the opposite way of Baker & Taylor—approximately 80% store and 20% library/institutional.

•• **Regional Wholesalers:** These wholesalers focus primarily on one region of the country and some have active marketing programs and specialized sales representation. They include The Bookmen (Midwest), Bookazine (New York), Southern Book Service (Southeast), Sunbelt Publications (Southwest), Washington Book Distributors (Mid-Atlantic) and others. There are about a dozen significant regional wholesalers.

●◆ **Specialized Wholesalers:** A larger number of wholesalers offer books in specific categories—children, computers, cookbooks, gift books, health, legal, medical, music, new age, outdoor, religious, scientific, travel and so forth. Some serve specific types of sales outlets, such as college stores, golf shops, school supply stores and truck stops.

●◆ **Library Wholesalers:** These companies find books for libraries. Up to 90% of the libraries buy from wholesalers. These intermediaries provide a valuable service by combining orders and saving librarians from thousands of single-title orders. Larger library wholesalers stock some books, but most order from publishers only when filling an order.

While there are many library wholesalers, only about a dozen do substantial business. Brodart, in Williamsport, Pennsylvania, is the largest of the library wholesalers, with a warehouse stocking more than 100,000 titles. Other library wholesalers ranked by the approximate size of their inventories are: Emery-Pratt Company (100,000 titles), Ambassador Book Service (75,000), Midwest Library Service (75,000), Coutts Library Service (35,000), Blackwell Book Services (25,000), Academic Book Center (20,000), Book House (20,000) and Eastern Book Company (15,000).

And don't forget the earlier-mentioned wholesaler Baker & Taylor (B&T), which does 68% of its business in library sales.

Library Distributors: There are two library distributors, Quality Books and Unique Books. Quality and Unique each have traveling sales reps who actively sell books to libraries. Both are worth the time for a smaller publisher to pursue.

Independent Distributors (IDs) carry magazines, trade books and mass-market paperbacks to serve drugstores, supermarkets, newsstands, hotels and some airport outlets. IDs are really magazine dealers who treat books the same as magazines: the books go on the rack for one month. Then if they don't sell, the IDs replace the selection and return only the covers from unsold books for credit. You probably will not deal with many IDs, although your national distributor may. The larger IDs are Anderson News Co., The News Group, Charles Levy Circulating Co. and Hudson-RPM Distributors. Through consolidation and attrition, the number of IDs has dwindled from more than 1,500 several years ago to fewer than 300 today.

Chain bookstores are stores that are related to each other and usually have a single central buying office.

For lists of distributors, wholesalers and chains, see Appendix 2.

SELECTING A DISTRIBUTOR

Now the major question is: *How do you find the right national distributor?* The secret is to match your book (or line of books) with a distributor that already offers titles of the same type. They'll have a relationship with stores that have major sections of that type of book, and they may be serving other appropriate stores outside the book trade. For example, if you have a business book, you might approach Midpoint Trade or NBN. If you have a health and fitness book, you might check with Nutri-Books. If you strike a deal with Nutri-Books/Royal, for example, they will get your book into bookstores with significant health and fitness sections and into health-food stores. You want a distributor or sometimes a wholesaler that is already plugged into the right markets for your book.

SELECTION CRITERIA: Distributors are very selective. Each may only present a couple of hundred new titles each year. Many of these new "front list" titles are from their existing publisher clients, so their acceptance of new publishers may only be a hundred, more or less, per year. They have to be choosy!

Distributors will consider the following when deciding whether or not to accept your book:

•• **Do they feel they can move this title?** Does it fit into their existing line of books? Is there a ready market for this type of book? Is there too much competition, both from other similar titles and from competing lines of books they already distribute?

•• **Is the book manufactured to accepted industry standards** in terms of binding, page and cover design, typestyle, size and so on? Cover design and a professional interior design and typesetting are especially important.

•• **Is the book backed by an advertising or promotion budget and marketing plan** that will bring the book to the attention of readers, libraries and/or bookstores? A substantial budget for marketing and promotion is important. A distributor can convince trade buyers to make the book available in bookstores, but the publisher in turn must make readers aware of the book and motivate them to buy.

•• **Does the publisher have more than one product?** Distributors like to open accounts with established, ongoing businesses. Many distributors are hesitant to deal with one-book publishers who may never publish again.

•❖ **Do they perceive the publisher to be a "problem client,"** that is, someone who will tie up their time with constant phone calls and naïve questions, not really market or promote, ask for constant explanations of the distribution process and sales reports, nitpick their contract terms and generally be more of a nuisance than the value of their potential book sales?

Your next move is to contact the distributors who appear to best match your book(s) and request submission procedures. For a current list of distributors and the categories of books they want and don't want, see Document 605, *Locating the Right Distributor,* at http://parapub.com/sites/para/resources/allproducts.cfm.

If a distributor turns down your book, it may be because the book is not right for their particular market, the book may be poorly written or produced or, in their brief evaluation, they may fail to see its sales potential. Distributors, like bookstore buyers, have little time to evaluate the dozens of books they receive every day. So try again. Wait a few months and build up a track record. Then resubmit the book and send along sales figures, reviews, endorsements, your marketing and promotion success—anything that will demonstrate that the book is selling and that customers are responding. If the book is moving, the distributors may want to get in on the action.

If you call a distributor and they don't feel your book is right for their line, ask them for a recommendation of another distributor or specialized wholesaler. They know the industry and will not consider noncompeting distributors as a threat.

PMA TRADE DISTRIBUTION PROGRAM: *Plan B.* Started in 1992, this is a special book program sponsored by the Publishers Marketing Association (PMA) and the Independent Publishers Group (IPG), a national distributor. Twice each year (in January and July), PMA members may submit books to a selection committee. Books are screened for suitability for general-interest bookstores by buyers from Borders, Barnes & Noble, Baker & Taylor, Ingram, Independent Publishers Group and independent bookstores. IPG has agreed to carry all the books selected. This is a great service for the chains, because they get access to pre-selected, pre-screened (otherwise unseen) books. It's also a great program for the smaller and newer publisher because it provides access to the chains, wholesalers and independent booksellers. See PMA's Web site at http://www. pma-online.org.

EXCLUSIVES are necessary in the book trade because sales reps want credit for their efforts. Stores prefer single vendors of record so they can cycle books back (via returns) and forth (through orders). The exclusive territory is only for the outlets covered by the national distributors. The sales outlets are usually wholesalers and bookstores, or what we call the "book trade." Give your distributor an exclusive to the book trade and then concentrate your time and money pursuing other areas such as the gift trade, catalogs and other outlets.

CONSIGNMENT: Most distributors operate on consignment inventory and pay you 90 to 120 days after they ship the books to the bookstore or wholesaler. This means they have very little invested in their operation. While publishers should avoid selling to small accounts on consignment, there are good arguments for these terms with national distributors. Book manufacture requires large print runs, so part of your inventory might just as well sit in another warehouse as your own.

Remember, however, title (ownership) to the books is still yours. If the books are lost or damaged and if the distributor doesn't have insurance, the loss could be yours.

BOOKSTORE CHAINS (See Appendix 2 for a complete listing.)

The large bookstore chains are important to publishers because they control the majority of the bookstore market. That means that a limited number of buyers have power over most of the books sold in bookstores. Chains are easier to reach since they have single central buying offices. Visiting one chain buyer to sell hundreds of copies is more efficient than sending sales reps to hundreds of individual stores.

The chain stores have their cash registers tied to the central computer to monitor sales. They purchase by category and demographics, matching books to the store's neighborhood clientele. Often the computer will throw a large number of books out to stores as a test, only to be sent back if unsold after a period of time. This instant access to sales information enables the headquarters to stay on top of fast-breaking books. They can reorder quickly to maintain inventory levels.

> *What really interests us are print runs and promotions. We want to know what is the publisher going to print? What is it going to put behind the book? Is the author good on talk shows? And is there going to be a tour?*
>
> **—Harry Hoffman, former CEO, Waldenbooks**

Although most chain buying is centralized, many local stores are authorized to make small purchases, and they are especially receptive to regional books and local authors. Though Walden does not permit local managers to make purchases, their headquarters does listen to them when they request a local publisher's book. Most chains expect a 40% discount, FOB origin, and many pay in 60 to 90 days.

The larger chains have stopped buying directly from smaller and newer publishers. However, you can still reach them through your distributor. So find a distributor and then let the distributor pitch the chains. You can also place your books with the various wholesalers and then encourage bookstores to order via the wholesalers.

The major bookstore chains account for the majority of national bookstore sales. If you add to that the percentage of books sold through warehouse and discount stores, the Internet, book clubs, mail order and other outlets, then independent bookstores and small chains (those with six or fewer stores in the chain) now make up only 15% or less of the total dollar volume of books sold. (This is why some distributors send reps only to the chains and major wholesalers, and then sell to the remaining independent bookstore market via catalogs and the telephone.)

Here is a breakdown of the major types of bookstore chains:

THE LARGER CHAINS: The three largest bookstore chains control the majority of the bookstore business.

•❖ **Barnes & Noble** is a national chain affiliated with BookStar, B. Dalton, Bookstop, Doubleday and Scribner stores. They have more than 1,500 bookstores, and are increasing their superstores, while decreasing the B. Dalton stores.

B&N buys by format and publisher rather than by subject category. The best way to approach them is to have a distributor's sales rep visit, as he or she will have an established relationship with the buyer. You could also try to contact the appropriate buyer yourself (but clear it with your distributor first). Send the buyer review copies, news releases and catalogs, and see if you can stir interest in your project.

•◆ **Borders**, which is affiliated with Waldenbooks, Brentanos and Library Ltd., is one of the most successful mall-based booksellers in the U.S., with more than 1,100 stores. Borders purchases books from approximately 7,500 publishers, but they prefer to deal with (fewer) distributors.

Borders buys by category. Your distributor should contact the Borders buyer for you or you can try yourself (clear it with your distributor first). Send review copies, news releases and catalogs to the appropriate buyer.

•◆ **Books-A-Million** has more than 100 stores, and 26 are superstores. Many are combination book and greeting-card stores operating under the Bookland name.

NATIONAL CHAINS: These include two larger chains that sell not only books, but also music and videos: Hastings (with about 150 stores) and Media Play (with about 80 outlets, including the Musicland and On Que stores). Other national bookstore chains include Little Professor Book Centers, Virgin Megastores (about 20 stores, also selling music and videos), Rizzoli and Waterstone's (about 20 stores in airports). Little Professor—based in Ann Arbor, Michigan—has no central buying; each store buys individually.

REGIONAL CHAINS: These include chain bookstores that serve specific regions of the country, such as Joseph Beck (including Davis-Kidd) and Reader's World in the Midwest, Harry Schwartz in the Upper Midwest, Olsson's in the Central Atlantic area, and Books Inc., Tower and Powell's on the West Coast.

CHILDREN'S BOOKSTORE CHAINS: These include chains that sell books, toys and other children's products, such as Books "R" Us, FAO Schwarz, Hammet's Learning World, Kidsmith and lots of stores with the word "Learning" in the name—Learning House, Fun, Place, Shop, Smith, etc.

INDIVIDUAL BOOKSTORES: Individual, but not necessarily independent, are a diverse group of retailers. They include the downtown bookstore, the college store, the religious bookstore and others. There are more than 15,000 stores that carry books. They come in all sizes. Some sell books exclusively, while others carry books as a sideline. Some stores are general, and some are specialized (computer, movies/TV, mystery, new age, science fiction, women's, etc.). Some are attached to museums or libraries.

Bookstores are a lousy place to sell books.

Modern booksellers are faced with trying to attract and sell to all kinds of different people. To do so, they have to locate in high-rent, heavy-traffic areas. Stores report an inventory turnover of two to five times a year, with an average of 3.3 times. If a book hasn't moved in four months on the shelf, it is usually returned. The newer and smaller publisher is trapped between the Scylla of wide exposure and the Charybdis of massive returns.

Bookstores are the frosting, not the cake.

Many small publishers tolerate, but don't pursue, small individual bookstores. The major challenges with the stores are that they order just a few books at a time, complain about the 40% discount, seldom pay in 30 days and often return the books for a refund—damaged. You wind up processing a lot of paperwork for many small orders and returns while making very few sales. The best approach is to let your distributor handle the stores.

If selling books through bookstores was good business, the bookstores might be paying their bills.

Try visiting nearby bookstores; it will be a good education. Tell them you're a local author and therefore local people will be interested in your book. Mention any local publicity such as talk shows that are planned. Stores want to know if the book is readily available through a wholesaler and if it will be promoted. Reviews and author appearances are more important than advertising. If the book is professionally produced, a sale should not be difficult. Be ready with a stock phrase such as: "I can offer you the books at a full 40% discount, without delivery charges, and they are fully returnable, of course." The whole pitch will probably run five to 10 minutes. You can also offer to do an author signing or mini-seminar.

BOOKSTORE PATRONS: Bookstore patrons consist of the book addict and the occasional buyer. These recreational readers are used to plunking down $24.95 for hardcover fiction. Fifty percent of the customers in a bookstore are looking for a particular book. These particular-book seekers are more likely to be younger and female. About 47% are looking for a nonfiction title, 27% for a particular book of fiction and 28% want textbooks. Although 20% do not find the book they are looking for, 54% buy one or more books before they leave. Then there are those people who never visit a bookstore.

COLLEGE, SCHOOL AND TEXTBOOK STORES also respond best to face-to-face sales calls. There are roughly 2,800 college stores serving 2,200 U.S. colleges and universities with more than 11 million students. Some of the major college-store chains are: Follett College stores (about 600 stores), Barnes & Noble (315), Wallaces' (60), Nebraska Book (50), Founders (20) and Dekalb (15).

College stores follow their own schedule, depending upon whether they are on the semester, quarter or early-semester system. Don't put too much energy into college stores. Many of them primarily stock textbooks and reference materials. Students generally don't spend money on much more than assigned texts, music and beer. Large textbook orders go to the publisher. About one-third of school-store orders are through wholesalers, so wholesalers may be a better way to reach this market.

THE LIBRARY TRADE

Libraries come in several types. There are almost 16,000 public libraries and 8,937 public library systems, some with branches. There are 50,000 libraries in elementary schools, 20,000 in high schools and 15,000 special libraries (including 1,700 law libraries). Other libraries include more than 3,000 in colleges, 1,897 governmental, 363 military and over 1,000 formal libraries exist in larger churches.

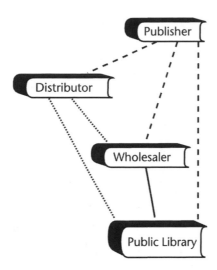

The library trade

The Library of Congress shelves 24 million books, Harvard University has 14 million and the New York Public Library has 11.5 million. For more library statistics, see http://www.ala.org.

Many librarians view the publisher as the money-grubber between the author and the reader.

More than 90% of the libraries that respond to your mailings or a review in *Library Journal* or the other library magazines will order from a library wholesaler, and 75% of those orders go to Baker & Taylor. Rather than place thousands of orders with individual publishers for single titles, libraries (just like the bookstores) save time by bundling the orders together and sending them all to a wholesaler. They are extended a 20% to 33% discount by the wholesaler, so they're not only saving time but also receiving both a discounted price and service.

Their challenge is money. The cost of ordering and processing a new title can cost as much as the book itself. Many libraries are spreading their already tight budgets even thinner now by adding audiovisual and other nonprint items. Most of the library budget goes for personnel; only about 15% is spent on books and other media.

LIBRARY MARKET SIZE: Libraries spend around $1.5 billion each year for books, buying some 14% of the books published. Of those, public libraries buy 23%, el-hi school libraries 33%, college libraries 27% and special (e.g., law, medical) libraries 17%. Many library purchases are for books with press runs under 5,000, which would not get published without their support.

If libraries bought one copy of every book published in the U.S., they would each need a budget of more than $2 million per year. Yet only about 2,600 public libraries have an annual book budget of $25,000 or more, and most have much less. They have to be selective in their purchases. Contact only those libraries that can afford to buy your book. Don't waste your energy and money pursuing the rest.

As could be expected, nonfiction, reference and technical books would be of greatest interest to college libraries (rather than children's books, for example). Send your brochures to the right type of library. If you have a special-interest book, target those libraries (and bookstores) with an interest in your subject.

Libraries don't buy "fill-in-the-blanks"-type books because librarians don't want people writing in their books. If your book has to be filled in, you must accept the fact that libraries will not buy it. Some fill-ins can be changed to lists. Or you might suggest that readers photocopy the page.

Many libraries are also averse to buying spiral- or comb-bound books, because patrons can easily rip out the pages. Additionally, spiral- and comb-bound books must have a printed spine so they can be shelved "spine out." Libraries almost never buy books in ring binders, and if they do, they rebind them for permanence.

Many libraries buy more for topic than quality. They have to justify their budgets to the community (if public) and try to offer something for everyone. It's said that better judgment is shown in the purchasing of children's books and fiction. One librarian recently explained, "When material is scarce on a topic and interest is high, we will often buy any reasonably priced new book through an ad in *Library Journal* or even a flyer. However, we usually don't buy if the book receives a bad review."

Libraries don't expect a discount unless they order several copies. Some publishers follow a universal discount schedule, giving 10% for an order of 5, 20% for 20, etc. Some big-city public libraries take advantage of quantity deals because they are buying for several branches simultaneously.

DO LIBRARY ORDERS KILL SALES? Some book publishers question the wisdom of selling to libraries, based on the theory that this one sale will kill several others when many people read the book free. They note that some magazines charge libraries a higher price for a subscription on the theory that more people will read the periodical.

Other book publishers feel that libraries are showcasing their book—and are paying to do it. Often orders for *The Self-Publishing Manual* are received with a note stating: "The library will not let me check the book out again, so I want to buy my own copy."

Library loans may hurt sales of fiction (which are read through less often), but not reference books (which are referred to over and over and people may need a personal copy). Mailing a free copy of a new book to the central buyer of major library systems (those with many branches) might even be a good promotional investment.

APPROVAL PLANS: Some wholesalers serve their library accounts automatically by sending collections of books in specific categories *on approval,* allowing the library to return the unwanted titles. Because the wholesaler has prescreened the books and matched them to the library's special collections, few are returned. Academic and special libraries might buy 30% of their books this way, whereas public libraries buy some 10% of their books through approval plans. Obviously, it's to your great advantage to have your book included in these computer-matched offerings, especially in the Baker & Taylor system.

ORDERING CYCLES: Libraries tend to do most of their ordering around the beginning or end of their fiscal year (usually December 31 or June 30), when they try to use up their old budget or break into a new one. This is when they may show slightly less buying discrimination. Your book might be selected at this time even if it's an afterthought, not a first choice. At the three-quarter point in their fiscal year, libraries are often out of book-purchasing funds. School libraries usually use the slow summer months to work on ordering.

ACQUISITION LIBRARIANS: Some libraries have acquisition librarians, while committees select books in others. Because more than one person is often involved in acquisitions in the larger libraries, it's wise to send more than one copy of your promotional material.

Don't send your promo package to the head librarian or acquisition librarian. In large libraries, it's best to direct mailings to the subject-area supervisor who makes the actual buying decisions. These supervisors are in charge of areas such as children's books, adult fiction, reference, etc. Ask about these categories at your local library, and always list the category at the top of your sales flyer. You could also check the correct category and person's name for each specific library on your mailing list before sending the material off.

Since libraries want to order from wholesalers, you must let them know which wholesalers carry your book by listing them on your sales flyer. Make ordering easy. Librarians want all the numbers: ISBN, LC control number, Dewey classification, copyright date, number of pages, trim size, binding, etc.

It helps if you build consumer demand, because most libraries respond when a library patron requests a title. For example, school libraries are responsive to the wishes of their faculty. Mailings to teachers often result in school library orders.

BOOKS WEAR OUT: A book can be lent out only so many times. A softcover book is good for about 18 cycles. The life span of most books is 1.5 to 2 years. Unless a worn-out title has seen a lot of recent use, it usually isn't reordered. On the other hand, if the book has been very popular, the library may order several copies. Books are also stolen. Despite electronic security systems, about 20% of a library's collection is lost each year.

IN DEMAND ON THE LIBRARY SHELF

In 1979, when *The Self-Publishing Manual* was first presented to a librarian in Santa Barbara, she said, "We'll have to order several of these. This is the type of book our patrons keep." During the next few years, the library went through more than 30 copies, despite the fact that the book is available for sale in several bookstores, copy shops and office supply stores around town.

HARDCOVER OR SOFTCOVER BOOKS? Do libraries want hardcover or softcover books? Actually, more and more, they want *electronic books*, because they don't have shelf space for printed books. Fiction is still being stocked in print form, but reference materials may be sought on CD-ROM or be accessed online by library patrons. Now when people want to take research material home from a library, they may download it to a floppy, rather than photocopying or printing out a hard copy. The world of electronic books is not coming; it's here!

LOCAL SALES: Your local library should buy your book just because you're part of the community. Some even have a special private room for books by indigenous writers. If so, it would be appropriate for you to donate a copy to this reference section. If you do make such a donation, be sure the local paper is notified with a news release so you can get some promotional mileage out of your largess.

HONORED IN A SPECIAL ROOM

I donated a couple of my new books to the local public library when I lived in Quincy, Massachusetts. The books were placed in a special room reserved for local books. This was quite an unexpected honor in the hometown of two U.S. presidents.

SELLING TO LIBRARIES: The best ways to approach the library market are to be accepted by Quality Books, become a stock publisher with Baker & Taylor, let all the library wholesalers know where to find you by sending them a brochure, join the PMA library mailings, make your own mailings to libraries with special collections, patronize selected library co-op exhibits and prepare a great review package for *Library Journal*. Be organized and persistent.

QUALITY BOOKS: The secret to having your book accepted by Quality Books is to notify them of the new title early. Quality has to get the jump on the regular wholesalers if they're to be effective in moving books for you. The selection committee turns down 700 to 800 titles each month. Some books don't meet the selection criteria, but most rejects are older books from larger publishers.

A SECOND LOOK

Quality rejected *Parachuting: The Skydiver's Handbook* when it was initially published. The selection committee just didn't believe the library market was large enough for such a specialized sport. Quality was handling a number of my other books and gave the handbook another look soon after Tom Drewes (then owner) took up skydiving in 1983. Everyone was pleasantly surprised— Quality moved several hundred copies.

The ideal time to send in the New Book Information form along with a sample copy and promotional materials is before you go to press. Then books can be shipped directly to Quality from the printer. It's a great feeling to go to press knowing some books are already sold. If you cannot submit an advance sample copy prior to printing, then submit the book, forms and promotional materials immediately after printing. The sooner the better. An initial stocking order from Quality is usually 50 to 100 books.

UNIQUE BOOKS: Unique Books operates like Quality Books—but on a somewhat smaller scale. They warehouse about 5,000 titles and accept not only adult nonfiction and children's books, but also fiction and university press titles. Like Quality, they send sales reps to libraries and exhibit at library conferences. Your book can be carried by both Unique and Quality—a usual opening order from Unique is 30 to 60 books.

BAKER & TAYLOR: Become one of their *stock publishers.* Library sales account for 68% of B&T's business. You should have made contact as you worked through the previous section on Wholesalers and Distributors.

OTHER LIBRARY WHOLESALERS: Notify other library wholesalers through a mailing. Some of the larger library wholesalers include Academic, Ambassador, Blackwell, Book House, Brodart, Coutts, Eastern, Emery-Pratt, Midwest and Yankee Book Peddler.

BOOK REVIEWS should be sought in library review magazines. Since a good review in *Library Journal* or *ALA Booklist* will move around 1,200 copies of most books, book reviews are worth some extra effort.

Book reviews are the librarians' overwhelmingly most popular tool for making selection decisions. Acquisition librarians just don't have time to read and evaluate all the new books. They rely mostly on *Library Journal, Booklist, Publishers Weekly, Kirkus Reviews, Choice* and *The New York Times Book Review*. Ninety-four percent of librarians rely on reviews in *Library Journal,* while 91% read the reviews in *Booklist.* Only 44% believe the ads in *LJ,* and only 35% have confidence in the ads in *Booklist.* The figures for *Publishers Weekly* are 75% relying on the reviews, and 53% buying into the ads (notice that this is higher than the ads in the two other publications). For the addresses of the publications, see Appendix 2 under Magazines for Publishers. Also see the Book Review, Magazines and Serials sections of *Literary Market Place*.

Follow up on review-packet mailings to the above-mentioned library review magazines with a telephone call. Never ask if they plan to review the book, but rather if they have received the book. If not, or if they can't find it, get a name and send another book.

PMA CO-OP LIBRARY MAILINGS: PMA (the Publishers Marketing Association) periodically mails a flat envelope containing individual book flyers to 2,600 public libraries across the U.S. that have a purchasing budget of $25,000 or more. These are just public libraries, and only those that can afford to buy. Cost for participation is $145 plus your flat (unfolded) flyer on one or more books. For $165 per mailing, PMA also makes co-op mailings to 3,200 K-12 libraries, 3,300 college and university libraries and 2,600 special-interest libraries. See http://www.pma-online.org.

Consider the type of library that's most likely to buy your book. Maybe you just want school, medical or law libraries, or perhaps you have a regional book and just want public libraries in New England. You can make mailings either alone or in cooperation with other publishers.

SPECIAL COLLECTIONS: Look for special libraries or regular libraries with special collections. For instance, if yours is an aviation book, you could send brochures to libraries with an aviation section. Don't go to the expense of mailing to all libraries when you can isolate those that have a particular interest in your topic. Gale Research rents mailing lists of *libraries with special collections.* See their Web site at http://www.galegroup.com.

For a list of *special libraries,* contact the Special Library Association at http://www.sla.org.

Many individual library associations rent their mailing lists. For example, the American Association of Law Libraries can supply on labels a list of 2,300 law libraries. For more information on contacting special libraries, see *Marketing to Libraries through Library Associations* from the American Library Association at http://www.ala.org.

When you plan to make a mailing to specialized libraries, invite other publishers to join you. Co-op promotions can save a lot of money and help justify otherwise marginal mailings.

LIBRARY REVIEW MAGAZINES: *Library Journal, ALA Booklist* and other trade magazines run special editions and special sections throughout the year. Categories covered are travel books, children's books, metaphysical books, cookbooks, religious books, etc. Book listings (a few sentences about your book) are usually free. Advertising and listings should be planned for these special editions where attention is being drawn to a particular subject.

Contact each magazine for a list of upcoming special issues, ad rates and information about how to list your book. The addresses are in Appendix 2 under Magazines for Publishers.

SCHOOL MARKET

The school market spends more than a billion dollars each year for textbooks. While most of these books are developed especially for certain courses, many are regular books developed for other markets but adopted as supplementary educational aids.

ELEMENTARY AND SECONDARY SCHOOLS: In the U.S., there are approximately 64,000 public elementary, 24,000 public high and 1,800 combined schools in 18,000 school districts. Additionally, there are some 14,000 private elementary and 4,000 private high schools. Together they employ 2.3 million teachers.

In 22 states, schools purchase texts under a state adoption system, where a board approves titles for a five-year period. State adoption is a hunting license and allows the salespeople to try to sell the book to the schools. Even where there is no state adoption system, planning seems to follow a five-year cycle. In some areas, publishers have to ship to central depositories, where the schools draw on books as needed. This usually means a consignment inventory, and the publishers aren't paid for the books until requisitioned by the schools. The school market is tough and very competitive.

COLLEGES AND UNIVERSITIES: Colleges are changing. There are more students over 25, more women are going back to school and more people are turning to continuing education courses in their specialty.

There are three types of college bookstores: (1) those that are owned by the institution, (2) those that are private and (3) those college stores with a private lessee. As in the general bookstore business, large chain franchises are devouring independent college stores.

Textbook publishers concentrate on wooing the instructors, who select books for their courses in more than 3,000 schools. This decision is easier for some professors, because they pen their own textbooks. Normally, this purchasing is done by the local bookstore, and the instructor notifies them of his or her choice by April for the fall term. Of course, there are challenges. Sometimes the choice is made too late or the estimated number that will be needed is wrong. Some students avoid buying the text by sharing or making repeated visits to the school library. The result is a store-return rate on textbooks of more than 20%.

Teachers expect to get free examination copies of books, and while some treat this privilege with respect, others just collect books or sell them to the bookstore. The bookstore, in turn, sells the book to a student or returns it to the publisher for a refund. The bookstores even supply teachers with blank Desk Copy Request forms designed to be sent to the publisher for freebies. Often, young instructors are trying to build up their libraries. Older professors, who have more say in book selection, do much less collecting.

To check the validity of these requests for examination copies, some publishers request information about the size of the course, the requester's academic position, etc.

TWO LARGE DEALS ONLY; MANY SENT OUT

During the last 35 years, I have sent out scores of requested desk copies and so far only two have resulted in large school bookstore orders.

To attack the college market, analyze your book's subject and decide which course might find it useful. The teachers are easy to find, and direct mail advertising is the most effective method of reaching them. In fact, some publishers find the lists so specialized that they use them to send free, unsolicited examination copies.

More and more college students are avoiding the college bookstore. They are getting a better deal from online textbook dealers.

PREPUBLICATION SALES

These sales will bring in some money early and help you pay the printing bill. But it isn't wise to start too soon on the prepublication publicity for your first book. The first time around is a learning experience, and there will be countless delays in the writing, production and printing process. You do not want to find yourself spending all your time answering the question, "Where is the book I ordered?" On your first book, hold the announcement until it is on the press. The next time, adjust and start earlier.

Once you learn the promotion ropes, you should be able to sell enough books through prepublication sales—to both wholesale and retail customers—to pay the print bill.

Offer an early wholesale deal ("to be shipped directly from the printer") to associations and specialty dealers. It's nice to have a pile of orders on the desk when the book comes off the press.

If your book is specialized and you're able to find an appropriate mailing list, you should consider a prepublication retail offer. Tell potential buyers the book is being printed, and if they want one hot off the press they should send their money now because you'll be shipping on a first-come-first-served basis. Include an early-order deal such as "postage free if you order from this ad." This mailing should also be sent to all your friends and acquaintances; many will respond and be pleased that you thought of them. If a prospect is mentioned in the text or the acknowledgments, that person is sure to buy one. You can also autograph selected copies.

Never discount a brand-new book! Many new publishers feel they have to offer a deal to readers. Discounting a new book makes you appear to be in a distress situation. You're in a very strong position—you have a new book! And you need every penny of profit; don't give it away.

NONTRADITIONAL MARKETS

Specialty (nonbook) outlets offer many nonfiction publishers their largest market. For example, a book on mountain climbing will sell better in backpacking shops than in bookstores, and the size of the store's purchases will be larger. Sales to stores other than bookstores are often called "nontraditional sales" or "special sales."

AN EARLY PIONEER

Warner Publishing cracked a new market in 1978 when Karen Lustgarten's *Disco Dancing* was sold in record stores.

The common ground for nonfiction books is in their packaging; the subject matter of each book is unique. Nonfiction should be sold where customers for it can be found. Boating books should be placed in nautical shops, local geography–history books in tourist shops and football books in sporting-goods stores. Sell your books where the highest concentration of potential customers can be found. Most of your prospects probably never go into a bookstore. So make your books available through bookstores, but don't confine your sales efforts to these shops.

At Para Publishing we tolerate,
but do not pursue, bookstores.

SELLING TO SPECIALTY STORES: Many specialty stores will want a 40%, 50% or higher discount, but they usually buy outright. There are no returns.

In these shops, it's very important to establish, cultivate and maintain as close a personal relationship as possible with the management. It is of the utmost importance that they like you and your book so they will promote it at every opportunity. Selling them the first time often requires a personal visit to prove the sales potential of the book. When making a promotion to these shops, remember their peak selling seasons and the required lead time.

> *The smaller houses were relatively*
> *more successful in using nonbook retail outlets*
> *than the largest houses were.*
> **—Judith Appelbaum, How to Get Happily Published**

One innovative book marketer is Bruce Lansky of Meadowbrook Press. Bruce is good because he markets books the way he used to market candy. His wife at that time, Vicki, wrote a book on nutrition for babies called *Feed Me, I'm Yours*, and the Lanskys decided to publish it themselves.

First Bruce tried a local children's clothing store. They bought, so he approached a wholesaler of infant items but was turned down flat. He had to offer consignment and counter racks to let the wholesaler prove to himself the books would move. The wholesaler called three days later and ordered 12 dozen more—the Lanskys were in business. Next, Bruce created a mailing stuffer for the wholesaler to enclose with the statements he sent to his 1,000 accounts. Sales soared.

Bruce's secrets to special sales are:

•◦ **Play dumb.** Visit the account and learn all about their terms, key accounts, store or warehouse and the reps in their field. Think as the specialty wholesaler and retail outlet does.

➻ **Don't act like a publisher.** Pretend you're in their business. Bruce was in infant accessories that day. Act as they do. Your book is a "specialty product."

➻ **Use success to breed more success.** Do your research, run small tests and learn the industry. Subscribe to their magazines, join their associations, exhibit at their trade shows and get to know the players. Make a mailing to distributors and retailers, and follow up with calls.

Other nonbook retail channels include gift shops, hardware stores, garden shops, auto supply stores, etc. Many are establishing book corners for an additional profit center, as well as to lend prestige to their line.

Run a test in a few local shops. Develop your approach (posters, counter displays, price, etc.) before rolling out in a wider promotion.

Just as there are distributors and wholesalers serving the bookstores, there are other distributors and wholesalers catering to the nonbook outlets. Check these stores and look for books. Find out who distributes them to the store. That distributor could get your books to other stores of the same type in their territory.

Those stores that don't carry books will have to be accessed through sales reps of other types of products. Ask the local store manager for names of hot sales reps and rep groups who handle other lines of products. These sales reps may take on your book. They will want a sales commission of 10% to 15% of the net-billed amount (that is, a commission on the books after discount and not including the shipping charges).

For counts on the number of businesses in many categories and the number of stores in each chain, see http://www.vendorpro.com/stores.htm.

If the specialty shop is a franchise, make a pitch to the headquarters. Many franchisers do not control the buying for their individual franchisees, and, even if they do, the sale will not be easy. However, the hope of making one large sale to the whole chain is worth some of your sales time.

A SURPRISE MARKET

Years ago, I was in a local photocopy shop when the owner began asking about *The Self-Publishing Manual*. Forty percent off sounded good to him, and he wanted to put some books on the counter. I doubted the books would sell, but brought in eight copies in a counter display (cut-down carton) to humor the owner. Three days later, he called for more. Apparently, the people who frequent photocopy shops are the type who work with the written word—a good market after all. This lesson resulted in an expansion into other copy shops. Some outlets for books may not be obvious at first.

If you receive an inquiry from a market you never thought would be interested in your book, draft a letter to similar stores or groups saying, "This [store or group] ordered the book and we thought you might be interested too." The mailing might just go out to 100 places—no great investment—and there's a good chance of a payoff.

A SURPRISING DEAD END

A few years later, I thought I might capitalize on desktop publishing by selling *The Self-Publishing Manual* through computer stores. I placed books in several stores and there they sat. Very

> few were sold. Sometimes the seemingly obvious outlets for a book don't work.

If the Appendix of your book has a source directory, do a mailing to each firm saying, "You're mentioned in the book. We thought you would like to know and that you might like to offer this book to your customers." Build up a strong, reliable dealer network.

TARGET YOUR MARKETS

Audience specialization is accomplished by concentrating your promotional efforts on those people most likely to buy. Before you wrote your book you analyzed your potential audience, and then you slanted your text toward them. In producing your book, you considered how it might be marketed and made your product attractive in this medium. Perhaps you put extra effort into the cover. The selection of your marketing channels is very important. For example, the chains seem to concentrate on fast-moving books. If your book is very technical and is aimed at a very narrow audience, you don't want to send it to the chains. The unsold books will only come back. Even if you get your book into a nonbook market where there aren't any returns, you want the books to sell, not to sit on the shelves forever. You want dealers who are repeat customers. So consider who patronizes each of the various outlets, and be objective in considering whether they are your buying audience.

There is no secret formula for success.
It's simply a good item for which there is a need,
at the right price, offered to the right market.

In analyzing the market, you'll consider your principal marketing concerns, your customers (individuals, schools, libraries, international markets, subsidiary rights, industry, government, etc.) and your distribution channels (distributors, wholesalers, bookstores, specialty stores, book clubs and catalogs). Your marketing tools are book reviews, news releases, articles, direct email advertising, exhibits, sales representation, etc.

With a specialized nonfiction book, you can avoid the expensive, traditional, big-publisher methods of marketing to everyone by identifying and locating only those people vitally interested in your subject matter. Work smarter, not harder. Define your core audience, and then get to work. Select your special audience and find a way to reach them. You'll find that magazines, stores, catalogs, broadcast interviewers, mailing list servers, specialized book clubs, columnists, associations, conventions and others serve your target group. For example, if my book is on skydiving, I know I can reach my customers through the U.S. Parachute Association, the Para-Gear catalog, *Skydiving* magazine, at the national championships and so on. Who are your customers? What is their profile? Where can you find them? Where do they congregate with others who have like interests? Where is your customer?

You don't have to attack the whole group; you can skim the cream off the top. Mail to the libraries with the largest purchasing budgets, visit the buyers of the larger chain stores and target the larger category catalogs.

Hedge your bets by balancing your markets. Put most of your energy into selling your primary target group. Next, attack your secondary group, then your tertiary group and so on. Sell to anyone outside those groups who approaches you too, but don't spend a lot of time courting him or her. Invest your time and money where they'll bring the greatest return.

Focusing on where you can sell the most books most effectively is the same strategy used by many of the national book distributors who primarily court buyers at the major bookstore chains and wholesale operations, where a single order can be placed for hundreds or thousands of copies. Then smaller book outlets that buy only a few copies are called on maybe once or twice a year or just sent a catalog and contacted by telephone.

REPETITIVE AUDIENCE CONTACT is your mission once you have identified your marketing area. Establish and maintain a presence in your marketplace. Join associations, attend conventions, read magazines, take part in mailing list servers and so on. If you're a *participant* in your book's subject matter, you probably already do.

Love what you write; write what you love.

It helps, as well, to have more than one product, because each customer who buys is a prime target for similar books and products. People who buy how-to books on a specialized subject often collect them all. Slowly build your clientele and your product line.

SEASONS AFFECT YOUR SALES

You should plan your major marketing efforts around the prime selling seasons. The big publishers bring out most of their new titles in the fall, targeting them at the December holidays. Their second major season is in the spring. June graduates are a good market. Business books move best in the late spring and late fall, not during the summer. Outdoor books do best in late winter, when people are confined indoors and are thinking about the activities of the coming summer. Travel books will do well a few months before the applicable travel season.

Most publishers find December and late August to be slow. In December, it's because of the many competing end-of-the-year activities; in late August, it's because people are concentrating on the transition from summer activities/vacations (play) to fall (work/school). Business picks up again after the first of the year and after Labor Day.

SELLING TO THE GOVERNMENT AND MILITARY

There are 2,300 libraries in the federal government library system and 80 agencies that purchase books, according to *Publishers Weekly*. Most of the libraries come under the Department of Defense.

Some of the army's libraries must be approached through central offices, but others can be approached directly. For example, the Army Library Program procures hardcover books for army libraries around the world and softcover (or paperbacks) for distribution in the field. Of the about 60 hardcover titles chosen monthly, some 60% are nonfiction. About 100 softcover titles are procured each month and distributed in 900 kits; selections are highly recreational. Centralized purchases are made under annual contracts with wholesalers.

Navy libraries spend more than $3 million each year on books. The International Communications Agency (formerly the U.S. Information Agency) runs 129 libraries in 110 countries with 6,000 to 25,000 volumes each and devotes about $2 million each year to procurement. They like to see brochures and review copies.

Sending brochures to military buying-offices is not nearly as successful as sending information to *specifiers*. For example, a brochure I might have on a parachute book should be sent to parachute lofts in the army, air force, navy, Coast Guard and Marine Corps. The parachute riggers in lofts know how useful the book can be and will tell the buying offices how many they want.

For more detailed information see Document 637, *Selling Books to the Military Market* by Michael Sedge, at http://parapub.com/sites/para/resources/allproducts.cfm.

PREMIUMS AND INCENTIVES

First, let's define some terms. *Premiums* are products that are given away or sold at a discount to promote business. Premiums may be given away by a store or other business to attract customers. (An *ad specialty* is an imprinted product, such as a pen or key chain, which is given away.) Meanwhile, *incentives* are given to salespeople as prizes for achieving sales goals.

The premium/incentive market is a $20 billion per year business. Books are in eighth place with $500 million in sales. According to *Potentials in Marketing* magazine, 16.8% of the companies using premiums also use books. Books make especially good premiums because you can customize their covers and they have a higher perceived value than some other premium trinkets. (Interestingly, in some areas, regulated industries such as banks are prohibited from giving away certain items or the value of those items is limited.)

Look for a company with products or services that closely match the book's subject matter. If your book covers a regional topic, try local businesses. The books can be digitally imprinted with "Compliments of...," for example. If you cover a subject with wider appeal, such as a book on beer-can collecting, contact the beer, aluminum, can and packaging companies. Such a book would make an ideal corporate gift or could be worked into a promotion. A tour guidebook might be sold to a motel chain.

A PREMIUM SUCCESS STORY

Judy Dugan was working in a graphic arts shop when the first edition of *The Self-Publishing Manual* was being typeset. As she pasted up the pages, she read the book and became increasingly interested. She had been toying with two manuscripts (one on Santa Barbara highlights and history; the other a children's book) for years. She began asking me all sorts of questions about the possibilities for her books. One challenge she had was a lack of money to invest.

I noticed that Valley Federal Savings was moving into downtown Santa Barbara. I explained that it was a prime candidate for a regional book such as her Santa Barbara book, because it would tie the out-of-town bank to the local community. A premium could be used to lure potential patrons into the new bank.

In two short visits, she walked out with a purchase order for 5,000 copies in softcover and 1,000 copies in hardcover. She was paid one-half on signing and one-half on delivery—at full list price. The money allowed her to print 11,000 books so she could serve the local tourist market with her own 5,000.

The bank's copies had special back-cover printing that said, "Compliments of Valley Federal Savings." The bank advertised in newspapers, on radio and television. They invited people to come into the bank for a free, autographed copy of the book. They set up Judy with a table and a sign and she spent the week greeting people and signing her name.

Publishers have sold premium books to doctors, dentists, chiropractors and other health-care professionals (both individual and group practices), and to those in finance, real estate, insurance and other fields. The possibilities are endless.

Premium orders are large, usually 1,000 or more books, and the customer can ask for 60% off or more. Such a discount can be justified for a large order that eliminates the problems of financing, storage and individual shipping. A typical premium discount schedule might look like this:

# Copies	Discounts
25-99	20%
100-499	40%
500-999	50%
1,000-14,999	60%
15,000 up	Cost of printing plus 10% of list price
Terms: Nonreturnable, net 30 days, FOB warehouse/printing plant, freight collect	

Discount schedule for premiums

If you can strike some premium deals before going to (or back to) press, you might increase your press run and achieve a lower per-unit cost. Making a premium sale is time-consuming, but the payoff is big.

Don't forget to capitalize on a premium sale. For example, you might use "Official Recipe Book of the Pillsbury Company" or "Recommended by Radio Shack." Premium deals are not just sales; they are also endorsements for the quality of your book.

SPONSORED BOOKS are those you are almost commissioned to write. There may be an institution that wants your book printed and will offer a large advance order. For example, when we wrote our book on the Frisbee, the Wham-O Manufacturing Co., which makes flying disks, might have wanted to help the publication of the book, thinking the publicity could help their sales. With this sponsorship, they might have asked for some sort of cover credit, such as "Published in Association with Wham-O." Such an endorsement is to your advantage, because it lends credibility to the book.

Some industries need favorable publicity and find that sponsoring a book is much less expensive than placing full-page ads. They may pay for much of your production, printing, marketing and publicity. A book is also much more effective promotion because it appears to be more objective.

You may write a book for them or spin off a customized version of your existing book.

FUND-RAISERS

Nonprofit organizations are always running sales to raise money for their cause. These *flea markets, bake sales, street fairs, etc., promoted by church and civic groups can provide you with an opportunity to move some books.*

Every nonprofit has a constitution and bylaws. In the document is a mission statement. The primary mission will be education—to spread the word on what the organization does. All you have to do is match your book to their mission statement.

Find a group that agrees with the subject of your book. Offer to sell them books by the carton at 40% off. They can sell them at list price (or offer a slight discount to their members) and put the money into the club's treasury.

THINKING OF THE UNOBVIOUS

Leila Albala in Quebec wrote and published *Easy Halloween Costumes for Children*. When writing the book, she included a short chapter on UNICEF, since it's traditionally connected with Halloween in Canada. After the book was printed, she sent copies to the UNICEF branch in Calgary. The branch liked it and ordered 10 copies on consignment. Leila capitalized on the order by sending a press kit to the *Calgary Herald*. The story on the book mentioned UNICEF, and 400 copies were sold in just a few days.

Next she contacted UNICEF Canada. They were impressed and agreed to take the book for the whole country. Then she sent press kits to all the major daily newspapers. UNICEF Canada has sold more than 3,000 copies in English and 1,000 copies in French.

Leila thought of a market that was not so obvious, placed the books and then created the demand for them. Who cares that UNICEF had never sold books before?

Try approaching some local organizations first to get a feel for the way they operate. A gardening club might sell a gardening book, for example. If you're successful, consider contacting similar groups nationwide. Don't forget to tell them of your past good track record for sales and assure them that the unsold books can be returned—they can't lose!

When an organization buys your book, they are giving it an implied endorsement. You can mention this in your promotion materials.

CATALOGS

More than 7,000 print catalogs are published in the U.S., and each year 11.8 billion are mailed. For our purposes, there are two types of catalogs: (1) general book catalogs, which are not interesting, and (2) special-interest catalogs, which are. Catalogs can move a lot of books, and they're committed to you for the life of the catalog—usually one year. If your book sells well, it may appear in issue after issue.

Special merchandise catalogs feature a line of merchandise but devote a page or two to related books. Since you're already in the field (having written about it), you probably know who they are. See the various catalog directories at your public library.

For more information on catalogs, see Document 625, *Selling Books to Catalogs*, at http://parapub.com/sites/para/resources/allproducts.cfm.

SUBSIDIARY RIGHTS

Essentially, subsidiary rights give someone else permission to reproduce (repackage) your material. They include book clubs, mass-market paperbacks, film rights, translations, etc. The two major classes of subsidiary rights are *print rights* and rights to *nonprint adaptations.*

> *The bottom line makes it abundantly clear: subsidiary rights have become less and less subsidiary.*
>
> **—Nancy Evans**

Subsidiary rights are so important to the big publishers that the rights are often auctioned off before the original book is printed. Such a sale is also a great morale booster for both the author and the publisher—not only because of the money, but also because someone else obviously likes the book.

The main reason publishers can sell the subsidiary rights for so little is that they're not paying production costs to their printers—or, more important, royalties to their authors. Most author–publisher contracts call for a 50/50 split of subsidiary-rights revenues. Some contracts give 90% of revenues to the author on any nonprint (e.g., film) subsidiary rights. The publisher gets 10% as an agent.

> *A publisher's attitude toward a manuscript ought to be similar to a coal-mine operator's attitude toward coal: get every last bit of value out of it.*
>
> **—Sol Stein, president, Stein and Day**

MASS-MARKET REPRINT RIGHTS are for those pocket-sized books selling from $1 to $5 in the supermarkets. This is the one market where it is easier to sell fiction than nonfiction. Mass-market publishers like seven-year contracts with renewal options and initial print runs of 30,000 to 50,000 copies. Mass-market publishers offer 4% to 7.5% in royalties; the cover price is low and the royalty scale does not slide up until sales reach 150,000 copies. Advances are usually just a few thousand dollars. Unless you have a *very* popular book, the mass-market firms won't be interested.

The secret is to match your book with a publisher that has experience with that type of material. Look at other books and search for publishers who have produced the same subject matter. Not every editor in every house is interested in everything. Mass-market publishers can be contacted after your book has been out for a year or so.

> *Without subsidiary rights,*
> *publishers would operate in the hole.*
>
> **—John Dessauer**
> **Book Publishing: The Basic Introduction**

PERIODICAL RIGHTS may be serializations or condensations.

Serializations and excerpts by magazines and newspapers may be *first serial rights*, if before publication, or *second serial rights*, if afterward. Both generate a lot of good publicity. Big periodicals pay more than small ones, and first rights are more valuable than second rights. The subject matter has to be of great interest to the periodical's readers.

Always request that the periodical include the ordering information for your book in the article. Place the exact wording in your contract or letter as well as on the material submitted, such as:

Reprinted with permission from *The Self-Publishing Manual* by Dan Poynter, copyright © 2006. See http://ParaPublishing.com.

Such a notice will generate book sales. Anyone who reads the whole article will be a prime prospect.

Magazines will probably contact you regarding serializations after receiving a review copy of the book. However, you should make the offer to the most appropriate magazines prior to going to press. Send advance information to those magazines most closely related to the topic of your book.

Condensations in magazines do not normally pay a lot, but the publicity they provide will sell more books. Make sure the magazine is a quality product, one you will be proud to be associated with. Check their past condensation work, and call the publishers of the subject books. Ask if they are happy with the way they were treated and with the quality of the condensation, and compare the price they were paid with the one you've been offered.

The magazine normally farms out the rewrite, and the work should be a true condensation, not a reprint of two meaty chapters. You can expect them to offer a couple of hundred dollars, up to several thousand, depending upon the publication and circulation. Expect an offer of $600. Remember, they have to rewrite the text and that costs money. Sell the condensation rights on a nonexclusive basis; the magazine will be first in print, but you want to retain the right to sell again to other publications. Always retain text approval, because their writer could completely miss your point when making the condensation. Read the draft over carefully and make corrections; your name is on the piece, and the condensation will be a major sales tool for your book. You want it to be right. Make sure the condensation includes information about where the original book can be purchased. See the example in "Serializations," above.

Magazines will probably contact you regarding condensations after receiving a review copy of the book. However, you should make the offer to the most appropriate magazines prior to going to press. Approach just a few magazines with a good book-to-readership match.

ANTHOLOGY RIGHTS: An anthology is a collection of writing selections from one or more authors, usually on the same theme. You may be able to sell a chapter or two of your book for a compilation. Editors of anthologies may offer you a flat fee or a percentage of a normal royalty. If 10 authors are each contributing a chapter, each might be offered 1% of the list price or one-tenth of a 10% royalty.

You could also spin off a piece of your book into your own anthology by contacting other authors in your field for submissions. Many times "experts" in a field who have not authored many books will contribute a chapter to an anthology for only a small fee or even free copies of the final book that they can use for promotion and to impress their peers.

BOOK-CLUB RIGHTS: Book clubs offer you some money and a great deal of prestige. Since they were established in the mid-1920s, the Book-of-the-Month Club (BOMC; at 3.5 million members) and the Literary Guild have been helping their members by selecting the best books of the thousands available at lower than normal prices. Now there are more than 200 national book clubs moving over $500 million worth of books each year, most of which cater to highly specialized groups. There are also a growing number of community book clubs or *reading groups* serving specific regions and cities. Some local book clubs have several thousand members.

A book not submitted is a book not chosen.

The usual book club royalty is 10% of the list price, plus production expenses. For example, say it costs you $2 to print the book and the list price is $20. The clubs like to discount the book to their members, so knock off 20% and you have $16 as the membership price. You will receive $3.60 per book, representing $2 for production and $1.60 as a 10% royalty on the $16 membership selling price. If the book club invests in the printing, you get just the *royalty* of 10% of the club's selling price. Book club purchases are usually nonreturnable.

Larger clubs will make their own printing or join you in your original print run. Smaller clubs will want to buy from your finished stock. Those doing their own printing or joining yours should benefit from a 10% royalty deal. Book clubs buying 500 to 1,000 books from your stock should be treated as a large dealer and be given a discount of 55% or 60%.

The larger clubs usually want an exclusive; they don't want other clubs to carry the book too—at least not at the same time. Smaller and specialized clubs aren't so particular, because their memberships do not overlap.

SEPARATING THE CLUBS BY SPECIALTY

When Alan Gadney and Carolyn Porter placed their contest/grant book with seven national book clubs, they were able to separate the clubs by specialty—film and video, writing and photography book clubs. Each group didn't care about the others because there was little overlap. The two large photography book clubs also agreed to split the book itself—one took hardbound, the other softbound (they considered them separate books at separate prices). And they each offered the book as a Special "ALA Award Winning" Book Club Selection, which meant featured promotion in the club mailings. All of this took considerable negotiation among the seven clubs—that's where the fun came in!

A book-club sale is an important endorsement. If you can make the sale before going to press, the endorsement can be noted on the back cover as well as on all your promotional materials. For example, on the back cover of *Is There a Book Inside You?* it says, "Writer's Digest Book Club, Main Selection."

Do sales to book clubs hurt regular sales? Absolutely not! They help you start off with a large number sold, provide you with a valuable endorsement and draw a lot of attention to the book via the book-club promotions. Your per-unit printing cost is lower because of the additional book-club copies added to the print run, and you can make some money on the deal.

Approach book clubs when you have a completed manuscript or galley to show them. If they don't respond, write them again after publication and enclose photocopies of your reviews. They have to be convinced it is a desirable book, and that is where clippings of reviews can help. Send a letter to every club that might possibly be interested. Check *Literary Market Place* for book clubs and make up a list for a mailing. Also, see Book Clubs in Appendix 2.

PERFORMING RIGHTS cover stage, motion pictures, radio and television.

The usual royalty rate is 15% of the *net*, and this is usually a bad deal. Film companies are notorious for their creative accounting procedures that result in a very small net, if any; some have been known to write off everything possible against the film. Always insist on a smaller percentage of the *gross*; the gross figure is much more objective. Another possibility is a fixed fee or percentage each time the book or film reaches certain pre-established performance levels. For example, when the book becomes a best-seller or receives a major award, the film is sold to television, major cable, video, foreign distributors or it achieves high box-office grosses.

Performing rights involve complex contracts and should not be negotiated without advice from a book attorney. See one immediately if you receive a firm offer.

TRANSLATION RIGHTS: A publisher in another country may wish to buy the translation rights. The foreign publisher will pay you an advance, take care of translation, production and distribution and pay you a royalty on sales. Normally, you supply the text and photo files and a couple of copies of the book with late changes noted. Royalties might be 5% to 7% for hardcover rights and 5% to 10% for softcover. Usually measurements are changed by the publisher to metric.

Foreign publishers and foreign-rights representatives are listed in *International Literary Market Place.*

> *It is easier to sell another edition of an existing book than to write a new book.*

When negotiating a foreign-rights contract, consider the number of copies to be printed, the printing schedule, cover price, royalties for both hardcover and softcover editions, the advance and the government tax, if any. Some countries impose a tax on exported royalties. Japan, for example, charges 10% of the remitted amount. Generally, you should negotiate as high an advance payment as possible, because with certain publishers in certain foreign countries policing your royalty payments and actually getting paid may prove difficult. Always get references on foreign publishers, distributors or wholesalers you're not familiar with.

For complete details on foreign sales, see *Exports/Foreign Rights: Selling U.S. Books Abroad* under Para Publishing Special

Reports in Appendix 2 or at http://parapub.com/sites/para/ resources/allproducts.cfm.

THE INTERNATIONAL MARKET: Foreign sales of American-language books exceed $2 billion annually, with most going to Canada, Great Britain, Japan, Australia, Mexico, Singapore, South Korea, The Netherlands, Taiwan and Germany—in that order.

The most common way to cater to the international market is to fill and mail foreign orders the same way you fill domestic ones. Most of your export sales will come via email. Most of the foreign bookstores get your address from R.R. Bowker's *Books in Print*.

Ship small quantities of books via the Postal Service's Global Priority Mail.

Adding a country to your U.S. distribution will not double your sales. For example, expanding from the U.S. to Canada may increase sales only 7% to 10%. You must compare the sizes of the English-speaking populations.

For more details, tips and contracts, see *Exports/Foreign Rights: Selling U.S. Books Abroad* in Para Publishing Special Reports in Appendix 2 and at http://parapub.com/sites/para /resources/allproducts.cfm.

MERCHANDISING RIGHTS: If the subject of your book suddenly becomes hot, customers will beat a path to your door with offers to make T-shirts, decals and coffee mugs. They will want to license your title or logo to put on their products. Note all the *Chicken Soup for the Soul* products.

RECORDINGS AND BRAILLE EDITIONS are published for the visually impaired. If your book is well received, you may be approached for permission to translate *your book* into Braille or to put it on tape. When you fill out the copyright form for your book, you'll have the opportunity to give the Library of Congress a nonexclusive right to reproduce your book in recorded or Braille form. In a recent year, Recordings for the Blind & Dyslexic distributed nearly 225,000 recorded and computerized books to 45,000 members. See their Web site at http://www.rfbd.org.

See *Literary Market Place* for more subsidiary-rights possibilities. For subsidiary-rights wording, see *Publishing Contracts* on disk under Para Publishing Special Reports in Appendix 2 or at http://parapub.com/sites/para/resources/allproducts.cfm.

OPPORTUNITIES WITH OTHER PUBLISHERS

CO-PUBLISHING is a way for two firms to spread the risk and the reward in a new book. Usually, one publisher is large and the other small, or the two concentrate on different markets. The larger publisher typically handles the bookstores and libraries, while the smaller one sells directly to user groups and fills the individual mail-order sales.

Get an agreement on who decides, performs and pays for the following: book and cover design, editing, page and cover production, printing, marketing strategy, promotion and sales to the book trade versus special markets, fulfillment and accounting. Be wary of supposed co-publishing deals where you pay for everything, and the co-publisher uses their ISBN (so all sales go to them), and they market the book and handle accounting without you being able to monitor their performance or break the contract. Don't let a co-publisher take advantage of you.

For a co-publishing agreement, see *Publishing Contracts* on disk under Para Publishing Special Reports in Appendix 2 or at http://parapub.com/sites/para/resources/allproducts.cfm.

SELLING OUT TO A LARGER PUBLISHER: Many new author–publishers publish their first book and then sell it to a large publisher—and many sell too cheaply.

Acquisition editors from major houses make the rounds of the booths at book fairs such as Book Expo America (BEA) in the spring. These editors are hunting for good books to add to their lines. Small publishers are usually thrilled to be courted by a big house and often make the mistake of selling for the same 10% (or less) royalty an author gets for a manuscript.

Ten percent of the net receipts is small reward after expending so much time and money to package and pro-mote a book as well as to test the market. The big publisher is exploiting the little publisher at 10% because all the risk has been removed. Successful books should cost more. The large publisher must understand that even though your company is small, the book is coming from another "publisher"; this is not just an untested manuscript from an author. A fee should be paid to the small publisher for packaging, market exploration and establishing a sales record, as well as a royalty to the author.

When a large publisher buys a book from a small publisher, the price should be two or three times the production costs, plus 10% of projected sales. They should pay for all your time, work and financial risk. The deal should be made "royalty inclusive," which means receiving your money up front—not waiting until months after their books are sold.

Sell only the *North American rights* to the *book trade.* Retain all rights except those to bookstores and libraries in the U.S. and Canada. Always keep the nonexclusive individual sale, mail-order rights. The big publisher will not be interested in individual sales anyway. Make sure you can buy books for resale for the printing cost plus 10%. Normally, you'll be required to buy in lots of 500 or more, but this is a bargain because you don't have to invest in a large print run. Make sure all rights revert to you once the publisher lets the book go out of print. In evaluating a contract, consider the advance, the royalty, when you will get paid, who gets what part of other subsidiary rights, the duration of the contract and free copies to the author.

Give the publisher the rights for only what they are publishing in-house. For example, if they publish audio, give them the audio rights. But if they try to tie up the eBook rights and only intend to look for a buyer, give them a 90-day option on the electronic rights.

Small publishers and self-publishers are better off cutting a distribution deal or co-publishing with a larger publisher. In a distribution arrangement, the big publisher buys several thousand books for 60% to 70% off list price on a non-returnable basis with an advance to cover your printing—the remaining payment upon delivery or 30 days after delivery—and they have an exclusive in the book trade (that is, bookstores and libraries). Insist on a large quantity so the large publisher is in deep and has to promote the books.

With the book trade covered, the author–publisher is now free to concentrate on retail mail-order sales and the nonbook markets. But be forewarned: If you do sell out to a larger firm, you'll probably make less money and lose control of your book.

BOOKSHELF BOOKS: Offering other books in the same line as your anchor product will spread costs and make you the "information center" for your interest area. Find other books that complement yours. If the other publisher is small, offer to trade cartons of books. Now both of you have another product to sell—at no additional cost. The other books cost you what your books cost as you just traded inventory.

Since you paid printing cost for the traded books, you can even afford to wholesale them to your (nonbook trade) dealers.

FLYER EXCHANGES: Some publishers in your specialty field may be interested not in buying and reselling copies of your books, but rather in a simple cross-promotion—you include their sales flyers in your consumer mailings and/or book shipments, and they do the same with your sales flyers. You can locate similar publishers in the *Publishers Marketing Association Resource Directory* and at book fairs and publishing events.

BOOK EXHIBITS

Specialty shows—such as sport and boat exhibitions and trade shows—are rarely worthwhile for a small author–publisher with a single title, because the costs to exhibit (booth space, travel, food, lodging and shipping) are expensive. However, you can make sure that your book is carried and offered for sale by someone in the show. Find one or more booths with related merchandise and offer them some books on consignment; sign them up as a dealer. Give them a carton of books and an examination copy for the table. They will get a 40% piece of the action and you get the exposure while moving your books. Place your book in as many booths around the show as possible.

BOOK FAIRS provide important exposure for your book. The major national U.S. shows are sponsored by the following:

•❖ **Book Expo America (BEA):** This is the most important book-trade convention in North America. It's often held in late May and gets an attendance around 35,000. BEA is a book-industry event, not for the general public. See http://www.bookexpo.reedexpo.com.

•❖ **American Library Association Book Fair:** This major library conference is held in late June and gets an attendance of about 25,000. The ALA also holds a midwinter exhibit in January, with an attendance of around 10,000. See http://www.ala.org.

•❖ **National Association of College Stores Book Fair:** Usually held midspring, this fair is attended by college bookstore managers. See http://www.nacs.org.

•❖ **Christian Booksellers Association Book Fair:** This fair is usually scheduled in July, and a midyear expo in January. See http://www.cbaonline.org.

•❖ **Frankfurt Book Fair:** The world's largest international rights convention, this fair is usually held in early October with a location of Frankfurt, Germany. http://www.frankfurt-book-fair.com.

•❖ **London Book Fair** is usually held in March. See http://www.lbf-virtual.com/.

Contact these organizations about the fairs and then attend a nearby one yourself to assess how you might fit in and use it to your advantage. The big associations sponsor regional and local book fairs. Also, many cities throughout North America sponsor book fairs open to the general (buying) public. *The Los Angeles Times* Festival of Books held at UCLA each April is becoming one of the largest, with a weekend attendance of 150,000.

International book fairs are held all over the world, the most important being in London and Frankfurt for all types of books and in Bologna, Italy, for children's books. They can give your products good exposure and may lead to foreign-rights sales, but are not worth your own exhibiting effort yet. Use a co-op exhibit service instead.

Conventions and conferences of professional, academic and trade associations will present you with a targeted or "qualified" audience for your books if you match your subject matter to the show. Educational books do well at educational exhibits, and these conferences are especially fun because they provide you with an opportunity to meet with authors as well as customers. For more ideas, consult *National Trade & Professional Associations of the U.S. and Canada Directory* and *Gale's Encyclopedia of Associations*, available in your public library.

Exhibiting at a book fair is often an inspiring experience; it will recharge your batteries. You'll learn more about the industry, meet some great people, make valuable contacts (distributors, wholesalers, retailers, reviewers and the media), sell a few books and perhaps even sell some subsidiary rights. Typically, the show's management provides a space measuring about 10' x 10', a draped table, curtained side and back panels, a sign, carpet and a chair or two. Check their brochure closely. Get some book stands, mounted blowups of your book covers, and take a good supply of books and brochures.

THE POWER OF BANNERS & LOCATION

Find out what promotional opportunities the book fair offers. One-On-One Book Marketing was able to secure a 10' x 30' book-banner space for their publisher clients above the main entrance to the BEA in Chicago. They reserved the space in advance, after hearing that, because of construction, all 30,000 people attending would enter the BEA main hall through one set of escalators past the banner. With traffic in and out six to eight times a day for three days, they estimated well over a half-million advertising impressions during the show. And they know the banner worked. There was constant activity at the booth, buzz around the floor, and the authors were mobbed at their book signings. The banner turned heretofore unknown authors (and books) into stars of the convention.

EXHIBITING SERVICES will put your books on display with those of other publishers very inexpensively, and some do a very good job of representing your wares. Some of the larger co-op exhibit services are: Combined Book Exhibit (CBE) and PMA for library and book-trade events, Association Book Exhibit (ABE) for professional conferences and Academia Book Exhibit and Scholar's Choice for academic meetings. Write to several of them to compare prices and see which fairs they plan to attend; some offer package deals if you sign up for the whole season.

For more information on book fairs, see *Book Fairs: An Exhibiting Guide for Publishers* under Para Publishing Books & Reports in Appendix 2 or at http://parapub.com/sites/para/resources/allproducts.cfm.

Selection is directly related to sales.

—Jon Glazer, Little Professor Book Centers

It's much better to have reps selling the list to 1,000 buyers across the country, making independent decisions, than having five buyers at the chains deciding what is or isn't a worthwhile or viable book.

—Sales Director of a major publishing company in Publishers Weekly

Self-publishing was the only form of publishing for 400 years between Gutenberg and the Victorian era. It is not only honorable, it is historic.

—Godfrey Harris, author and publisher

9

ADVERTISING YOUR BOOK

USING ADS SMARTER & THINKING BEYOND THEM

I t's said that advertising will make a good book sell better, but it can't turn a poor one into a success. Don't spend money on advertising until all the free publicity is exhausted. Advertising is just too expensive and rarely pays when selling books. You're selling a $20 or $30 book, not a $20,000 or $30,000 automobile. You have to sell a lot more product to pay for the ad, and you can't even justify as much need to your buyer.

When in doubt, do not advertise.

The secret to successful publishing is not to publish more and more books but to effectively market those books already published.

YOUR WEB SITE

Your *Web site* is the center of your promotion program. You want to sell your books there, post all your press-kit materials, let visitors register for your mailing list and so on. Make your company "Websitecentric." All of your promotional materials should start on your site.

Expensive (to print and distribute) four-color brochures may no longer be necessary, but you do need ways to get people to visit your Web site. Your business card and most promotional materials should be designed to drive eyeballs to your Web site. The Web site is your new brochure, and it is also your storefront—open to the world 24 hours a day.

Try to get URLs incorporating your company name, your name, your book titles, etc., and point them all to your Web site. Dot com is the default extension. Even with the proliferation of dot extensions, only .com counts. Most people try .com first when searching for a site and .com can make you appear to be more established. Spend money on Web site optimization or learn to do it yourself.

DIRECT MARKETING

Direct-response marketing is any promotion or advertising that provokes a measurable response or order from the individual it was targeted to reach. In book publishing, direct marketing consists of order blanks in books, catalogs, package inserts, radio, TV and direct email.

Don't confuse "direct mail" with "mail order." Direct mail is a form of advertising that competes with space ads and television spots, whereas mail order is a delivery method or form of distribution that competes with storefronts.

TARGET MARKETING: This is the Age of Specialization—of the narrow focus. For example, years ago we had general weekly magazines such as *Look, Colliers* and *The Saturday Evening Post.* They are gone. Today we have specialized magazines such as *Graphic Arts Monthly, Publishers Weekly* and *Parachutist* magazine. We also have specialized newsletters, Web sites, ezines and cable-TV programs. As consumers, we have the advantage of buying only those products that are specific to our wants and needs. As entrepreneurs, we must *tailor* our products to special segments of the population and then *tailor* our pitch to bring the product to their attention.

A book will not sell unless people know about it.

—Bob Greene, Esquire

DIRECT EMAIL ADVERTISING allows you to pinpoint your target market with a specialized pitch. For example, the people I target with a mailing might be skydiving instructors. The instructors have different needs and desires than skydiving students, or jump pilots, or parachute riggers, or drop-zone owners. Each is involved in skydiving in general, but each requires a different pitch.

Direct-mail advertising is a targeted shot at the customer. This is not a shotgun blast at every household in the neighborhood, hoping to find a couple of people interested in your books.

Tell not what the recipient can do for you, tell what you can do for the recipient.

Use email, not postal mail. You won't have to wait several days for the mail house to assemble the packages and for the Postal Service to deliver them. And email is cheaper. You don't have to spend money on envelopes, stuffing or postage. Email also provides feedback sooner. Responses often start within 30 minutes. Then you can test another pitch. Most broadcast email costs you some time, but little money.

SPAM: Don't rent email lists; you won't want to be accused of spamming recipients. Build and maintain your own email contact lists. You'll use them over and over. You can collect email addresses by offering a free InfoKit on your Web site and building an ezine subscriber list.

> *The ad worked because it reached the right audience... because it aroused curiosity and because it offered a reward.*
>
> **—John Caples**

DIRECT MARKETING TECHNIQUES: What makes direct marketing successful is: (1) the offer of the right products, (2) via the right medium, (3) with the most enticing propositions, (4) presented in the most effective formats, (5) with proven success as a result of the right tests. The successful direct-mail campaign is made up of planning, list selection, copy, layout, timing and testing.

Creating Ad Copy: You'll need a good, basic description of the book that will appeal to the consumer. Start with Copying/Pasting your back-cover sales copy. This material, altered as required, will then be used over and over. Come up with very few words to describe the book. This becomes its "handle" and can even be the subtitle for the book. Once this is done, the future copywriting will be easier because you won't be starting from scratch each time.

If you include a FREE offer, be sure there are no strings attached. People get mighty fed up with "free" offers that wind up costing them money.

Repetition: Many publishers send a weekly email memo or ezine to their clients. The memos contain news and often some humor. These periodic messages help you to keep in touch; they are constant reminders.

Timing: The best time for your email offer to arrive is midweek, on a Tuesday, Wednesday or Thursday. A lot of email arrives on Mondays and the day after holidays, and your piece could be lost in the clutter. Friday's messages are often put aside because the recipient is about to leave for the weekend. Fortunately, it's easier to time the delivery of email than it is with bulk-rate postal mail.

The best times of year for offers to arrive, according to some experts, are after the start of the New Year or well after Labor Day. Conversely, some say that March to April (income tax time?) and May to June are the worst months for offers to arrive. Other experts warn against the summer months, when people are away and the messages pile up. Most agree December is bad because the potential customer is busy with family and holiday activities.

The truth is that it's the subject of your books that will determine the best months for your efforts. For example, if your books are on outdoor sports, the best months are January through May, with a peak in March, and September through November. During the summer, the prospects are more likely to be out doing what they were reading about during the winter. The best time to email to federal libraries is March and April, when they're preparing for their next fiscal year. May appears to be the best month for schools. Professional books seem to sell better in the first quarter of the year; the third quarter is second-best. All factors must be considered in relation to your specialized subject and audience. On the other hand, you may have a reference book that people need throughout the year.

> *I know that half my advertising is wasted*
> *but I don't know which half.*
>
> **—William Wrigley**

INTERNATIONAL MAILINGS: The U.S. is a culturally influencing country. The world consumes great quantities of U.S. information and thought. With the increase in both the standard of living and purchasing power in many other countries, the potential for book sales worldwide is good. There's a demand for books on leading-edge subjects.

English became a world language in the last century. In fact, although 6,000 languages are spoken in the world, more than 40% of the knowledge base is in English. English has replaced German as the scientific and technical language, replaced French as the diplomatic language and is the international language of aviation, business, computers and the Internet. Business books from the U.S. have done very well in the last few years with the surge of worldwide interest in U.S. management thought.

Naturally, books in English should be promoted with sales copy in English, and prices should be quoted in U.S. dollars (with checks drawn on a U.S. bank) since it is customary to settle international accounts in U.S. currency. Converting foreign money into dollars is expensive.

As you build your house email lists, don't delete the international clients.

ECHO EFFECT: Every promotion campaign you wage for a book will bring in some sales that are not directly attributable to that campaign. Some people find it easier or faster to buy your product somewhere else, such as dropping by a retailer's store. There are many ways people can get the book besides responding to your email. For instance, college professors who receive interesting mailings often request their libraries to order the book.

> *The "echo effect" is difficult to measure, but some direct marketers claim these indirect orders often exceed the direct orders.*

Since more than 75% of libraries use wholesalers, most of the orders from an emailing to libraries will come to you through Baker & Taylor, and you won't know the name of the actual purchasers. Sometimes publishers even help the potential customer in this direction and, in effect, give him or her choice of purchasing by mail or visiting a bookstore. The promotional message might say, "Available at your local Waldenbooks or direct from the publisher."

WHITE MAIL: Orders not traceable to any promotional effort or source are called "white mail." The longer you're in business, the more orders you'll receive that are not traceable to any specific promotion. The marketplace is a vast web of connections. A brochure sent to one source generates a multibook order from another. A review book sent to a single reviewer winds up syndicated in newspapers across the country. That's what makes the book business so constantly exciting—the always unexpected response.

SINGLE LINE OF BOOKS: Publishers should concentrate on a single line of books, such as aviation, regional subjects or wastewater treatment. Then all the books on your Web site will relate to each other. Think like a specialized book club and define your audience. Stay in one field with your books, related products and services.

TESTIMONIALS: People today are overwhelmed with exaggerated claims and hype from the media. Therefore, it's important to incorporate a confidence factor into your promotional copy. Testimonials from readers and reviewers will help justify your claims for the book and draw attention to your customer service. Testimonials help build the reader's perception of believability, stability, honesty and value. Shorter testimonials can be placed in your email letter, promotional materials and on the book itself. Longer ones should be on your Web site.

> *Your book is a success when people who haven't read it pretend they have.*

To be valuable, the endorsement must be from someone who has a name or title recognizable and important to the reader. For example, if you have a book on golf, you might want a few nice words penned by Tiger Woods or a testimonial from the executive director of the PGA. Buyers respond first to quotations from well-known people (if appropriate), then to people who have professional credentials (doctors, lawyers, educators, authors, Ph.D.s, etc.) or who are connected with well-known organizations.

For more information on gathering testimonials, see Document 609, *Blurbs for Your Books: Testimonials, Endorsements and Quotations*, at http://parapub.com/sites/para/resources/allproducts.cfm.

CO-OP ADVERTISING

Co-op ads are a popular way the big publishers direct sales to bookstores with local-space advertising. Typically, the publisher pays 75% of the ad cost (but no more than 10% of the value of the books shipped to the store), and the bookstore pays 25%. If the store is a regular advertiser in the local papers, they usually get a slightly better rate. The procedure is to have the store place the ads, but the tear sheets of the ads and bills go to the publisher. Then the publisher credits the store with 75% of the ad bill toward book purchases.

To justify co-op advertising, you have to anticipate that the store will move a lot of books. And while the stores may be a major outlet for a big publisher, they're usually a minor one for a small firm that concentrates on nontraditional markets.

The Federal Trade Commission (FTC) regulations insist that any deal offered to one dealer must be made available to all. Small publishers who test co-op ads with one store could find themselves in great financial difficulty, being obligated to advertise for everyone else.

Many small firms feel that co-op advertising is just too complicated and too time-consuming, and they routinely answer all inquiries in the negative. This saves time and money, and avoids related problems with the FTC.

On the other hand, some online booksellers provide an advertising credit to the publishers based on their sales. The publishers can use the credit to match a title with another well-selling book on the bookseller's site. This placement increases exposure.

POINT-OF-PURCHASE SALES AIDS

These sales aids include bookmarks, dumps, posters, etc. *Posters* can be very useful in specialty shops and at exhibits, but there just isn't any room for them in a bookstore, where every inch of space is used as efficiently as possible. Librarians like posters, but they rarely buy more than one book. Free *bookmarks* with advertising printed on them are used 30% to 38% of the time by bookstores. *Dumps* are special shipping cartons/display units, which are used by 38% to 40% of the stores, depending on the available counter and floor space. Many larger stores suggest and request them. Some clever publishers have designed small tabletop dumps with directions for detecting counterfeit bills on the back. This ensures premium display space on the counter near the cash register.

RECYCLE & BENEFIT

Dumps can often be found for recycled use in trash bins behind bookstores. Many publishers ship their books in counter dumps, floor dumps and shippers (cartons). Bookstores don't need all of these dumps because they have shelves, so they end up tossing dumps and shippers into the dumpster. You'll find a variety of colors, sizes and shapes. Use the dumps for testing new (non-traditional) markets.

ONLINE ADVERTISING

Some online booksellers will sell you ad space on their Web site just as chain bookstores sell ad space in their stores. For example, see *Paid Placements* at Amazon.com.

You can also buy *adwords* on search engines such as Google. Adwords match your book to items that people are searching for on the Internet.

A strong book market must rely on the prospect that many different writers may have their works appraised and published by numerous competing firms and sold by numerous competing bookstores in diverse markets.

—Richard Howorth, president
American Booksellers Association

Try to submit to an agent or a publisher and you will be dead before you hear back.

—Denny Hatch, author and columnist

10

FULFILLMENT

MOVING YOUR BOOK OUT THE DOOR

Book-order fulfillment consists of inventory storage, invoicing, picking, packaging and shipping. These routines involve opening the orders, keyboarding the invoices, wrapping the books, affixing the shipping label, applying postage to the package, making the trip to the post office (or other delivery system) and maintaining a record of the sale. Inventory management includes storage and stock-monitoring, so you'll know when to order another printing.

Fulfillment is expensive. According to publishing consultant John Huenefeld, most small to medium-sized publishers spend about 10.5% of their gross on fulfillment. All costs, including labor, storage and shipping materials, average $2.44 per order handled, or 66¢ per book. If your business is mostly whole-sale (many copies of the same book to fewer customers), you may be able to drop your fulfillment percentage to 6% or 7%. If all your orders are for individual books at retail, your fulfillment costs may be as high as 14%.

MAIL-ORDER SELLING

Mail-order selling offers you the opportunity to run a high-volume, worldwide business without a large cash investment in multiple facilities. To compete with larger companies, all you need is a better product and more efficient promotion. Since we're far from most of our customers, book publishing is primarily a mail-order business for us.

Mail-order businesses deal with their customers at a distance, without face-to-face delivery. Orders might come via email or telephone. The product might be delivered via the post office or a large shipment might go by truck. Mail order is particularly appropriate for the distribution of books. In fact, *over half the business and professional books are sold and shipped directly from the publisher to the ultimate consumer.*

Smaller publishers are attracted to mail-order selling because it's easier than getting into bookstores. They ship to wholesalers and stores, but they don't spend money visiting them. In fact, there are many stories about books that did poorly earlier in the bookstores but—when properly promoted—sold well through mail order.

Mail-order buyers probably do not frequent bookstores, and it's likely they don't even think of themselves as book buyers. Some of these customers are ordering from online bookstores and some get their books directly from the publishers. A *Publishers Weekly* article about Bantam noted that, geographically, mail orders equate proportionally to population figures. The majority of orders come from the most populated states, California and New York—not from the states with fewer bookstores.

Mail-order purchasing is a habit. Many people prefer to buy informational books this way. Once they begin, these customers often collect everything they can find on a subject. Many Amazon customers love the convenience of ordering from home with speedy 1-Click® processing.

*For smooth-running fulfillment, you must have
a well-thought-out system.*

ORDER TAKING

Initially, you will take, process and fill orders yourself to keep it simple. You want to streamline the workload to avoid any duplication of effort. For example, keyboarding an invoice and then typing a separate label is a waste of time and money (cost of label, etc.). Just print out three copies of each invoice and use one copy for the shipping label/packing slip (see "Order Processing" a little further into this chapter for more instructions). This one-time writing also avoids transposition errors in figures and addresses. Once your business grows to the point where you have several titles and employees, you'll require a more elaborate fulfillment system.

To enable you to visualize the distribution system, the fulfillment process will be discussed in sequence.

ORDERS: Most of your orders will arrive electronically via telephone, fax and email. These orders are usually charged to a credit card. A few orders will arrive in the mail with enclosed checks or money orders. Since many orders will be received electronically, you will need *"merchant status"*—the ability to accept credit cards.

Many of your orders will be generated by your *Web site*. If most of your promotional efforts are on the Web, most of your orders will arrive via email and most of your correspondence will be via email.

Draft stock paragraphs that can be copied and pasted into an email to answer questions, to announce new products and services and to take care of routine business matters.

Today, more and more people use the telephone to order. Not only is it easier and faster—if they're paying 10¢ per minute or less for telephone service, a three-minute call is cheaper than a stamp.

Telephone contacts are important opportunities for sales and increased sales. They take place when you have the attention of the prospect. Consequently, an untrained employee should not handle telephone calls. Make sure everyone knows who is to take calls, except in case of overflow, or train every staff member to take calls. Have an order form ready, or route orders to the order-entry computer operator for direct punch-up. Order forms prompt questions, making it easier to obtain all the necessary information (such as the *ship to* address).

Be sure to ask for their email address. Retain it for your mailing list and use it if there is a question about their order.

For a free copy of our Telephone Order Form, see Document 147 at http://parapub.com/sites/para/resources/allproducts.cfm.

VOICE MAIL ORDERS: Answering machines are very useful in business because they can take orders after business hours. They're a great convenience to both you and the customer. Clients don't expect you to answer after hours but they do expect to be able to leave a message at any time. It's nice when you return after a weekend away to find a number of orders waiting for you on your answering machine or voice mail.

OUR ANSWERING-MACHINE MESSAGE

Many people like our recording, which says: "Para Publishing, this is Dan Poynter. If you would like an information kit on publishing or parachuting, please leave your name and address. If you would like to charge a book to your VISA, MasterCard, Discover or American Express card, please leave your name, address, telephone number, the name of the book, type of charge card, the card number and the expiration date. Thank you." *(beep)*

FAX ORDERS: Fax transmissions don't replace the telephone, but they can replace the Postal Service for delivering purchase orders. Some of your orders will come in by fax.

Get a fax machine and install it on a separate telephone line. List your fax number on your Web site, business card and order blanks. Get a plain-paper model.

TOLL-FREE PHONE NUMBERS AND CREDIT CARDS: It's generally accepted that a (800/888/877/866) toll-free order number will increase the response to an offer. Some clients will respond to your solicitation via email, but some would rather call than send their credit-card numbers into cyberspace. Toll-free numbers raise the confidence level and the level of customer service.

Try to get an 800 number as opposed to one of the other toll-free area codes. When people see "toll-free," they think "800." Though their eyes see 888 or 877, their fingers may still hit 800.

The best 800 numbers are those that tie into your company such as Para Publishing's 800-PARAPUB. To find if a number is available, just call it. If someone answers—it's not!

Toll-free numbers work best when paired with credit-card charge arrangements.

There is more to fulfillment than immediately comes to mind.

CREDIT-CARD ORDERS

TAKE CREDIT CARDS—GET MERCHANT STATUS: To increase sales and size of sales, publishers must accept credit-card payments. Getting Merchant Status used to be difficult. Local banks were told not to accept merchants who engaged in telephone and Web site sales or who operated from home rather than a storefront.

Some publishers have found that getting Merchant Status through Costco is a good deal. Others have been conned by Independent Sales/Service Organizations (ISOs). ISOs make their money when they sell or lease you the terminal and printer, often at exorbitant rates with a long-term contract. ISOs don't process your charges. They find a bank and get a commission on all your sales.

We've made a deal with QuickBooks (the processor we have used for 10 years) to make an offer available to book publishers, and it can save you money. There are no setup fees, no application fees and no service fees for two months. The credit-card feature works with the QuickBooks accounting program. You'll process the credit-card numbers when you cut the invoice.

To get Merchant Status, call toll-free 1-888-335-4541. To get the savings, mention "Dan Poynter, Para Publishing, 1-805-968-7277."

We have been accepting credit-card payments for more than 20 years. We used hand-operated imprinters, MiniTerminal with printers, credit-card software and now QuickBooks. QuickBooks saves us a lot of time and desk space.

In addition, Publishers Marketing Association (PMA) has a Merchant Status program that its members can apply for through First National Merchant Solutions. The rates for credit- and debit-card processing are low, and there's no monthly minimum transaction requirements. For more info, see http://www.pma-online.org/benefits/creditcard.cfm.

If you still want to try to work through a bank, get merchant card packets from several banks and compare prices and restrictions. The merchant card packets from most banks list the prohibitions (such as no telephone orders, no mail orders, no working from home), but they also have lists of exceptions. Some have higher start-up and monthly fees than others. Ultimately, the bank may send a representative to check out your place of business.

Credit cards boost sales and increase the size of sales while cutting down on collection problems. VISA and MasterCard are used the most in telephone orders, American Express is third, with Discover and the others used to a much lesser extent. Credit cards increase your cash flow and may decrease your need for expensive short-term loans.

Credit-card orders take more time to process, but the sale always comes out even. As a result, there's no additional billing or difference to refund.

ORDER PROCESSING

Get an inexpensive order-entry/accounting program such as *QuickBooks* (http://www.intuit.com/) or *PUB123* (http://www.adams-blake.com/).

Print out two copies of your (accounts receivable) *invoice* or (cash-with-order) *sales receipt*. One copy of your invoice is folded in thirds and slipped into a 4.5" x 8.5" clear packing-list envelope (Stock #45-3-23, Associated Bag Co., http://www.associatedbag.com). This copy serves as the invoice, packing list and shipping label. The second copy is stored in a binder. This is your hard-copy backup. A third copy can be generated and sent separately to the customer if requested. Many wholesaler orders (libraries, schools, government, etc.) require that the invoice be sent separately from the actual shipment.

From:

Para Publishing
Post Office Box 8206
Santa Barbara, CA 93118-8206 USA

Invoice

DATE	INVOICE NO.
5/26/1999	2680

BILL TO	SHIP TO
Borders Inc SPO Dept 100 Phoenix Drive, AP Stores Ann Arbor, MI 48108-2202	Borders Books & Music #23 9108 Metcalf Avenue Overland Park, KS 66210

P.O. NO.	TERMS	SHIP VIA
K-1133C	NET 30	UPS-GRO...

ITEM	DESCRIPTION	QTY	EACH	AMOUNT
PSH7	Parachuting, The Skydiver's Handbook 1-56860-045-3	1	19.95	19.95
40	40% Discount		-40.00%	-7.98
SHIPPING	Shipping charges		4.00	4.00

PLEASE REMIT FROM THIS INVOICE. THANK YOU.

Total $15.97

ISBN: 0-915516- & ISBN 1-56860- ; SAN: 215-8981; DUNS: 09-141-9358; Fed. ID: 95-6532235; Seller's Permit: SR AR 15-633785
Tel: (805) 968-7277; Fax: (805) 968-1379; Street Address: 530 Ellwood Ridge, Santa Barbara, CA 93117-1047 USA
winwprd:com\invoice.doc

Sample invoice

Individual orders come from readers and are usually paid for in advance, cash-with-order (CWO). Enter the sale into your computer and print out a sales receipt. The sales receipt looks like an invoice but shows a zero balance. Set the check aside for deposit or process the credit-card number.

Save envelopes with their orders enclosed. At the end of each week or month, rubber-band the envelopes and date the pile. Save them for 12 to 18 months, in case a customer contacts you about the order or the package is returned as undeliverable. If a book is returned by the Postal Service as undeliverable, check the postmark to determine when the shipment went out and then go through the envelopes to find the original order. The book may have been sent to the address on the check rather than the one on the envelope, numbers may have been transposed, etc.

If a customer complains that the wrong book was shipped, he or she did not order the book or a missing check was actually enclosed, looking up the original order will confirm or deny the claim. When replying, enclose a photocopy of the original order so the customer can see what he or she did.

ORDERS NOT RECEIVED: Occasionally, a customer will contact you saying that he or she has not received the book. Check back through the original order envelopes and computer record to make sure you received and processed the order and that the book was sent out and on what date. Then contact the customer, stating the date the book was shipped and how it was sent. Slower, but cheaper, Media Mail can take up to 30 days in the U.S. and 120 days to foreign addresses. Remind the customer that the package had a return address and it was not returned to you. Rarely does the Postal Service lose books. Tell the customer that if the book doesn't arrive in a couple of weeks more, you'll ship out another book. This is a good way to keep a potentially valuable customer happy.

When you ship the second book, write up the transaction on an invoice, make three copies and mail one to the customer. Note on it that if the customer receives two books, he or she should refuse delivery of the second one. If the customer does that, the Postal Service will return the book to you with only postage due. If the customer accepts delivery, he or she may never get around to sending the book back and you'll be out a book. Explain that you're sorry for the inconvenience and don't wish to trouble him or her further by having him or her rewrap and reship the (second) book. Once the customer receives a book, the chances are very good he or she will refuse delivery of the second one because there's no need for two copies.

One way to avoid most of these "books not received" challenges is to ship most books via *Priority Mail*. You can use the free cardboard Priority Mail envelope and the package arrives in two or three days.

UNDERPAYMENTS: Short slips can be used to collect small amounts due. Some customers, ordering by mail, will not send enough to cover the book, shipping and sales tax.

Sometimes the shortage is too small to bother collecting. Very small improper payments (high or low) are not worth haggling over as it costs more to process a short slip than the amount you might collect. Just ship the book.

If you decide to use short slips, set certain limits such as:

0 - .40:	Forget it!
.40 - $4.99:	Enclose a short slip.
Over $5.00:	Cut an invoice for the balance.

Short Slip

Your order was short $_____ .

We know you'll appreciate our sending the books now rather than holding up the shipment pending payment of this small amount.

Please return this slip when you next contact us—now OR with your next order or payment. THANK YOU.

Your name:_____

Check number:_____

Send to:

Para Publishing, Accounting Department, PO Box 8206, Santa Barbara, CA 93118-8206 USA
orders@ParaPublishing.com; 805-968-7277

Sample short slip

Collect these small payments as they come in and bank them once a month. The small amounts add up and are worth collecting. But you must compare the costs of collecting small amounts with the amount that can be collected. Most people are good about short slips and will pay; however, it's not worth badgering them for 30¢ if they have to use first-class postage to send it to you.

OVERPAYMENTS: If the customer sends a little too much, ship the book a faster way, such as UPS. If he or she sends a lot too much, issue a refund check for the balance. Fortunately, credit-card orders come out even.

BAD CHECKS: Checks to book publishers rarely bounce, and it's not worth the record-keeping and loss of customer goodwill to delay shipments until checks clear the bank. When a check is returned, look at the original order envelope to make sure you have the correct address. Then send off a photocopy of the returned check and the bank notice that came with it. Write across the photocopy: "Please send another check" and circle the bank charge and the new total amount. Most of these customers will make the bad check good. You can always include a short, direct letter, but this photocopy technique is faster and simpler. Since books have a high markup, it's probably not worth your time to expend more effort trying to collect these few small debts from "check bouncers."

SHIPPING INSURANCE: Insuring book shipments is a waste of your time and money. The shipper should replace books lost or damaged in the mail. Your only alternative is to insure each parcel. It is far cheaper to *self-insure* by replacing the occasional lost or damaged book. There will not be many lost books, and the cost of replacement is small compared to the price of insurance and the paperwork and hassle involved processing a claim—to say nothing of the value of a happy customer.

REFUNDS: Refunds should be handled promptly. *The customer is always right.* A cheerful, fast refund will let customers know they can trust you, and there is a good chance they will be back.

Unlimited Guarantee

We guarantee your satisfaction. Order any book and look it over. You may return it at any time if not satisfied and your full purchase price will be refunded, no questions asked. There is no 10-day or 30-day limit; you may return it even after a year.

Sample guarantee

Set up as few barriers to ordering as possible. If your product is good, most customers will keep it. Since there is no limit on the free trial period, most unsatisfied customers will put off the return—forever.

> *The customer usually pays the shipping on an order and on a return. This means that you will refund or issue a credit (against future purchase) only for the price of the book.*

SALES TAX: Sales tax will have to be added on to the invoice on those *retail sales made within your state* to an end user (the reader). Don't collect sales tax on books sold *for resale* to bookstores and other resellers in your state because they will collect the tax.

When you sell to other resellers in your state, you must record their state *resale number.* The point is that the ultimate reseller will collect the tax (either to you or to the store). You must either collect the sales tax or get a resale number that indicates who will collect it. In most states, libraries are not exempt from sales taxes; after all, they don't resell the books. Usually, the sales tax is not collected for any sales made out of your state. The sales tax is calculated on the merchandise only, not the shipping charges. Record the dealer's resale number on the invoice or in the customer's record in your accounting program. QuickBooks provides a box for the resale number. (Also see the discussion on Sales Tax in Chapter 3.)

Keep in mind that the bottom of the invoice can be used for any other pertinent information or even a nice personal note.

SHIPPING LABELS: Labels are not needed for most shipments; you'll use a copy of the invoice, as this has the "ship to" address at the top. However, you do need labels for sending out review copies and other promotional material.

Labels come in rolls or sheets, and small quantities can be generated on your laser printer. Here's an example of a 3" x 5" label:

Sample shipping label

Custom-printed labels are available from label manufacturers in various sizes, colors and typestyles. One is Discount Labels at http://www.discountlabel.com. Do not order labels on slick gloss stock. Addresses will smear and the ink takes much longer to dry.

CREDIT AND INVOICING

Dealer orders come from your distributor, commercial wholesale customers and those individual retail customers (such as libraries and large companies) that must be billed. These customers are usually extended credit and invoiced.

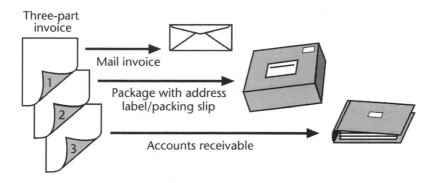

The invoice route

ACCOUNTS RECEIVABLE: When payment arrives, match the check with the invoice and date-stamp the invoice to give yourself a record of the date payment was received. Then move the invoice to a binder of a different color for storage. Update your computer file.

EXTENDING CREDIT: The customer may send a check, authorize you to charge his or her credit card or you may extend him or her credit (e.g., net 30 days). Most publishers require a check or credit card from individuals and extend credit to bookstores, libraries, their distributor and wholesalers (as long as the orders are not unusually large and the purchase order looks professional).

Individual contracts are rarely required with dealers such as bookstores. That's because the terms of sale (net 30 days, consignment, etc.) are printed on the invoice in the box marked "Terms."

DELAYED ORDERS

"Back orders" are those that cannot be completely filled when the order is received. Notify your customer immediately via email of the status of the order.

Most publishers use a common code of abbreviations to cover the most frequent back-order problems: OS (out of stock), TOS (temporarily out of stock), OP (out of print), TOP (temporarily out of print), NOP (not our publication) and FP (future publication). If you use these abbreviations, make sure they are explained somewhere on the invoice. Only librarians and bookstores will already understand the codes.

THE FEDERAL TRADE COMMISSION (FTC) has some strict rules for CWO (cash-with-order) mail-order operations. If you receive money for books:

•• You must ship the order within 30 days of receiving it (or charging their credit card), unless your offer clearly stated that shipping would take longer.

•• If it appears the order will not be shipped when promised, you must notify the customer before the promised date, giving a definite new date, if known, and offering him or her the opportunity to cancel the order with a refund or consent to a definite delayed shipping date or an indefinite delay.

•• Your notice must contain a self-addressed, stamped card or envelope for the customer to indicate a preference. If there is no response to this notice, you may assume agreement to the delay but must ship the order within 30 days of the original shipping date promised or required, or the order will be automatically canceled. A prompt refund must be made if the order is canceled.

•• Even if the customer consents to an indefinite delay, he or she retains the right to cancel the order at any time before the item is shipped.

➤ If the customer cancels an order that has been paid for by check or money order, you must mail a refund within seven business days.

➤ If the customer cancels a credit-card order, you must issue a credit within one billing cycle following the receipt of his or her request. The customer can stop payment pending settlement of the matter if the purchase is over $50 and he or she is within 100 miles or within the same state.

➤ Credits toward future purchases are not acceptable.

➤ If the book ordered is unavailable, you may not send substitute merchandise without the customer's consent.

This FTC discussion regarding credit-card rules may be redundant, because your contract with the credit-card company probably says if the customer purchases by mail or telephone (that is, without physically handing you the card) and later contests the bill, you must issue a credit.

See *A Business Checklist for Direct Marketers* and *A Business Guide to the FTC Mail or Telephone Merchandise Order Rule* from the FTC. Search for them at http://www.ftc.gov.

As long as you guarantee satisfaction by offering to send a refund for any merchandise returned for any reason, you shouldn't have any run-ins with the FTC. Just treat your customers right and keep in touch with them. Use email and keep printouts.

PROMPT SHIPMENTS: Orders should be shipped as soon as possible after receipt, usually the next day. The sooner the orders are processed, the sooner the money will be deposited; this is the best incentive for speedy fulfillment.

Customers want their books as soon as possible. A few who are not familiar with mail order will even call two days later asking about their package, but this is rare.

UNORDERED BOOKS: Customers receiving unordered merchandise cannot be pressured to pay for it or return it. They may use it or discard it as they see fit. So be careful where you ship books. See the *Postal Service Domestic Mail Manual.*

QUALITY CONTROL

One way to avoid shipping errors is to employ as few people as possible in the order-entry and packaging functions. Having fewer people in the loop provides accountability. The second secret is *cross-training* so everyone understands the system (and can fill in during absences). If an error is made punching up an order, the packer may spot it if he or she understands the system. In very small companies, one person will perform all these functions, but as you hire staff, be sure to cross-train. If the same person handles mail opening or order entry and accounts receivable, he or she will remember the bad debts and other challenges and will flag the questionable new orders.

> *Your most unhappy customers are your greatest source of learning.*
>
> **—Bill Gates**

COMPLAINTS: A complaint must be viewed as an opportunity, not a problem. Complaints can be expensive if not handled quickly, and they mean a lost sale unless you can make a substitute or convince the customer you are worthy of a future order. Complainers can also spread their hostility to others. Some mail-order companies, such as Quill (the large office supply company), enclose a return form with every order to emphasize how easy it is to do business with them.

Complaints should be answered promptly. Even if the book has probably arrived by the time you get the complaint, you should answer. You must maintain credibility.

Written complaints should be handled with a call, unless a lot of photocopied documentation is required. Customers can be cooled down more easily over the telephone.

When customers call in a complaint, you have an opportunity to wrap up the problem on the telephone at their expense so don't offer to get back to them. Remind the caller or writer that you guarantee satisfaction. You will try to work out the problem, and if you can't, you will refund the money. Most customers want the book, and the problem works itself out.

Find out what the customer wants before suggesting a solution. Ask, "What do you want?" The answer is usually much easier and less expensive than you would have offered.

A checklist form letter can be used to handle common small problems. However, because they're impersonal, they should not be used for major complaints.

INVENTORY AND STORAGE

Book storage cannot be taken lightly, because books are not light. If your floor will not support a waterbed, don't haul in a ton of books.

Often the best place to store your new product is in the garage, alongside a shipping table. This way, the books can be off-loaded in the driveway and stacked in the garage, wrapped as needed and placed back in the car for the post-office run. All these operations can be done with a minimum of carrying. Hauling books down steep steps into a cellar, only to wrap them and haul them back up, gets very old very soon and makes no sense at all. This is heavy work.

Tell the printer you want the finished books plastic shrink-wrapped in stacks of two or more books each. The plastic wrap will keep the books clean, dry and dust-free, and the books will not rub on the carton. Small publishers need shrink-wrapping and tightly packed cartons because they often store the books in places without climate control, such as in an unheated garage. If the cartons are not tightly packed (filled to the top), they will crush and tip, rather than stack well.

Don't stack cartons directly on top of each other. Stack them to overlap like bricks (this is the way your boxes are usually stacked on the wooden pallets from the printer). The alternating stack will be solid and will not tip over. Very little shelving is required in your shipping area, because you should store books in their original cartons.

If your state has an inventory tax, you can avoid most of the bite by careful ordering or by having your printing done in another state. Then, keeping an eye on the tax date, have the printer ship you a pallet of books as needed.

As noted above, the books should be shrink-wrapped at the printer, boxed and sealed. Then the cartons will be palletized, banded three ways (with straps or plastic wrap) and trucked to you as a unit. This keeps the books from shifting in the cartons, which can scratch the covers. Palletized and banded cartons are less likely to be broken open en route, but always expect to find at least one torn carton (perhaps a curious trucker has opened it to check out the contents).

New titles can be "drop-shipped" directly from the printer to your wholesale accounts in various quantities. This cuts down on reshipping. There is no reason to expend the time and money to route them, for example, from Michigan to you in California and then back to your distributor, wholesaler, book clubs and other major accounts.

Books must be kept in a cool, dry, dust-free place. Dampness can ripple or curl the pages, make covers stick together and rust wire-stitches (staples) in saddle-stitched books. Depending upon your location, moisture and type of flooring, it might be wise to stack the cartons on pallets, so air can circulate under the boxes. Always leave an air space between the stack and a wall. Sunlight will fade and yellow paper. Dust will scratch the covers and dirty the edges of the books.

Fire is always a concern, but insuring the inventory in a noncommercial (hence non-fire-rated) area may be impossible. Ask your insurance agent.

If your books become damaged, slowly or quickly, you're out of business. Therefore, your inventory must be protected, and this means leaving the books in their protective cartons and bags and opening only one carton at a time as needed. Unbelievably, some publishers unpack their books and place them on shelves, exposed to sun and dust.

If the pages of the books ripple due to high humidity, they may straighten out when the moisture returns to normal. Again, leaving the books stacked in their cartons will hold the pages flatter.

INVENTORY CONTROL is simpler if all the books are stored in a single place. When you have cartons of books scattered around your garage, in the office, at the printer, with friends and in your distributor's warehouse, some will disappear and you'll have trouble counting them. If you don't have a garage or spare room available, try renting storage space at a self-storage facility. These storage centers are quite common now; check the *Yellow Pages* under "Storage." Then try to store books in one place, or no more than two: the bulk in the rented storage space and a few cartons in the shipping area.

Physical inspection is the easiest way to get stock information. If you quickly count the books on hand monthly, you'll be able to plot a good inventory chart. These figures will be a great help in your planning next year. Reorders must be scheduled so the reprints will arrive just before the previous supply is exhausted. Having to report a delay in filling an order costs money in terms of paperwork, and time is money. The decision to reprint will be determined by the rate of sales, stock level, seasonal sales expectations (outdoor books sell better in the spring), the time required to print and, in some states, the date of the inventory tax.

Dun & Bradstreet reports that 9.5% of all business failures are due to excessive inventory. Keep the inventory low and order more often.

PICKING AND PACKING

The Shipping Area is where you do the picking, packing and posting. It should be arranged so as to require as little motion as possible; books, bags, cartons and other materials must all be within easy reach. Position the fast-selling books closer to the shipping table.

Packing involves the placing of the books in a protective wrapper so that your customer receives the clean, non-mutilated goods he or she is paying for. Books must be packaged well enough to arrive in good condition the first time. It costs too much to ship them twice.

Single orders can be prepackaged and stacked to wait for a label. When this is done in front of the TV set, the time passes quickly.

Priority mail flat-rate envelope

Books can be safely shipped in Priority Mail *flat-rate envelopes* (two pounds or more). Flat-rate envelopes are mailed at the two-pound rate, regardless of the total weight. These envelopes are provided free from the Postal Service. The Postal Service will even ship quantities of these envelopes to you at no charge. Just call 800-222-1811.

Get the right type and size (EP 14F-flat rate) and fold the envelope to immobilize the book(s). If the envelope is too large, the book(s) will slide around inside and the covers will be scuffed. (See the Postal Service Web site at http://supplies.usps.gov.) Put the book(s) into a plastic bag before inserting them into the cardboard envelope.

PADDED BAGS: Review copies can be sent in padded bags at the Media Mail rate (formerly Book Rate and Special Standard Mail), which is less expensive than Priority Mail.

Fiber-filled padded bags are heavy, dirty and can only be stapled closed. The plastic-bubble Jiffy-Lite® bag, on the other hand, is clean, light and waterproof when sealed. Compared with other plastic-lined bags, the Jiffy-Lite is not as smooth inside, making it difficult to stuff large books, but it offers the best protection. We have tested every type of plain and padded bag, lightweight and heavyweight, and have found the Jiffy-Lite bubble bag to be the best.

Jiffy-Lite bags cost more than fiber-filled bags, but you'll save on postage. A standard 6" x 9" hardcover book measures a half-inch wider and longer and is a quarter-inch thicker than its paperback edition. Both fit the #1 Jiffy-Lite bag when they have less than 200 pages. Contact Sealed Air Corp. for the name of the local paper dealer who handles their Jiffy-Lite bags. See http://www.sealedair.com.

Also contact Quill Corporation for a catalog and compare bag prices. Call 800-789-1331 or see http://www.quill.com. Remember to add in shipping charges when comparing prices.

Shipping bag

STAPLERS AND HEAT-SEALERS: The shipping bags can be stapled closed (get the heavy, hand-grip type of stapler); some have their own adhesive strips or are heat-sealed. Sealing machines come in several sizes and provide a moisture-tight closure.

OVERSIZED PAPERBACKS: 8.5" x 11" softcover books can be shipped in Postal Service Priority Mail envelopes. Put the book(s) into a plastic bag before inserting them into the cardboard envelope.

Vari-depth mailer

Some thinner 8.5" x 11" books require more protection for the spine and require a Vari-depth mailer. Vari-depth mailers are die-cut, flat shippers that can be folded around one or more books. The mailers cost more than padded shipping bags but offer excellent protection when the books are first placed in a plastic bag. Amazon.com uses this packaging for individual books.

CARTONS: Three or more books require a carton for protection. Check the *Yellow Pages* for nearby paper-goods dealers, and purchase standard 5.5" x 8.5" or 6" x 9" cartons (as applicable) of various depths. They ordinarily come 25 to the bundle. Many times, large-box manufacturers and distributors will give you free samples so that you can select the right-sized carton for your books.

Bookstores are a good source of shipping cartons. They usually get more than they can recycle, and disposal is expensive. Ask the storeowner and check the dumpster.

If you standardize the trim size of all your books, you'll minimize the carton and bag sizes required for shipping. The best measurements for books are 5.5" x 8.5" and 8.5" x 11", because they will stack together (two of the smaller-sized books, side by side, over one of the larger books).

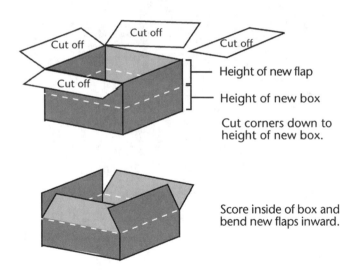

How to cut down a carton

Incidentally, some states, such as California, don't charge sales tax on shipping supplies such as cartons and tape. This is probably to encourage exports. Check on this with your office-supply store or state sales-taxing authority.

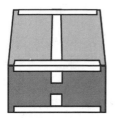

Sealing a carton with nonreinforced paper tape

PAPER TAPE AND DISPENSERS: The least expensive way to seal cartons is with 3" nonreinforced brown-paper tape. Reinforced paper tape is strong, but it's also dirty and hard to cut with inexpensive tape dispensers.

Fancy paper-tape machines cost several hundred dollars—quite a shock—so look around for a used one. Check used office-equipment stores and swap meets. Compare the prices at Quill at http://www.quill.com. Also contact Arrow Star Discount for a catalog at 800-645-2833.

The water will flow onto the paper tape more easily if you add a little vinegar to the reservoir in the tape machine. You may, alternatively, use a couple of drops of detergent, but detergent can gum up the machine more quickly than vinegar will.

PLASTIC TAPE: Plastic sealing tape costs more to use than paper tape and is harder to apply, but the handheld dispensers are much less expensive. The lightest-weight plastic tape is sufficient; buy the cheapest, lowest-mil thickness available. But be very careful of the special sales on rolls of plastic sealing tape, because the rolls vary in length and some offers are no bargain.

You will need ½" reinforced "strapping tape" for large cartons, so you should also use it on the small ones. Don't waste money buying wider tape.

Don't use twine; UPS does not allow it anymore. String takes too long to put on and it catches in mail-handling machinery.

PLASTIC BAGS: Take a carton and 20 books to your paper-goods store. Pick up some large garbage-can liner bags to line large cartons. Measure the bags against the carton. Then stack some books in one pile to fit the smaller cartons you're buying, and get some smaller plastic-bag can-liners to match. You have to run these packaging tests each time you buy, because the bag manufacturers are continually changing the measurements, mil thickness and gussets.

RAZOR KNIFE: Get a common razor knife for opening cartons, and keep it sharp. A sharpening stone will prolong the life of the blades. Be very careful when cutting open cartons. It's common to score the covers of the top books by cutting too deeply.

RUBBER STAMPS: The common rubber stamps you'll need are pictured in the illustration. Order them from your local office-supply store. Some are commercially available, and others must be made to order.

Rubber stamps

When shipping a package by air, stamp the "air mail" notice *near the address* on the package so that it will be more noticeable to the mail sorters. A red air-mail stamp over in one corner of the carton might be missed, resulting in a high-priced, slow delivery.

Rubber stamps come with a variety of inking mechanisms: (1) nonrefillable (not very economical), (2) refillable (with the ink held in a reservoir) and (3) those that use a stamp pad. If using a stamp pad, turn it over every night to make the ink flow to the top of the pad.

LADDER: Get a short, sturdy ladder or step stool so you can stack cartons higher and retrieve them more easily.

SCALES fall into two categories—spring and electronic— and two general ranges. Electronic scales are more accurate.

The two ranges are 0-2 lb. or 0-5 lb. *letter scale* and 0-50 lbs. (or more) large *parcel scale.* The larger scale need only read from 0-50 lbs. Packages heavier than 40 lbs. do not protect their contents well (will be dropped) and should not be shipped.

Book publishers don't need fancy zone and rate-computing scales since books shipped by Media Mail and in flat-rate Priority Mail envelopes are not zoned. A simple scale and a rate chart are all that are needed.

The scale should be accurate, but don't be obsessed with it being perfect. The Postal Service rarely checks the postage on a stamped package at the loading dock.

THE PACKING PROCESS

There are two important steps in successful book packaging: (1) keep the books clean and (2) keep them immobilized.

Start with cartons that are close to the size of your book. If you have 5.5" x 8.5" books and can get 5.5" x 8.5" cartons in several depths, the fit will be perfect and there won't be any sliding and scuffing between books. Slip the books into a plastic bag and slide them into the carton. For the best fit, cut down the top of the carton rather than fill it with dunnage. The books will be kept clean by the plastic bag and immobilized by the perfect-fitting carton.

STUFFING MATERIALS: Foam peanuts and disks are greasy, gritty and will work their way between the pages of a book if not separated by a plastic bag. Reuse any peanuts sent to you, but don't buy them. The best shipping carton is a perfect fit or one that has been cut down to fit. The next best choice is to stuff with newspaper; however, remember that newspaper is dirty—another reason to place the books in a plastic bag first. Other stuffing materials include cheap newsprint paper in sheets or in rolls, plastic bubble wrap and inflatable plastic and rubber balloons. Uline offers a wide range of shipping supplies; phone 800-295-5510, or visit http://www.uline.com.

LABELING: Once the bag is stuffed or the carton is wrapped, it's time to apply the packing list/shipping label. This copy of the invoice is simply folded and inserted into a large, pressure-sensitive, adhesive-backed clear envelope and placed on the bag or carton. (Stock #45-3-23, Associated Bag Co., http://www.associatedbag.com) Now the person receiving the shipment will have exactly the same information as the person receiving the bill.

Occasionally, the person receiving the separate bill will not want the person receiving the books to know the prices and terms (such as in a drop shipment). In this case, simply use scissors to clip off the pricing information. When the *ship to* address is not the same as the invoiced address, cross out the latter and circle the former with a felt-tip pen, or use a common 1" x 3.5" address label to cover the *sold to* address.

TAPING: Using nonreinforced paper or plastic tape, seal the ends of the carton as well as the long flaps. Sealing the ends will make the carton far sturdier. Place the shipping label/packing slip in its self-adhesive, clear envelope on top. Place this envelope over the carton closure, so the recipient will have to remove the envelope to open the carton. Then reinforce the carton by banding in at least two directions with reinforcing tape. Run the tape over the clear packing slip envelope to secure it to the carton. Then if another heavy package is skidded across this one, the label will not be spindled off.

When assembling cartons with paper tape, cut the tape long enough to hang over the carton by 2" to 3" on each end. Since folding down the four flaps and taping is a three-hand job, try this: With all four flaps closed, place the tape on the far long flap. Pull the carton up against you, and seal the tape over the near long flap and the ends of the carton.

The wrapped and addressed carton

SHIPPING RATES

Obtain both the domestic and international rates from the Postal Service at http://www.usps.gov and make up postal charts for both the invoicing and wrapping areas. Inflate the figures on the chart for the invoicing area to allow for the price of the shipping bag, invoice, tape, envelope, the first-class postage of the invoice and self-insurance (because you'll replace any books that are lost or damaged in transit). It's cheaper to replace a lost book than to pay for postal insurance.

For Postal Service publications and Web sites, see Postal Books, Manuals & Web Sites in Appendix 2. For the most current rates, see http://www.usps.gov.

MEDIA MAIL (BOOK RATE): Books can be shipped via the Postal Service's Media Mail (formerly called Book Rate and Special Standard Mail). To qualify, books must have at least eight pages, contain no advertising and be permanently bound. Media Mail is cheaper than regular parcel post, and there are no postal zones to compute. The same low rate applies to any destination with a zip code from Guam to the Virgin Islands, including APOs and FPOs.

If, however, you're shipping a heavy parcel in the nearest postal zones to yours, compare the Postal Service's Media Mail rate with their regular parcel-post rate, and with UPS, courrier for the lowest rate available.

Get a copy of the Postal Service *Domestic Mail Manual* from the post office or print it from the Postal Service Web site at http://www.usps.gov. For a free comparison chart, send a self-addressed, stamped envelope to Upper Access Books, PO Box 457, Hinesburg, VT 05461; 800-

310-8320, 802-482-2988; Fax: 802-482-3125; or print it from their Web site under "Publishers Services" at http://www.upperaccess.com.

PRIORITY MAIL: Flat-rate envelopes (EP-14F) can be shipped for just $4.05, regardless of the weight. And since you save 30¢ because the envelope is free, your cost is really just $3.75. You can get up to four books in the envelope, or just over four pounds. Eighty-four percent of Priority Mail is delivered anywhere in the U.S. within two days. See http://supplies.usps.gov to order free supplies. We ship virtually every single book via Priority Mail. Customers love the quick delivery.

> *Among other things good and bad that modern civilization has produced, surely the postal system which covers the whole world, is one of the most beneficial activities.*
>
> **—Jawaharlal Nehru**

Postal Rates for Book Publishers—January 8, 2006

Media Mail – Books – Surface

Lbs.	U.S.	Canada	Foreign**	Library Rate-USA	First Class Oz.	Rate
1	1.59	2.85	See Rate	1.51	1	.39
2	2.07	Rates in	Group	1.97	2	.63
3	2.55	4-oz.		2.43	3	.87
4	3.03	increments		2.89	4	1.11
5	3.51	——4-lb. Limit——		3.35	5	1.35
6	3.99			3.81	6	1.59
7	4.47			4.27	7	1.83
8	4.81			4.59	8	2.07
9	5.15			4.91	9	2.31
10	5.49			+.32/lb.	10	2.55
11	5.83				11	2.79
12	6.17				12	3.03
13	6.51				13	3.27
14	6.85				14	3.51
15	7.19	11 lbs. and over: Use			15	3.75
16	7.53	"Direct Sack of Prints."			16	Use Priority Mail
17	7.87	Economy (Surface) M-Bags				
18	8.21					
19	8.55	*Canada:*	*Other Countries:*			
20	8.89	1.00/lb.	See Rate Groups			
21	9.23	(11.00 min.)				
22	9.57					
23	9.91					
24	10.25					
25	10.59					
26	10.93	Packages over 40 lbs. are			**Priority Mail**	
27	11.27	difficult to handle &			Lbs.	Rate
28	11.61	are subject to damage.			1	4.05
29	11.95					
30	12.29	41	16.03		(No weight limit on "Flat-Rate" envelopes)	
31	12.63	42	16.37			
32	12.97	43	16.71		2+	Zoned. See
33	13.31	44	17.05		http://postcalc.usps.gov/.	
34	13.65	45	17.39			
35	13.99	46	17.73			
36	14.33	47	18.07			
37	14.67	48	18.41			
38	15.01	49	18.75			
39	15.35	50	19.09			
40	15.69	+.34/lb.				

**Consider Global Priority (air) Mail at $7.50 to North America and the Caribbean and $9.50 to the rest of the world.

To get the latest rates and explanations, see http://postcalc.usps.gov/.

Para Publishing, Dan Poynter, PO Box 8206, Santa Barbara, CA 93118-8206

Tel: (805) 968-7277; Fax: (805) 968-1379; orders@ParaPublishing.com; http://www.ParaPublishing.com

© Dan Poynter, promo\144-Postal Rates.doc

UNITED PARCEL SERVICE: UPS provides excellent service, including daily pickup, but their prices for single books are not competitive with the Postal Service, and their shipments require more paperwork. Daily pickup service starts at only $7 per week. Contact your local UPS office for prices and a UPS Customer Materials Kit or see http://www.ups.com.

By way of comparison, a 1-lb. parcel shipped coast to coast in the U.S. in early 2007 cost the following:

Postal Service

Media Mail (surface):	$ 1.59
Library Mail (surface):	$ 1.51
Parcel Post (surface):	$ 2.96–$3.95 (depending on zone)
Priority Mail (air):	$ 4.05
Express Mail (air):	$18.80

See http://www.usps.gov

United Parcel Service

Surface:	$ 6.59
Second Day Air:	$14.51
Next Day Air:	$33.08

See http://www.ups.com

Federal Express

Ground:	$ 5.40
Second Day:	$16.73
Overnight:	$35.40

See http://www.FedEx.com

OVERNIGHT DELIVERY SERVICE: Some customers want the books right away, and they'll pay the extra cost, so it's wise to offer the option overnight delivery. Federal Express is the largest of the overnight companies, followed by UPS, Airborne, Purolator and Emery. UPS, the U.S. Postal Service and Federal Express are the three largest second-day delivery services. Most offer pickup service, but charges are lower if you drop off the package at their office or drop box. Check the *Yellow Pages* and contact all the overnight services listed for supply kits of envelopes, cartons and bills of lading.

Overnight and fast deliveries to foreign countries vary greatly in price. Always call for prices before selecting a carrier. DHL is the oldest and largest international carrier.

See the Web sites of these delivery services in Appendix 2 under Shipping Services.

INTERNATIONAL SHIPMENTS: International parcels of printed matter are limited by the Postal Service to 5 kg (11 lbs.). Larger shipments must be broken down into 5 kg increments or wrapped in a larger carton weighing over 15 lbs., inserted into a mail sack and shipped as a *direct sack of prints* in *M-bags*. Visit your post office for some No. 2 sacks and PS 158 tags. Also take some time to read section 225.953 of the *International Mail Manual*.

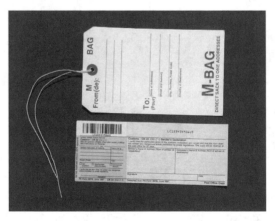

PS tag 158 & PS form 2976

To ship in *direct sacks of prints*, line a carton with a heavy plastic bag and insert the books. Make sure the books are tightly packed and that they fit the cartons perfectly. Seal and reinforce the carton in all directions to guard against splitting. Then "double-box" by inserting the package into another carton and seal this with paper or plastic tape. Copier-paper cartons are slightly larger than the cartons holding four stacks of 5.5" x 8.5" books and work very well. Affix the shipping label with the added words "Postage paid—direct sack of prints." Then band with reinforcing tape in all three directions. Weigh the package at this point and affix postage to a PS 158 tag. (Postage is paid on the contents, not the weight of the bag.) Turn the carton on end and slip a No. 2 mail sack down over it. Attach a shipping label to the PS 158 tag and attach the tag to the cinch clip on the mail sack. The Postal Service will pull the package out of the sack at the border, keep the sack and let the package continue by itself.

Most international shipments weighing more than 1 lb. require a "customs sticker." The type (PS2976 or PS2976A) depends on weight and/or shipping method.

Neither rain, nor snow, nor heat, nor gloom of night stays these publishers from the swift completion of their appointed rounds.

POSTING

If your shipment weighs less than 1 lb., you can drop the weighed and stamped package off at the loading dock at the rear of the post office or the counter up front. There's no need to wait in line. Most postal employees don't know much about classes and rates (just quiz one about direct sacks), so they aren't much help after a long wait in line. If you have a postage meter, you can drop off heavier packages at the loading dock because the meter imprint has a serial number and is traceable to you. If you don't have a postage meter, you have to hand over packages that weigh more than 1 lb. to an employee inside the post office because of the Unabomber rule.

Mail is usually sent from each post office to a centralized mail-handling facility before it is shipped out of town. If you drop the packages at this central facility, they will move out faster and will be subjected to less handling. For the address of your nearest mail-handling facility, consult the white pages of the telephone directory under the U.S. Government listings.

A LESSON LEARNED

Some years ago, I dropped off a load of packaged books at the branch post office where I have my postal box. Six days later, I was dropping off another load at the central mail-handling facility and discovered the previous shipment. It had taken the books six days to travel 10 miles at book rate (now Media Mail).

If you like the large 3" rubber bands used by the Postal Service, you can get a box free. Just stop by the bulk mail office (ask your local post office about its location) and tell them you're planning a large mailing. While there, pick up some mail bins and some No. 2 mail bags. The bins can be used to carry many small parcels to the post office, and the sacks will be used for Direct Sack shipments. Don't be bashful about asking for bins and sacks. The Postal Service wants to lend them to you, because they make it easier for them to handle the mail.

Designs in connection with postage stamps and coinage may be described, I think, as the silent ambassadors on national taste.

—*W. B. Yeats*

ALTERNATIVES TO LICKING AND STICKING

POSTAGE METERS: Metered mail travels faster and is handled less. Stamped parcels are taken out of the bins at the post office, canceled and thrown back in. Another advantage is that whereas the postal clerks may compare stamps with weight, they rarely return metered mail for more postage.

This Pitney Bowes meter includes a letter scale.

Once your business has grown and there's the potential temptation for employees to walk off with stamps, you might consider a meter. You can never stop employees from running a few personal letters through the machine, but this is better than losing a couple of $1 stamps every day.

A meter imprint makes your publishing company appear more established by eliminating that "postage-stamped, loving hands at home" look. The meter also allows you to print an advertising message on the outgoing mail.

On the other hand, postage meters cost money. There's no discount on postage, and the machine must be rented from a meter company.

Most postage meters come in two parts: the meter and the base unit. The base unit can be purchased outright, but the meter (the part holding the postage) can only be rented. Shop for a base unit that imprints on both envelopes and tapes for packages. Make sure your base is for an electronic meter. Mechanical meters have been phased out.

There are other meter companies besides just Pitney Bowes but PB has the best deal currently. See the Mailstation™ at http://www.PB.com.

ONLINE DIGITAL POSTAGE is more expensive and more time-consuming than having your own meter. You must go online to type in the address of your customer and then print out the postage on your laser printer. Online postage is not yet as fast or as easy as a meter. See the online demonstrations. Compare the monthly service charge with the cost of a meter, and the time each involves.

For details, see http://www.usps.com/onlinepostage/welcome.htm?from=home&page=onlinepostage.

METER SUPPLIES: Address labels are cheaper than buying meter tapes from the meter company.

Some newer meters use a thermal print-ribbon instead of ink, which has the advantage of a consistent imprint, no smearing and no inking (you just have to replace the ribbon). If your meter uses ink, don't use just any ink. The postal machinery that turns the envelopes face up recognizes the fluorescent red ink supplied by the meter companies.

RETURNED BOOKS

Processing returns is not the best part of the book business. Anytime you're feeling depressed over a returned book, remember that some large publishers get a lot of their books back. The industry considers 20%, or a little more, to be normal. Smaller publishers rarely suffer such a high return rate.

When a book comes back, make out a receiving slip. This doesn't have to be a fancy form; a note on a scratch pad or your notation on the packing slip will do. But you need some written record. Note the date received, the sender and the condition of the book. Determine whether any damage was caused in mailing, or before shipping, by the condition of the package.

Bookstore shipments almost always arrive damaged, because books usually aren't packed correctly. Most bookstores dump the books in a carton without a protective plastic bag or cushioning material, so the books rattle around and become scuffed and bent. Or they throw three books in an oversized Jiffy bag, and the books rub against each other as they journey across the country.

On receipt, the good books should be returned to the storage area and the bad ones set aside in their box, pending settling up with the customer. Return the damaged books with an invoice for the shipping and an explanation regarding the condition. Be sure to mark the books so they'll be easy to spot if returned to you again. One publisher places a small black dot with a fine felt-tip marker on the bottom edge of the book near the spine.

One well-known Eastern book wholesaler frequently orders books and returns them from different departments on the same day.

The object is to get your books into the stores. If the store has tried your book on the shelf and it hasn't sold, they should not be penalized for returning it. If, on the other hand, the book is not just shelf-worn but was obviously damaged in return transit due to poor packaging, the store or wholesaler should eat the cost.

Books returned by the customer because they were received damaged should be replaced at once. This is a cost of doing business and keeping clients happy.

Damaged books can be offered to acquaintances as *selected seconds* and donated to institutions. Some publishers offer them to the walk-in traffic at a 50% discount with the explanation that "all books look like this after a week."

When an individual retail order is returned by the Postal Service marked "Undeliverable," check the original order to verify the address. If the address is wrong, type a label with the correct address, then slip the whole book and package into another, larger package so the addressee will see what happened and why the shipment took so long. If the address is correct, date the package and put the order and book aside and wait for your customer's anxious letter or call.

Some publishers have "order from" addresses that are different from their "return shipping" addresses. That's because it's expensive and disruptive when cartons of books are delivered to the editorial offices. Be specific about your receiving address in your returns policy.

ORDER FULFILLMENT ALTERNATIVES

There are many ways to fulfill your orders besides doing it yourself. The alternatives are listed below.

Remember, however, that even with outside fulfillment for orders, you'll still need a small shipping facility yourself for review copies, sales samples and other mailings. Keeping your fulfillment in-house will provide better inventory control, faster shipping of orders, fewer shipping errors, fewer damaged books and lower fulfillment costs.

JOINT REPRESENTATION: This is where a large publisher accepts a smaller one with similar titles. Commonly, the big firm takes over all the marketing, distribution and billing functions as well. The cost can be high: 25% or more of the net sale. Like the commissioned sales reps, the firm gets credit for all the sales regardless of who generates them. Not only does the arrangement cost more than doing it yourself, but you also never learn the ropes. You become more dependent than ever, and the large publisher may push its own titles (which are more profitable) before selling yours. Unless you simply don't have the time or the will to do your own marketing and fulfillment, joint representation should not be considered until you have operated long enough to make an educated decision and draft an ironclad contract.

FULFILLMENT WAREHOUSES: If you are unable to spend the time picking, packing and posting, lack the necessary space or would rather concentrate on writing and marketing, there are commercial fulfillment firms that will do the job for you. Typically, they have a price list of charges for packaging and many other services, plus postage and packing materials. Some charge a percentage of the order. They may also charge per month per skid of books for storage.

Figure roughly 1¢ per book per month for warehousing. You can send your orders and invoices to these fulfillment warehouses (or they will cut the invoices for you). Most also accept credit-card orders from your customers via a toll-free telephone number and offer accounting, invoicing, order tracking, returns and sometimes even collection services. The best have 24-hour order taking via email, postal mail, phone, fax and their Web site.

Fulfillment firms are listed at http://parapub.com/sites/para/resources/supplier.cfm.

Remember, fulfillment houses only store, take orders and ship; they do not *sell*. They will not get your books into bookstores or sell subsidiary rights. Moving books from your garage to someone's warehouse does not mean your books have been turned into cash.

For more information on fulfillment, see *Book Fulfillment* at http://parapub.com/sites/para/resources/allproducts.cfm or under Para Publishing Special Reports in Appendix 2. Also, see the list of fulfillment services in Appendix 2.

REMAINDERS

Remainders are overstock books that are sold off to remainder dealers at greatly reduced prices. The big publishers are only interested in books while they're maintaining a certain level of sales. When the demand drops for a title, out they go. Your situation is different, because you're storing the books at home, have a lower overhead, like the prestige of having a current book and can get by on the occasional sales. Initially, each book adds to your size. You'll have to have several titles before you drop any. You can always run off another 500 copies or print single copies on demand; there's no reason to go out of print. If it's a good how-to book and you have kept it up-to-date with revisions at each printing, it should continue to sell indefinitely.

Typically, a remainder dealer will offer you 1% to 3% of the list (cover) price of the book. On a $19.95 book, that would be just 20¢ to 60¢ each. Don't remainder a book until the value of your storage space exceeds these amounts.

Publishing consultant John Huenefeld offers the following rule of thumb for determining when to drop a title. Multiply the quantity on hand by the list price. Then divide by 20 to get 5% of the list price value of the stock. Now compare this 5% figure with the net sales for the last 12 months. If the sales were not greater than this 5% figure, it's time to call the truck.

Remaindering is big business. More than 20,000 titles go out of print each year, and 25 million copies are remaindered. A lot of large companies are in this business. Many wholesalers carry remainders or "bargain books," which can account for one-third of a bookstore's gross. Some books see their sales pick up once they have been remaindered. The new price and marketing effort have turned books completely around. Remaindered books have sold out and then gone back to press.

Notify your distributor before remaindering a book and offer to take back their stock.

Lists of remainder dealers can be found in *Publishers Weekly, Literary Market Place* and the *American Book Trade Directory* at your library. Write to a number of remainder dealers (some of them specialize in certain types of books, sold to special markets), indicating the quantity, list price, title, hardbound or paperback, condition, location, whether they are prepackaged and, if so, in what increments. Enclose a copy of the book and your sales materials. Establish a closing date and announce that you'll accept the best offer for any quantity. Shipping is FOB your warehouse, terms are net 30 days and the books are not returnable. Once you have selected the highest bidder, call them and make sure you have a deal.

Most remainder dealers want 1,000 to 5,000 books, minimum, and they want your entire stock so they have an exclusive. Some will take your slightly damaged stock or "hurts" (scratched copies returned by bookstores).

For detailed information on remainders and other forms of inventory reduction, see Document 633, *Beyond Remainders*, at http://parapub.com/sites/para/resources/allproducts.cfm. Hopefully, you won't have to deal in remainders.

HURT BOOKS: Remainder or donate damaged returns (hurts) to a charity. You can deduct the value of the book at its original acquisition cost plus your storage and handling costs and the postage out. Prisons, foreign libraries and church bazaars will be very happy to accept your books. By donating your scuffed books, you recover your original investment in them.

A book has but one voice,
but it does not instruct everyone alike.
—Thomas Kempis

11

COPING WITH
BEING PUBLISHED

OR WHAT DO I DO NOW?

Once you become a published author, your life will change. Being in the limelight may not always be as much fun as your earlier dreams about it. This chapter discusses some of the interesting challenges you'll face, and it provides suggestions on how to deal with them.

YOUR NEW STATUS

Your status will change from that of a private person, the "writer," to a public person, the "expert"—possibly even the "celebrity." Your friends will treat you differently once you're published. Some will be very happy for you, and some will be jealous—envious because they didn't write the book. People new in your field will treat you like an idol, while those who have been around for years may feel threatened and be rather unkind.

Many new authors do not foresee their new popularity, their growing celebrity status. There is little you can do about your new treatment, except be prepared for it. Be nice, and in a few years your reputation will be so solid that no one will take swipes at you anymore.

AUTHORS FACE THE CHALLENGES

Gary Glenn spent 27 years working as a fire investigator. When he and his wife, Peggy, wrote *Don't Get Burned! A Family Fire-Safety Guide*, life at work changed. The new firefighters put him on a pedestal—they followed him around the firehouse, hoping he might drop a few pearls of wisdom. Meanwhile, some of his contemporaries in the very status-conscious firefighting community were cool toward him.

Bob Johnson wrote the first book on the triathlon. When he was 62, Bob took off for Hawaii to practice for the IronMan competition. He found himself followed by a covey of young groupies. This was quite a problem—while Bob had an obligation to his public, he wanted to get away to practice alone.

HOW TO AUTOGRAPH BOOKS

Autographing books is something you will be asked to do both in person and by mail. It's surprising how many prolific authors have never given much thought to how they might autograph a book. Confronted with an admiring fan, they're suddenly at a loss for words. Most authors simply sign "To Kathy, with best wishes," then add their signature and sometimes the date. However, it's a good idea to think of a more clever standard line to use that relates to the topic of your book. At times, you'll want to be more personal, such as thanking a contributor for his or her help and support on a book. And if there's something special about a particular buyer, I recommend including it in your autograph. Yet, often there's a question of time. At a well-attended autograph party with many people standing in line, it's difficult to think of a few well-chosen words while trying to give witty answers. And, by the way, especially when rushed, make sure you spell your buyer's name correctly. In all the hustle, it's easy to draw a blank and misspell the simplest name or word, ruining a book.

> *To autograph your book to a stranger is easy, to autograph for a friend is difficult.*
> **—Rex Alan Smith, Moon of Popping Trees**

Make up a sign for book signings and exhibits at events. They prompt people to buy now rather than delaying their purchase. One author takes the sign below along with him.

Autographed books are more valuable. Ask the author to sign your book.

Sample sign for book events

Some authors autograph a number of books before an event so all they have to do is add the name of the individual.

WRITING ARTICLES

Once your book is published and you become better known, editors will contact you for material. Usually they will ask you to write an article on your subject—something you probably will not have time to do. Additionally, once your book is in print, you will find new, pertinent information and will devise unique ways of explaining your program and methods. Your solution to these two challenges is the "interview article."

> *Other people are the pioneers and make the history.*
> *I just write it down—and sell it back to them.*

As you think of a point you want to make, draft it in the form of a question and answer. Let these questions and answers build until you have several pages of them entered into your computer. Then when editors call, just say you are too busy to generate a specific piece, but that you have this Q&A article with all the very latest information. Tell them they may select the Q&As most likely to be of interest to their readers, and to call if they need any more. Editors love this system and rarely can think of any more questions. Some editors run the Q&As as is, while some reporters use them to generate an original article. What's important is that you have supplied an interviewer with written, well-thought-out answers. This system gets editors off your back, saves you a lot of time, fulfills your obligation to the media and generates a lot of publicity for your book.

THE SPIN-OFF is an important concept. Repackaging the same information for various markets or in various formats (expanded and condensed versions, various sizes and bindings, etc.) will bring in more money while promoting the original book. Magazine articles can be extracted from the book, book chapters can be used as a basis for conference workshops, a series of magazine articles can be combined into a new book or the book can be rewritten and directed toward a new audience. With a computer, it's easy to pull out part of the book, add an introduction and a conclusion and turn the piece into an article, or add new material and turn it into a special report.

Always end your article with an "Editor's note," where you mention that the article was extracted from your book, and then give ordering information. Do not simply ask the editor to do this for you; place the words at the end of the article yourself.

> *The lover of letters loves power too.*
> —**Ralph Waldo Emerson**

Continue to recycle. After an article is printed, post it in an article bank on your Web site. Then alert other editors that you have articles available to them. For an example of an article bank, see http://parapub.com/sites/para/resources/articlebank.cfm.

CONSULTING

Many authors consult on their area of expertise. For example, I consult as a technical expert in parachute and skydiving legal cases. If you decide to sell your time, set your fee schedule early, so you will be ready with figures when you receive a call. Be advised that most beginning consultants price themselves too low. For guidance on legal consulting, see *The Expert Witness Handbook* at http://parapub.com/sites/para/speaking/edutrain.cfm. Wring more value out of your expertise.

SPEAKING ENGAGEMENTS

As a published author, you'll be asked to address all sorts of groups. Make sure the gathering will be large enough to make the trip worthwhile. Even if they guarantee a large group where you might sell a number of books ("back-of-the-room sales"), you should require an honorarium.

Place photographic blowups of your books at the front of the room when you speak. They will act as *continuous communicators* because your audience will look at them all during the speech.

Make sure your book can be sold in the "back of the room." Don't try to handle the money yourself; you'll be too busy fielding questions. Try to get the organization sponsoring the event to sell the books, and give them a 20% commission on each one they sell. That way, you'll gain their support and an implied endorsement for your books, possibly even some extensive promotion. If they don't wish to sell the books, draft an assistant to sell them for you. Compensate this helper with a free book.

Another approach is to have the room set up classroom style, with long tables in front of the audience members. Put books on the tables at every other sitting place, with an order form. Explain that the books are not part of the course but may be purchased and that you put them out for inspection because there's not enough time to look at them during the break. Tell the audience: (1) all they have to do is to fill out the form (you accept cash, check and credit cards), (2) to turn in the form and (3) to then take the book. This procedure is a self-service and honor system. Process the credit-card numbers when you get home. You'll sell a much higher percentage of the room.

Your book may become a springboard to professional speaking at a higher rate; you could emerge as a sought-after expert who speaks. For more information on professional speaking, see http://www.NSAspeaker.org. For an example of a speaker's Web site, see http://parapub.com/sites/para/speaking/.

AUTHOR PROMOTION

Once your book is out, you will have to switch gears and put on your promotion hat. Your creativity will be redirected to drafting copy for your Web site, sending out review copies, writing articles, etc. When sales slow down, you'll then have time to write the next book. Remember that writing the book is just the tip of the publishing iceberg. The real work begins after you send the disk off to the printer, because books will not sell without constant promotion.

YOUR WILL

Your books are valuable assets. Draw up a living trust or have your current trust amended. You will eventually die, but you want your work to live on. Name an executor who understands publishing so that your books and papers will continue. The cost of a living trust is very little compared to the expenses of taxes and litigation, not to mention the time and the heartache a trust could save your family and friends. By doing this, you insure that your "intellectual property" will continue its life.

STAY IN YOUR FIELD OF EXPERTISE

It is nice to have your eggs in more than one basket, but you might spread your talents too thin. You are primarily an expert in one field—that one in which you are a *participant*. You can stay in that field and become a "super expert," or you can branch out into another field and run the risk of being unable to keep up with both of them adequately. So spin off your current message into speeches, articles and more books. Do more of what you do best.

PUBLISH MULTIPLE BOOKS: Distributors will be more interested in your publishing company if you have a line of books. With more books, you can pursue repeat business. It is much easier to sell additional product to an existing customer than to find a new prospect. Spin off your information into multiple products (books, reports, audio and video tapes, CDs, electronic books, etc.).

> *Your big day arrives when your second book*
> *is out, someone calls to order a book*
> *and you get to ask, "Which one?"*

PRODUCT-LINE PACKAGING: Maintain consistent and appropriate packaging. If your books look similar, you will have a recognizable product line. They will look as though they are members of the same family. Standardize your measurements to facilitate shipping. You want to stock as few shipping cartons and bags as possible.

LOCAL STORES

Place your books in local stores. Then, when traveling fans call up asking where they can purchase your book, you can send them to one of these stores. This approach avoids the awkward situation where fans try to talk you into a free book, and it limits their later-hour visits. A one-hour visit for a one-book sale is not very cost-efficient. The store is a more objective sales rep. You don't have to try to talk the customer out of his or her money, and the customer doesn't have to decide whether to make the purchase with you standing there.

> *There is probably no hell for authors in the next*
> *world—they suffer so much from critics and*
> *publishers in this.*
> **—Christian Nestell Bovee**

THE HONOR OF BEING COPIED

When you do research to revise your book, you may get a surprise. Other books may have come out on the same subject after yours was published. In reading them, you will find many interesting (though familiar) ideas. Many will be copied directly from your own work. Remember that when you are writing you are *committing history*— you will be quoted, or at least copied (but hopefully not completely plagiarized). See Document 619, *Write It Once— Sell It Forever*, at http://parapub.com/sites/para/resources/allproducts.cfm.

Next, see "Your Book's Calendar" in Appendix 1 of this book. Its purpose is to assure that you're doing everything possible for your book and that you're performing the tasks in the right order. Also, review "The New Book Model" at the end of this chapter.

> *The book that he had made renders its author this service in return, that so long as the book survives, its author remains immortal and cannot die.*
>
> **—Richard de Bury**

Once you have published, you'll know what it's like to be an author. Before or after publication, treat yourself to a copy of *Successful Nonfiction* for tips and inspiration for the journey. See http://parapub.com/sites/para/resources/allproducts.cfm.

> *The chief glory of every people arises from its authors.*
>
> **—Samuel Johnson**

The New "Book" Model

© Dan Poynter

Creating the Content → PDF →

A. Set up.
Idea for your book
Qualify project according to the Six Musts. WN
   See *Writing Nonfiction: Turning Thoughts into Books*
Research the subject, title and competition.
   Stores, Amazon, Ingram 615-213-6803
Get a Model Book.
Draft back cover sales copy. Doc 116, WN Ch 6.
Select a working title. *Writing Nonfiction*, Ch 5.
Set up the binder for the manuscript. WN Ch 7&8
Assemble research materials into chapter piles.

B. Build the content. WN, Ch 8.
1st draft. Assemble the elements
Write text in MS-*Word* in page-layout format.
Import digital photographs
  PhotoShop, Paint Shop Pro or PhotoSuite
Import scanned drawings
Add art from Web
  http://www.ClipArt.com
Find quotations on Web. See quotation sites.
Request stories from colleagues with email
Add URL hyperlinks to references

2nd draft. Content edit. Fill in the blanks.

3rd draft. Peer review for feedback. Use email.
  Get testimonials for back cover, etc.

4th draft. Copy edit (punctuation, grammar).
  Fact check
  Proofread

C. Convert to: (Writing Nonfiction).
  1. PDF file with Adobe *Acrobat*.
  2. LIT file, MS-Reader with RosettaMachine.com

D. Get cover art
http://parapublishing.com/sites/para/resources/supplier.cfm

Producing the "Work" →

Publish: print & electronic versions.

A. pBooks (Photos & Dwgs: 300 dpi TIF)
  1. Press (ink on paper)
  2. PQN (toner - digital).
  Need 300-500 to test the market & for reviews.

B. eBooks (72 dpi. Photos: JPG; dwgs: GIF). Interactive
  Downloadable. See Doc 615
    From your site
    From other sites
  Portable eBook readers. PDF and LIT files.
  Also in Palm & MobiPocket
  CDs & DVDs

C. Large PRINT books. See Doc 642.

Media Asset Management
Multi-purpose your core content.
Wring maximum value out of your Work.

A. Versions (downloadable) from your Web site
  Audio version (Digital)
  Special reports (spin off from book)
  Articles (spin off from book)
    Pricing pBooks & eBooks

B. Sell from Web site (not downloadable)
  Seminars/Speeches
    Record and sell the audio
  Consulting
  Expert witness testimony
  Compatible (non-information) products

Help:
http://parapublishing.com/sites/para/resources/supplier.cfm

Codes: WN: *Writing Nonfiction*; SPM: *The Self-Publishing Manual*

For more information, contact
DanPoynter@ParaPublishing.com http://ParaPublishing.com

Promoting the Editions

Make your company "Website-Centric".
  Set up pressroom.

A. Book industry. Send sample books to:
  Agents (if you wish to sell out)
  Publishers (if you wish to sell out)
  Distributor/bookstores/online bookstores
  "Galleys" to pre-pub reviewers-SPM
Industry and early review copies. SPM
Book clubs. See LMP & SPM
Foreign rights-translations. See ILMP & SPM

B. Nontraditional markets. ID and Locate buyers.
Make Dealers (wholesale)
  Specialty stores (think products not books).
  Associations
  Magazines
  Events

Catalogs. SPM
Premiums. SPM
Fundraisers. SPM
Military and government. SPM

C. Disintermediation: sell directly to individual
reader/buyers (retail).
Promote your book with:
  Review copies to magazines. SPM
  Lists: http://parapublishing.com/getpage.cfm?file=/bookprom.html
  News releases to magazines. SPM
    Services
    http://www.book-publicity.com
eMail announcements (broadcast email)
eZine: Newsletter/List.
  Business cards (no brochures)
  Postcards (invite to Web site)
  Online : email lists, chat rooms & news groups
  Autographings/mini-seminars. See Doc 639
    Posters & buttons
Radio and TV interviews. See Doc 602

AFTERWORD

We *learn by doing,* and your first book will be your hardest. *We learn from our mistakes* and, hopefully, through the use of this book, your mistakes will be small ones. Learn the entire business by doing everything yourself before you begin to farm out some of the work, because doing it all yourself will provide you with a better understanding of publishing. I hope it introduces and guides you to a richer, more rewarding life.

The first step, the next one, is up to you. I hope you will take it. Then as you write, publish and market, refer to this manual. As you learn the business, make notes in its pages. Also, tell me your experiences, and let me know where this book could be improved. When you do get that first book into print, please send me a copy—autographed, of course.

Dan Poynter

> *The world is before you, and you need not take it or leave it as it was when you came in.*
> **—James Baldwin (1924–1987)**

I'm all in favor of keeping dangerous weapons out of the hands of fools. Let's start with typewriters.
—Frank Lloyd Wright (1868–1959), architect

Appendix 1

YOUR BOOK'S CALENDAR

WHAT TO DO

Now

While Writing Your Book

When Your Manuscript Is Nearly Complete

When the Manuscript Is Ready to Be
Delivered to the Typesetter

While the Book Is Being Typeset

While the Book Is Being Printed

When the Books Arrive

At Publication Date

Ongoing Promotion

CALENDAR

One of the biggest pitfalls in small publishing is the lack of sufficient planning, especially the first time around. You don't want to tie up funds by purchasing materials too soon and you don't want to miss some important publicity because you missed a filing date.

This checklist will help keep you on track. Follow this schedule for your first book. On your second, you'll want to move some items up, and skip others.

Chapter and Appendix references below are to *The Self-Publishing Manual*. Refer back to the explanations of each resource for Web addresses. Some forms and applications are available online. Documents numbered 1xx or 6xx are available from http://parapub.com/sites/para/resources/allproducts.cfm.

Now (these are the things you should do right now.)

☐ Get the InfoKit on book writing at http://parapub.com/sites/para/resources/infokit.cfm.

☐ Join the Publishers Marketing Association. Call 310-372-2732 for a copy of the newsletter and an application. One co-op marketing program will pay for your membership. See Professional Organizations in Appendix 2.

☐ Get copyright forms from the Library of Congress. See Chapters 2 and 5. Get Document 112 (free) from http://parapub.com/sites/para/resources/allproducts.cfm.

☐ Subscribe to *Publishers Weekly* (or read it at your library). See Magazines for Publishers in Appendix 2.

☐ Review Appendix 2. Send for the books, magazines, brochures and catalogs that interest you. Join those associations that can help you. See http://ParaPublishing.com.

☐ Choose a company name. File a fictitious name statement, if required. See Chapter 3.

☐ Purchase some office supplies. See Chapter 3 and Office & Shipping Supplies in Appendix 2.

☐ See the Bowker Web site for ABI Information. See Chapter 5.

☐ Apply for a post office box. See Chapter 3.

☐ Read the latest edition of *The Self-Publishing Manual* completely and highlight important areas.

☐ Visit the library and study the book *Literary Market Place*. Order a copy now or wait until you're finished with your manuscript.

☐ Contact the Small Business Administration about its services. Call your local office. See Chapter 3.

☐ Apply for any local business licenses. Ask other nearby small businesspeople for advice. Do not call the city licensing offices for information. See Chapter 3.

☐ Draft your book-cover sales copy. See Chapter 2.

☐ Decide on your audience and what you promise to give them. See Document 116 (free) at http://parapub.com/sites/para/resources/allproducts.cfm.

☐ Get *Writing Nonfiction: Turning Thoughts into Books*. See http://ParaPublishing.com.

☐ Add a signature to your email program. See Chapter 7.

While Writing Your Book

☐ Review Chapter 2.

☐ Learn about the CIP Office of the Library of Congress. See Chapter 5.

☐ Contact R.R. Bowker for ISBN/SAN information. See Chapter 5 and Document 112 (free) at http://parapub.com/sites/para/resources/allproducts.cfm.

☐ Solicit stories for your manuscript. See Chapter 2 and consider making a request in my *Publishing Poynters Marketplace* newsletter (http://parapub.com/sites/para/resources/newsletter.cfm).

☐ Get *The Book Publishing Encyclopedia: Tips & Resources for Authors & Publishers* by Dan Poynter. See http://parapub.com/sites/para/resources/allproducts.cfm.

When Your Manuscript Is Nearly Complete

☐ Get the InfoKit on book writing at http://parapub.com/sites/para/resources/infokit.cfm.

☐ Send requests for quotations to the 20+ digital and/or the 40+ offset printers. See Document 603 at http://parapub.com/sites/para/resources/allproducts.cfm.

☐ Purchase a set of ISBNs from R.R. Bowker. See Chapter 5 and Document 112 (free).

☐ Hire a cover designer to produce the book's cover. See http://parapub.com/sites/para/resources/supplier.cfm.

☐ Fill out the ABI form on the Bowker Web site. See Chapter 5.

☐ See the Library of Congress for your LCCN/PCN number. See Chapter 5 and Document 112 (free) at http://parapub.com/sites/para/resources/allproducts.cfm.

☐ Send a printout of your ABI form to Baker & Taylor Co., Academic Library Services Selection Dept., PO Box 6885, Bridgewater, NJ 08807.

☐ Research your title to make sure it's not being used. See *Books in Print* and *Forthcoming Books* at the reference desk of your public library. Also, see an online bookstore such as Amazon.com and make a Google search.

☐ Get any needed permissions from people pictured or quoted in the book.

☐ Send your manuscript out for peer review (content feedback) and copyedit. See *Writing Nonfiction* by Dan Poynter.

☐ Select a distributor. See Special Report *Book Marketing* for a discussion of distributors and lists of what categories of books they want. Or see Document 605 at http://parapub.com/sites/para/resources/allproducts.cfm.

☐ Solicit testimonials. See *Blurbs for Your Books*, Document 609 at http://parapub.com/sites/para/resources/allproducts.cfm.

When the Manuscript Is Ready to Be Delivered to the Typesetter (or when you are about to typeset it or about to finalize your typesetting)

☐ Set the publication date. It will be at least four months in the future. See Chapter 7 and Document 608 at http://parapub.com/sites/para/resources/allproducts.cfm.

☐ Assign the ISBN(s). See Chapter 5.

☐ Prepare a news release. See Chapter 7 and Document 150 (free).

☐ Contact book clubs. See Chapter 8.

☐ Apply for a resale permit. See Chapter 3.

☐ Prepare a CIP data block. Contact Quality Books for help in processing your application: http://www.quality-books.com. See Chapter 5 and Document 112 (free).

While the Book Is Being Typeset

☐ Get the InfoKit on book production at http://parapub.com/sites/para/resources/infokit.cfm.

☐ Set up storage and shipping areas. See Chapter 10. Get the Special Report *Book Fulfillment, Order Entry, Picking, Packing and Shipping* at http://parapub.com/sites/para/resources/allproducts.cfm.

☐ If you are subcontracting the typesetting, maintain a good proofreading schedule. Don't hold up your typesetter.

☐ If you don't have a Web site, start working on one.

☐ Contact *Contemporary Authors* for information. See Chapter 5 and Document 112 (free).

☐ Prepare mailing lists. See Chapter 9.

☐ Order shipping supplies and the rest of your office supplies. See Chapter 10 and Office & Shipping Supplies in Appendix 2.

☐ Send galleys to certain review magazines. See "prepublication reviews" in Chapter 7 and Document 149 (free).

☐ Send a book announcement to all wholesalers. See our Special Report *Book Marketing.*

☐ Send for Special Reports *Book Marketing: A New Approach, Book Reviews, News Releases and Book Publicity* and *Export/Foreign Rights.*

☐ Contact the *International Directory of Little Magazines and Small Presses* for an application form. See Chapter 5 and Document 112 (free).

☐ Prepare your prepublication sales offer. See Chapter 8.

☐ Print out book review slips and order rubber stamps. See Chapter 7.

☐ Pursue subsidiary rights. See Chapter 8 and Special Report *Book Marketing.*

☐ Develop your marketing plan using the *Book Marketing* Special Report. Also see Instant Report *Best-Sellers,* Document 612.

☐ Order bar code or make sure your cover artist is taking care of it.

☐ Select a book printer. See Special Report *Buying Book Printing* or see Document 603.

☐ Order business cards with a photo of the book's cover. See Chapter 7.

While the Book Is Being Printed

☐ Proof the "bluelines" (press proofs) carefully.

☐ Prepare review copy materials. Stuff and label the shipping bags, then put them aside until books arrive.

☐ Add the book information to your Web site or update it.

☐ Email your prepublication offer to individuals.

☐ Change the signature in your email program. Mention your new book. See Chapter 7.

☐ Notify your friends via email of your new book and ask them to forward your announcement to their friends. See Chapter 7.

☐ List your book with Para Publishing's *Success Stories.* See http://parapub.com/sites/para/resources/successstories.cfm.

When the Books Arrive

(Four months before the official publication date). See Document 608, *Your Publication Date,* at http://parapub.com/sites/para/resources/allproducts.cfm.

☐ Check the quality of the books. Make a count for your inventory. See Special Report *Book Fulfillment.*

☐ Fill orders.

☐ Photograph book. Add 300 dpi TIF to your picture file and the pressroom of your Web site.

☐ Pursue dealer sales. You want the books to be in the stores when all the promotion hits on the publication date.

☐ File copyright Form TX. See Chapter 5.

☐ Send books to reviewers. See Chapter 7.

☐ Pursue promotional possibilities in Chapter 7 and see *Best-Sellers*, Document 612.

☐ Send copy of book to CIP Office if your company has been enrolled into the CIP program. See Chapter 7 and Document 112 (free).

☐ Visit bookstores in your area.

☐ Submit request to *Publishing Poynters Marketplace* for reviews in Amazon.com, B&N.com and other online bookseller sites. See http://parapub.com/sites/para/resources/newsletter.cfm.

☐ Convert pages of your book into articles and send them to category magazines. See Chapter 7.

☐ Email your back-cover sales copy to everyone in your address book. Ask them to forward it to their colleagues. See Chapter 7.

At Publication Date

Traditionally, this is the date when your books are in the stores and your promotion hits. Your initial consumer promotion should be concentrated in the first few weeks after the publication date. See Document 608 at http://parapub.com/sites/para/resources/allproducts.cfm.

☐ Pursue consumer-oriented promotions such as autograph parties, talk shows, author tours, etc. See Chapter 7 and *Interviews: How Authors Get on Radio and TV*, Document 602.

Ongoing Promotion

Never give up. You have given birth to your book; now you have an obligation to raise it. Review what has worked and do more of it. Review what has not worked and cut your losses.

☐ Work on nontraditional or special sales. See Chapter 8.

☐ Implement your continuing review program.

☐ Consider more direct email solicitations.

☐ Look for spin-off ideas. Repackage your information into audiobooks, electronic books, large-print books, etc. Consider consulting in your area of expertise. See Document 615, *Electronic Books*.

☐ Make up a review/testimonial sheet. Paste up good reviews and reproduce them. See Chapter 7.

You are not just an author, a publisher or a publicist; you are an information provider. You must provide your knowledge in any form your buyer wants: books, reports, audiotapes, videotapes, CDs, seminars, speeches or private consulting.

Appendix 2

RESOURCES FOR PUBLISHERS

Appendix 2 is rich in resources that will be very valuable to you as a publisher and an author. Everything is here, from Dan Poynter's Special Reports on publishing issues, to distributors and wholesalers, to editors, writers, cover designers and typesetters, to printers and fulfillment houses. It is our wish that this section will serve you well, time and time again.

Note that we check every address just prior to going to press. Also, keep in mind that more than 20% of our population moves every year; so if you find an address that is no longer valid, make an online search for the new contact information. Web sites are continually updated and rearranged. If a URL is no longer valid, go to the opening page of the site and search. You could also try typing the company name, product or service into the search engines.

Be advised the R.R. Bowker Co. is a large firm with numerous functions, products and services. Although they have several offices, most of them are at the same New Jersey address; each office should be treated as a separate entity.

RECOMMENDED READING/BIBLIOGRAPHY

There are many good references on writing, publishing, printing, marketing, distribution and other aspects of book publishing. The latest and best are listed here. Find them in a bookstore.

A List of the Books, Reports & Other Documents from Para Publishing

Here is a complete alpha-sort listing of our books and other products. Go to http://parapub.com/sites/para/resources/allproducts.cfm to view their descriptions.

Books on Writing, Publishing & Promoting Books by Dan Poynter

▤ *The Book Publishing Encyclopedia: An A-Z Treasury of Tips & Resources for Authors & Publishers*

▤ *Writing Nonfiction: Turning Thoughts into Books*

▤ *Successful Nonfiction: Tips & Inspiration for Getting Published*

▤ *Is There a Book Inside You?: Writing Alone or with a Collaborator*

▤ *The Self-Publishing Manual: How to Write, Print & Sell Your Own Book*

Free Documents on Book Writing & Publishing (1xx series documents)

▤ 112: Poynter's Secret List of Book Promotion Contacts

▤ 113: List of attorneys who specialize in book publishing

▤ 116: Book Cover Layout

▤ 126: Article on the importance of reviews from *The Wall Street Journal*

▤ 134: Book Return Authorization: Example of the form we use

▤ 136: Dan Poynter speaking on book writing, publishing & promoting

▤ 137: Consulting with Dan Poynter

▤ 138: Dealer Bulletin: Discounts offered to dealers

▤ 139: Note to renters of mailing lists

▤ 140: Resources on Writing and Publishing Specific Types of Books

▤ 142: Mailing lists for promoting books

▤ 144: Postal rate chart for book shipments

▤ 147: Telephone Order Sheet

▤ 149: Layout example for a galley cover (prepublication review copies)

▤ 150: News release outline: Shows you how to construct a news release

▤ 155: Books That Were Originally Self-Published

▤ 156: Book Titles That Were Changed

▤ 167: Publishing workshops in Santa Barbara

▤ Speaking Forms Bank

Special Reports

Dan Poynter's series of Special Reports begin where *The Self-Publishing Manual* leaves off. With so much new and specialized book promotion material constantly appearing, these monographs fill the void by providing the most current, in-depth, complete information available. Called *Book Publishing Consultations with Dan Poynter*, each Report treats a specific area important to publishers and each is the latest word on its subject. Even if you were to collect every book and article on the topic, you would not find all the important details. Dan has combined extensive research with personal experience and condensed it all into a few highly concentrated pages.

▤ BR: Book Reviews

▤ NR: News Releases and Book Publicity

▤ DM: Direct Mail for Book Publishers

▤ BM: Book Marketing: A New Approach Is a Low-cost Marketing Plan

▤ BLP: Business Letters for Publishers: Creative Correspondence Outlines on Disk

▤ ForRts: Exports/Foreign Rights: Selling U.S. Books Abroad

▤ BF: Book Fulfillment: Order Entry, Picking, Packing and Shipping

▤ Print: Buying Book Printing

▤ FF: Financial Feasibility in Book Publishing

▤ PubCon: Publishing Contracts: Sample Agreements for Book Publishers on Disk

▤ SP-Note: Mr. Self-Publishing's Notebook (Publishing Poynters Archive)

Instant Reports from Para Publishing (6xx series documents)

These Reports provide you with the latest condensed answers to your book promotion questions. They're an inexpensive, instant consultation with Dan Poynter and other publishing experts.

▤ 602: Interviews: How Authors Get on Radio and TV

▤ 603: Book Printing, at the Best Price

▤ 604: How to Price Your Book

▤ 640: Book Promotion Made Easy: Event Planning, Presentation Skills & Product Marketing by Eric Gelb, MBA, CPA

▤ 641: Merchant Status: Credit Cards for Publishers

▤ 642: Large Print Books: Making Your Work Easier to Read

Publishing Books & Reports

Books can be ordered from your favorite bookstore.

Books on Book Publishing

▤ *1001 Ways to Market Your Book* by John Kremer

▤ *Beyond the Bookstores* by Brian Jud

▤ *Book Design & Production* by Pete Masterson

▤ *Book Fairs: An Exhibiting Guide for Publishers* by Dan Poynter

▤ *Book Marketing from A-Z* by Francine Silverman

▤ *The Book Publishing Encyclopedia* by Dan Poynter

▤ *Complete Guide to Book Marketing* by David Cole

▤ *The Complete Guide to Self-Publishing* by Tom & Marilyn Ross

▤ *The Complete Idiot's Guide to Self-Publishing* by Jennifer Basye Sander

▤ *From Book to Bestseller* by Penny Sansevieri

▤ *Is There a Book Inside You?: Writing Alone or with a Collaborator* by Dan Poynter & Mindy Bingham

▤ *Kirsch's Handbook of Publishing Law* by Jonathan Kirsch

▤ *Pocket Pal: A Graphic Arts Production Handbook* by Michael Bruno

▤ *Publishing for Profit* by Thomas Woll

▤ *The Publishing Game* by Fern Reiss

▤ *Putting It on Paper* by Dawn Josephson

▤ *Self-Publishing in Canada* by Suzanne Anderson

▤ *The Self-Publishing Manual: How to Write, Print & Sell Your Own Book* by Dan Poynter

▤ *Self-Publishing Simplified* by Brent Sampson

▤ *Selling Subsidiary Rights* by Thomas Woll

▤ *Small Time Operator* by Bernard Kamoroff

▤ *U-Publish.com* by Dan Poynter and Dan Snow

▤ *Wham! Bam! Publishing: The Strategic Marketing Plan for Authors and Publishers* by Janice M. Phelps & Joan E. Phelps

▤ *Writing Nonfiction: Turning Thoughts into Books* by Dan Poynter

▤ *Successful Nonfiction: Tips & Inspiration for Getting Published* by Dan Poynter

▤ *You Can Market Your Book* by Carmen Leal

Book Catalogs— with Books for Publishers

▤ R.R. Bowker Company
http://www.bowker.com
http://www.BowkerLink.com

▤ Direct Marketing Association
http://www.the-dma.org

▤ Dustbooks
http://www.dustbooks.com

▤ Gale Group
http://www.galegroup.com

▤ Information Today
http://www.infotoday.com/

▤ The Writer, Inc.
http://www.writermag.com

▤ Writer's Digest Books
http://www.writersdigest.com

Magazines for Publishers

Write for a sample copy and current subscription rates.

▤ *ALA Booklist*
American Library Association
http://www.ala.org

▤ *Bookselling This Week*
American Booksellers Association
http://www.bookweb.org

▤ *Canadian Author*
Canadian Authors Association
http://www.canauthors.org

▤ *Choice Magazine*
http://www.ala.org/acrl/choice/home.html

▤ *ForeWord Magazine*
http://www.Forewordmagazine.com

▤ *Horn Book Magazine* (children's books)
http://www.hbook.com/

▤ *Kirkus Reviews*
http://www.kirkusreviews.com/kirkusreviews/index.jsp

▤ *Library Journal*
http://www.LibraryJournal.com

▤ *Publishers Weekly*
http://www.PublishersWeekly.com

▤ *School Library Journal*
http://www.SchoolLibraryJournal.com
http://www.slj.com

▤ *Writer's Digest*
http://www.writersdigest.com

Newsletters

Write for a sample copy and current subscription rates.

▤ *Book Marketing Update*
http://www.rtir.com

▤ *Book Publishing Report* and others
Simba Information, Inc.
http://www.simbanet.com

▤ *PMA Newsletter*
Publishers Marketing Association
http://www.pma-online.org

▤ *Publishing Poynters.* News, tips & resources on books
Dan Poynter
http://parapub.com/sites/para/resources/newsletter.cfm

▤ *Publishing Poynters Marketplace.* A place to buy, sell & share
Dan Poynter
http://parapub.com/sites/para/resources/newsletter.cfm

Pamphlets & Reports

Pamphlets, reports and other help of interest to publishers.

▤ Library of Congress
Copyright Office
http://www.loc.gov/copyright

▤ Federal Trade Commission
http://www.ftc.gov
• *A Business Checklist for Direct Marketers*
• *A Business Guide to the FTC's Mail or Telephone Merchandise Rule*

▤ National Endowment for the Arts
http://www.arts.gov
Assistance, fellowships and residencies for writers

Reference Books & Directories

Most of these books can be found in the reference section of your public library. Write to the publishers for ordering details.

▤ American Booksellers Association
http://www.bookweb.org
http://www.spiders.com/portfolio/projects/bbh.jsp
• *Book Buyer's Handbook*

▤ American Library Association
http://www.ala.org
• *Membership Directory*
• *Marketing to Libraries through Library Associations*

▤ Bacon's Information
http://www.bacons.com
• *Newspaper/Magazine Directory*

▤ Broadcast Interview Source
http://www.yearbook.com
• *Yearbook of Experts, Literary Market Place*

▤ Columbia Books
http://www.columbiabooks.com/ntpa.cfm
• *National Trade & Professional Associations of the U.S.*
• *State & Regional Associations*

▤ Dustbooks
http://www.dustbooks.com
• *Directory of Editors*
• *Directory of Poetry Publishers*
• *Directory of Small Press/Magazine Editors and Publishers*
• *International Directory of Magazines and Small Presses* (A comprehensive listing of smaller publishers)
• *Small Press Record of Books in Print*

▤ Editor and Publisher
http://www.mediainfo.com
• *International Year Book*
• *Market Guide*
• *Syndicate Directory*

📃 EEI Press
http://www.eeicommunications.com/press
EEI Press has publications available on the writing, editing and production aspects of publishing, including:
• *CD-ROM Reference: Publications Project Management*

📃 Gale Group
http://www.galegroup.com
• *Business, Organizations, Agencies and Publications Directory*
• *Contemporary Authors*
• *Directories in Print*
• *Directory of Special Libraries*
• *Encyclopedia of Associations* (22,000 associations)
• *Gale Directory of Publications and Broadcast Media* (formerly Ayer Directory of Publications)
• *International Book Trade Directory*
• *International Organizations* (11,000 groups)
• *National Directory of Non-Profit Organizations* (273,000 associations)
• *National Fax Directory*
• *Newsletters in Print*
• *Publishers Directory*
• *Publishers International ISBN Directory*
• *Standard Periodical Directory* (Oxbridge)
• *World Guide to Libraries*

📃 Gebbie Press
http://www.gebbieinc.com
• *All-In-One Media Directory*

📃 Grey House Publishing
http://www.greyhouse.com
• *Directory of Business Information Resources*
• *Directory of Business to Business Catalogs* (5,700 entries.)
• *Directory of Mail Order Catalogs* (12,000 entries)

📃 Information Today
http://www.literarymarketplace.com
• *Literary Market Place*

📃 Online Computer Library Center, Inc.
http://www.oclc.org/dewey/
• *Dewey Decimal Classification and Relative Index*

📃 Oxbridge Communications, Inc.
http://www.mediafinder.com
• *Standard Periodical Directory*
• *National Directory of Catalogs*
• *College Media Directory*
• *National Directory of Magazines (21,000 magazines)*
• *National Directory of Mailing Lists*
• *Oxbridge Directory of Newsletters*

📃 PEN American Center
http://www.pen.org
• *Grants and Awards Available to American Writers*

📃 R.R. Bowker
http://www.bowker.com
• *American Book Trade Directory* (Lists 29,000 booksellers, wholesalers, etc.)
• *American Library Directory* (Lists 35,000 U.S. and Canadian libraries)

• *Books in Print* (Lists all books currently available by subject, title and author—annually)

• *Broadcasting & Cable Yearbook* (Comprehensive info on radio, TV and cable industries)

• *Forthcoming Books* (Books that will appear in the next edition of Books in Print)

• *International Literary Market Place* (Lists sources outside the U.S. and Canada)

• *Publishers, Distributors & Wholesalers of the United States* (A directory)

• *Publishers' Trade List Annual* (A compilation of 1,500 publishers' catalogs)

• *Ulrich's International Periodicals Directory* (Lists 120,000 newsletters and magazines)

• *Working Press of the Nation* (A three-volume reference covering many aspects of the media)

▤ SRDS, Inc.
http://www.srds.com
Direct Marketing List Source (list rental database)

▤ Writer's Digest Books
http://www.writersdigest.com
Writer's Digest Books publishes directories and many specific books on writing and getting published.

   • *Children Writer's and Illustrator's Market*
   • *Writer's Market*
   • *Writers Yearbook*

Postal Web Sites, Books & Manuals

The following Postal Service publications should be consulted for more information. They can be obtained from your local Postal Business Center (call 800-275-8777 for the one nearest you) or downloaded from the Postal Service Web sites.

Postal Service Web Sites

Business Center:
http://www.usps.com

Canadian Post Office General Web site: http://www.canadapost.ca

Domestic Zip Code Lookup:
http://www.usps.gov/ncsc

All Products: go to
http://www.usps.com/all/welcome.htm?from=doorwaybar&page=0019allproducts

then click Postal Explorer for

• *Domestic Mail Manual* (with rate calculator)

• *International Mail Manual* (with rate calculator)

Shipping supplies online:
http://supplies.usps.gov

Universal Postal Union (links to the Web sites of most countries):
http://www.upu.int

BOOK PRODUCTION & PROMOTION RESOURCES

Bar Code Suppliers

AccuGraphiX
http://www.bar-code.com

Bar Code Graphics
http://www.barcode-us.com

BookMasters
http://www.bookmasters.com/

FineLine Technologies
http://www.FineLineTech.com

Film Masters
http://www.filmmasters.com

Fotel
http://www.fotel.com

General Graphics
http://www.ggbarcode.com

J&D Barcodes
jdbarcodes@earthlink.net

Book Clubs

There are more than 200 book clubs
and most are very specialized. Only
three to six will be appropriate to
any particular book. For more clubs,
see *Literary Market Place*.

Bookspan
http://www.bookspan.com
30 clubs including:
• *Book-of-the-Month Club*
• *Children's Book-of-the-Month
Club*
• *Quality Paperback Book Club*
• *The Literary Guild*

Doubleday Book Club
http://www.DoubledayBookClub.
com

Writer's Digest Book Club
http://www.writersdigestbookclub.
com/

Book Designers
& Cover Artists

Book producers or book packagers
are graphic arts services that
specialize in the design, typesetting
and layout of book pages and covers.
Some will convert files to HTML
and PDF. Send for brochures with
prices.

Albertine Book Design
Dotti Albertine
http://www.DotDesign.net

Arrow Graphics, Inc.
Alvart Badalian
http://www.arrow1.com

Be It Now/Karen Ross Design
http://www.beitnow.com/
publishingdesign.htm

Casa Graphics
CasaG@wgn.net

Cypress House
Cynthia Frank
http://www.cypresshouse.com

Dunn + Associates
http://www.dunn-design.com

Foster & Foster
George Foster
http://www.fostercovers.com

Kleine Editorial Service
Walter Kleine
http://www.kleineedit.com

Knockout Design
Peri Poloni
http://www.knockoutbooks.com

Lightbourne
Allison Wildman, Shannon Bodie,
Bob Swingle
http://www.lightbourne.com

Linder Creative Services
Pat Linder
http://webpages.charter.net/
lindercreative

Lucky Press
Janice Phelps
http://www.JanicePhelps.com

MacGraphics
Karen Saunders
http://www.MacGraphics.net

One-On-One Book Production,
Editing and Marketing
Carolyn Porter & Alan Gadney
onebookpro@aol.com

Opus 1 Design
Pamela Terry
http://www.opus1design.com

Pro-Art Graphic Design
Robert Aulicino
http://www.aulicinodesign.com

Robert Howard Graphic Design
Robert Howard
http://www.BookGraphics.com

Sharp Spear Enterprises
Bob Spear
http://www.sharpspear.com

Write to Your Market
Susan Kendrick
http://www.WriteToYourMarket.
com

1106 Design, LLC
Michele DeFilippo
http://www.1106design.com

Book Fair Exhibiting Services

If you can't attend the fair yourself,
you might contract with an exhibiting
service to show your books. See the
discussion in Chapter 9 and read the
book *Book Fairs: An Exhibiting Guide
for Publishers* by Dan Poynter.

Association Book Exhibit
Mark Trocchi
http://www.bookexhibit.com

Combined Book Exhibit
Jon Malinowski
http://www.combinedbook.com

PMA Book Exhibits
http://www.pma-online.org

Scholar's Choice Exhibits
http://www.scholarschoice.com

Book Reviewers

Here is a short list of reviewers. For
more reviewers, see earlier chapters
of this book and *Literary Market
Place*. For a downloadable list of
reviewers in more than 90 book
categories see http://parapub.com/
sites/para/resources/maillist.cfm.

Midwest Book Review
Jim Cox
http://www.midwestbookreview.com

New York Review of Books
Barbara Epstein, Robert Silvers
http://www.nybooks.com/

Publishing Poynters Marketplace. A
place where you can request
reviews.
http://parapub.com/sites/para/
resources/newsletter.cfm

Rainbo Electronic Reviews
http://www.rainboreviews.com

Rebeccas Reads
http://www.rebeccasreads.com/

Washington Post Book World
http://www.washingtonpost.com

Book Shepherds

Book Shepherds are a particular kind of consultant. Each one is a virtual production and marketing director who is a mentor, tutor, coach and friend to author/publishers in the book business. Book shepherds specialize in taking a book project through all the necessary steps that may include editing, design, typesetting, locating the right printer, getting a distributor, marketing and promotion (including your Web presence). Shepherds work with the author/publisher to assure that the book is produced and marketed efficiently and economically. These godparents use their experience and contacts to make sure all the publishing bases are covered and that they are covered in the right order. Contact them to see what each one can do for you.

Alan Gadney
OneBookPro@aol.com

Barbara Florio Graham (Canada)
simon@storm.ca

Barbara Kimmel
nexdec@earthlink. net

Bob Goodman
rg@silvercat.com

Brian Jud
iMarketBooks@aol.com

Cynthia Frank
Cynthia@CypressHouse.com

Ellen Reid
sMarketing@MediaOne. net

Ernie Weckbaugh
CasaG@wgn.net

Gail Kearns/Penny Paine
Gmkea@aol.com

Janice Phelps
jmp@janicephelps.com

Jim Donovan
idonovan@ptd.net

Judith Briles, PhD.
judith@briles.com

Kira Henschel,
Kira@GoblinFernPress.com

Linda Radke
info@FiveStarSupport.com

Mindy Gibbons-Klein (UK)
infoC@bookmidwife.com

Patrick Ang (Singapore)
Patrick.Ang@pacific.net.sg

Serena Williamson Andrew Ph.D
(Canada)
sw@serenawilliamson.com

Shel Horowitz
shel@frugalfun.com

Shum F.P. (Malaysia)
shumfp@pd.jaring.my

Simon Warwick-Smith
sws@vom.com

Sylvia Hemmerly
PubProf@TampaBay.rr.com

Bookstores (Chain)

Here are the major chains. For smaller ones, see *The American Book Trade Directory*, available at your public library. Address the fiction or nonfiction, hardcover or paperback buyer. Also see our Special Report *Book Marketing.*

Barnes & Noble, Inc.
http://www.bn.com

Borders Group, Inc.
http://www.bordersstores.com/index.jsp?tt=gn

Books-A-Million, Inc.
http://www.booksamillion.com

Chapters, Inc. (Canada)
http://www.chapters.indigo.ca/Default.asp

Little Professor Book Centers, LLC
http://www.littleprofessor.com/

Bookstores (Online)

Contact the online bookstore's Web site for publishers' information.

Amazon
http://www.amazon.com

Barnes & Noble, Inc.
http://www.bn.com

Books-A-Million, Inc.
http://www.booksamillion.com

Borders Group, Inc.
http://www.borders.com

Consultants

Some consultants specialize in certain categories of books or specific markets. Contact each one for a list of specialties, services and fees.

Author's Publishing Cooperative
Dawson Church
http://www.AuthorsPublishing.com

Columbine Communications & Publications
Robert Erdmann
http://www.Bob-Erdmann.com

Cypress House
Cynthia Frank
http://www.cypresshouse.com

Five Star Publications, Inc.
Linda Radke
http://www.fivestarsupport.com

To Press & Beyond
Penelope C. Paine
http://www.topressandbeyond.com

Para Publishing
Dan Poynter
http://parapub.com/sites/para/speaking/edutrain.cfm#edutrain3

RJ Communications
Ron Pramschufer
http://www.selfpublishing.com

Smarketing
Ellen Reid
http://www.BookShep.com

Copywriters— Advertising/News Releases

AWM Books
Shel Horowitz
http://www.frugalfun.com

Brainstorm Editorial
Robin Quinn
quinnrobin@aol.com

Joe "Mr. Fire" Vitale
http://www.mrfire.com

Courses, Conferences & Seminars

There are many educational programs of interest to publishers. Some of the most important are listed here. For more, see *Literary Market Place.*

Santa Barbara Publishing Workshops
Dan Poynter
http://parapub.com/sites/para/speaking/edutrain.cfm

NYU Center for Publishing
http://www.scps.nyu.edu/departments/department.jsp?deptId=14

Publishing Institute, University of Denver
http://www.du.edu/pi

Simba Information, Inc.
http://www.simbanet.com

Stanford Publishing Courses
http://publishingcourses.stanford.edu

UC Berkeley Extension
http://www.unex.berkeley.edu/enroll

University of Chicago, Publishing Program
Graham School of General Studies
http://www.grahamschool.uchicago.edu

Discount Stores & Warehouse Clubs

Blockbuster Entertainment Corp.
http://www.blockbuster.com

Costco Wholesale
http://www.costco.com

Kmart
http://www.kmart.com/home.jsp

Sam's Wholesale Club
http://www.walmart.com

Target Stores
http://www.target.com

Tower Records and Books
http://www.towerrecords.com

Wal-Mart
http://www.walmart.com

Distributors to Bookstores

Distributors specialize in certain categories of books. You want a distributor with a strong line of books like yours. See their Web sites for the types of books they carry.

For descriptions of the distributors with lists of the categories of books they want, see the Special Report *Book Marketing*, or our Document

605, *Locating the Right Distributor*, at http://parapub.com/sites/para/resources/allproducts.cfm.

Advanced Marketing Services (AMS)
Advanced Global Distribution
http://www.advmkt.com

American Software & Hardware Distributors
http://www.ashd.com

The Antique Collectors' Club
http://www.antiquecc.com

Austin & Company, Inc.
(representation to the chains)
Rebecca Austin
http://www.AustinandCompanyInc.com

Biblio Distribution (NBN)
http://www.bibliodistribution.com

Booklines Hawaii
http://www.booklineshawaii.com

Canbook Distribution Services (Canada)
http://www.canbook.com

Charles E. Tuttle Company
http://www.tuttlepublishing.com

Client Distribution Services
http://www.cdsbooks.com

Consortium Book Sales & Distribution
http://www.cbsd.com

Cromland, Inc. (Computer books)
http://www.cromland.com

Distributed Art Publishers (DAP)
http://www.artbook.com/

Educational Book Distributors (Sells textbooks to schools)
orders@publishersservices.net

Faithworks (Christian books)
http://www.faithworksonline.com

Greenleaf Book Group
http://www.greenleafbookgroup.com

Independent Publishers Group (IPG)
http://www.ipgbook.com

International Publishers Marketing
http://www.internationalpubmarket.com

Independent Publishers Marketing
(Gift trade)
stjohns.ipm@blackhole.com

International Specialized Book
Services
http://www.isbscatalog.com/

Librera de Habla Hispaña
tomas@anet.comm

MBI Publishing Company
http://www.motorbooks.com

Midpoint Trade Books
http://www.midpointtrade.com

National Book Network (NBN)
http://www.nbnbooks.com

Origin Books
http://www.originbooks.com

Penton Overseas
http://www.pentonoverseas.com

Prologue, Inc. (Canada)
http://www.prologue.ca

Publishers Marketing Association
Trade Distribution Program
http://www.pmaonline.org/benefits/tradedistribution.cfm

Raincoast Book Distribution
(Canada)
http://www.raincoast.com

Red Wheel/Weiser
Samuel Weiser, Inc.
http://www.weiserbooks.com

Rights & Distribution, Inc.
http://www.fellpub.com

Samuel French
http://www.samuelfrench.com

Sandhill Book Marketing, Ltd.
(Canada)
http://www.sandhillbooks.com/
(Does not import from U.S.)

SCB Distributors
http://www.scbdistributors.com

Small Press Distribution (SPD)
http://www.spdbooks.org

Spring Arbor Distributors (Christian
books)
http://www.springarbor.com/

Wimmer Cookbook, R.R.
http://www.wimmerco.com/

Distributors to Libraries

Quality Books
http://www.quality-books.com

Unique Books
http://www.uniquebooksinc.com/default.asp

Editorial Services

Includes proofreading, copyediting,
editing and ghostwriting.

Brainstorm Editorial
Robin Quinn
quinnrobin@aol.com

Cross-t.i
Barbara Coster
bcoster@silcom.com

The Editorial Department
Ross Browne
http://www.editorialdepartment.com

GMK Editorial & Writing Services
Gail Kearns
http://www.topressandbeyond.com

Kleine Editorial Service
Walter Kleine
http://www.kleineedit.com

One-On-One Book Production,
Editing & Marketing
Carolyn Porter
onebookpro@aol.com

Media + (Media Plus)
Judith Kessler
jude001@earthlink.net

Penmark
Karen Stedman
Penmarkg@aol.com

PenUltimate Editorial Services
Arlene Prunkl
http://www.penultimateword.com

PeopleSpeak
Sharon Goldinger
pplspeak@norcov.com

Fulfillment Services

Send for prices. Also see Special
Report *Book Fulfillment*.

Book Clearing House
Nancy Smoller
http://www.bookch.com

BookMasters
Cathy Purdy
http://www.bookmasters.com

PSI Fulfillment
http://www.PSIfulfillment.com

Ghostwriters

Brainstorm Editorial
Robin Quinn
quinnrobin@aol.com

Penmark
Karen Stedman
penmarkg@aol.com

Word Wizard
David Kohn
WordWiz@gate.net

Electronic Lists

Online chats are the least expensive
consulting you can get. Several
interest groups serve book writing
and publishing. You can join and
learn—for free! You can ask questions,
and authors and publishers with
personal experience will answer you.
Sometimes you'll be able to contribute
to the list. See the various lists below,
visit their sites, select two or three
and join.

General
 • http://www.pub-forum.net/
 • http://finance.groups.yahoo.com/group/self-publishing/
 • http://www.publish-l.com/
 • http://finance.groups.yahoo.com/group/smallpub-civil/

Fiction
 http://www.webrary.org/rs/flmenu.html

eBooks
 • http://www.ind-e-pubs.com/
 • http://groups.yahoo.com/group/ebook-community/

POD Publishing
 http://finance.groups.yahoo.com/group/pod_publishers/

Publishing Design
http://groups.yahoo.com/group/
publishingdesign/

Book Signings/Mini-Seminars
http://groups.yahoo.com/group/
booksigners/

Publishing Law
http://groups.yahoo.com/group/
copyright-future/

Manuscript & Book Evaluation

Communication Unlimited
Gordon Burgett
http://www.SOPS.com

Office & Shipping Supplies

See their Web sites.

Chiswick, Inc.
http://www.chiswick.com

Drawing Board
http://www.thedrawing-
board.com

Grayarc
http://www.grayarc.com/

Paper Mart
http://www.papermart.com

Quill Corporation
http://www.quill.com

Reliable Office Supplies
http://www.reliable.com

Robbins Container Corp.
http://www.cornellrobbins.com/
1.htm

Order-Entry Software

PUB123
Adams-Blake Company
Alan Canton
http://www.adams-blake.com

Publishers Assistant
http://www.bookch.com

Quicken & QuickBooks
Intuit, Inc.
http://www.intuit.com

Printers, Offset (Ink)

These ink-on-paper printers specialize in manufacturing books. They will bid on manufacture and trucking; it doesn't matter where they're located. To get the best price, send a Request for Quotation (RFQ) to them all.

For more detail, see our Special Report *Buying Book Printing*, or our Document 603, *Book Printing, at the Best Price*, at http://parapub.com/sites/para/resources/allproducts.cfm.

Alumni Graphics, Inc.
Sonny Spencer
http://www.alumnigraphics.com

Bang Printing
http://www.bangprinting.com

Banta Book Group
Chip Fuhrmann, Dawn Binkley
http://www.banta.com

BookMasters
Shelley Sapyta
http://www.bookmasters.com

Central Plains Book Manufacturing
Becky Pate
http://www.centralplainsbook.com

C.J. Krehbiel Co.
Rick Hastings
http://www.cjkrehbiel.com

Color House Graphics, Inc.
Phil Knight
http://www.ColorHouseGraphics.
com

The Country Press, Inc.
Mike Pinto
http://www.countrypressinc.com

Cushing-Malloy
Thomas Dorow
http://www.cushing-malloy.com

Data Reproductions Corporation
Kimberly Colton
http://www.datarepro.com

Delta Printing Solutions
http://www.DeltaPrintingSolutions.com

Dickinson Press (Specializes in lightweight papers, also religious titles [Bibles, etc.] and educational)
Bob Worcester
http://www.dickinsonpress.com

Edwards Brothers
Joe Thomson
http://www.edwardsbrothers.com

Eerdmans Printing Co.
Matt Baerwalde
http://www.eerdmansprinting.com

Friesens Printers (Canada)
Jim Beckel
http://www.friesens.com

Global Book Printing
Brian Devany
http://globalbookprinting.com

Hignell Book Printing Ltd. (Canada)
Don Barnicki
http://www.hignell.mb.ca

Jostens
Ed Bohannon
http://www.jostens.com/commercialprinting/

Malloy Lithographing
Bill Upton
http://www.malloy.com

McNaughton & Gunn
http://www.bookprinters.com

Morgan Printing
Mark Hillis
http://www.morganprinting.org

Omnipress
Robert G. Hamm
http://www.omnipress.com

Patterson Printing
Linda J. Seaman
http://www.patterson-printing.com

Phoenix Color Corp.
http://www.phoenixcolor.com

Professional Press
http://www.profpress.com

Rose Printing Company (Can also print mini-books)
http://www.roseprinting.com

R.R. Donnelley & Sons
Chuck Harpel
http://www.rrdonnelley.com/wwwrrd/Home.asp

Sheridan Books
Mary Heim
http://www.sheridanbooks.com

Technical Communication Services
Ray Kiely
http://www.tcsbook.com

Thomson-Shore, Inc.
http://www.tshore.com

Transcontinental-Gagne Printing (Canada)
Denis Audet
http://www.transcontinental.com/en/index.html

United Graphics
Louis Segovia
http://www.unitedgraphicsinc.com

Van Volumes, Ltd.
Russell Tate
http://www.VanVolumes.com

Vaughan Printing Company
http://www.vaughanprinting.com

Von Hoffmann Graphics
Mark Bawden
http://www.vonhoffmann.com

Walsworth Publishing Co.
Joe Cupp
http://www.walsworthprinting.com

Whitehall Printing Company
John Gilbertson
http://www.whitehallprinting.com

Printers, Digital (Toner)

These printers produce books with digital printing in smaller quantities. They will bid on manufacture and trucking; it doesn't matter where they're located. To get the best price, send a Request for Quotation (RFQ) to them all.

For more detail, see our Special Report *Buying Book Printing*, or our Document 603, *Book Printing, at the Best Price*, at http://parapub.com/sites/para/resources/allproducts.cfm.

aa Printing
William Ashby
bAshby@PrintShopCentral.com
http://www.PrintShopCentral.com

Adibooks
Thomas G. Campbell
tcampbell@KingPrinting.com
http://www.adibooks.com

Alexander's Print Advantage
Doyle Mortimer, Barry Merrell
eprint@alexanders.com
http://www.Alexanders.com

BookJustBooks.com
Ron Pramschufer
customerservice@rjc-llc.com
http://BooksJustBooks.com

BookMasters, Inc.
Info@BookMasters.com
http://www.BookMasters.com

BookMobile.com
Nicole Baxter
nbaxter@bookmobile.com
http://www.bookmobile.com/

Books-On-Demand
Dave Shannon, CSS Publishing
http://www.CSSpub.com

C&M Press
Beth Chapmon
info@cmpress.com
http://www.cmpress.com/

DeHart's Media Services
Don DeHart
don@deharts.com
http://www.DeHarts.com

DigiNet Printing
Guillermo "William" Perego
gPerego@DigiNetPrinting.com
http://www.DigiNetPrinting.com

Documation LLC
lburchell@documation.com
http://www.documation.com

Document Technologies
Diane Gimbel
info@xrcdti.com
http://www.xrcdti.com/

Fidlar Doubleday
Lisa Mallory
lisam@fidlar.com
http://www.FidlarDoubleday.com

Gorham Printing
Kathleen Shaputis
kathleens@gorhamprinting.com
http://www.gorhamprinting.com

Morgan Printing and Publishing
Terry Sherrell
terry@morganprinting.org
http://www.MorganPrinting.org

On-DemandPress.com
Walter Fuller
editor@saintbartsbooks.com
http://www.on-demandpress.com/

P.O.D. Wholesale
Mark Gregory, VP Operations
info@podwholesale.com
http://www.podwholesale.com

Sir Speedy-Scottsdale, AZ
Mike Bercaw
mBercaw@SirSpeedyScottsdale.com
http://www.SirSpeedy.com/scotts
dale

Sir Speedy-Whittier, CA
Tim McCarthy
tim@ssWhittier.com
http://www.ssWhittier.com

Starnet Media Group
jeff@starnet-media.com
http://www.starnet-media.com

TPC Graphics
Len Metz
TPClen-Pat@erols.com

Tri-State Litho
Kumar Persad
kumarp@tristatelitho.com
http://www.TriStateLitho.com

Printers, POD

These printers produce books
one at a time (on-demand).

LightningSource/Ingram Book Group
http://www.lightningprint.com

Replica Books/Baker & Taylor
http://www.baker-taylor.com

BookSurge, LLC
http://www.BookSurge.com

Printorium Bookworks (Canada)
www.printoriumbookworks.com

Publishers, POD

These publishers produce books
one at a time (on-demand) and
publishing services.

Authorhouse
http://www.Authorhouse.com

Infinity Publishing
John Harnish
http://www.InfinityPublishing.com

Trafford Publishing
http://www.Trafford.com

iUniverse
http://www.iUniverse.com

Xlibris
http://www.xlibris.com

Professional Organizations

Write for an application and inquire
about benefits and dues. Many
associations publish a magazine or
newsletter. For a list of writers'
associations, see *Writer's Market*.

American Book Producers
Association
http://www.abpaonline.org/

American Booksellers Association
(ABA)
http://www.bookweb.org

American Library Association (ALA)
http://www.ala.org

Arizona Book Publishing Association
http://www.azbookpub.com/

Association of American Publishers,
Inc. (AAP)
http://www.publishers.org

Association of Canadian Publishers
http://www.publishers.ca

Authors Guild, Inc.
http://www.authorsguild.org

Bay Area Independent Publishers
Association
http://www.baipa.org

Book Industry Study Group
http://www.bisg.org

Book Publicists of Southern
California
http://bookpublicists.org/

Book Summit
http://www.BookSummit.com

Catholic Press Association
http://www.catholicpress.org/
index.htm

Christian Booksellers Association
http://www.cbaonline.org

Colorado Independent Publishers
Association (CIPA)
http://www.cipabooks.com

Direct Marketing Association
http://www.the-dma.org

Florida Publishers Association, Inc.
http://www.Flbookpub.org

Independent Publishers Guild, UK
http://www.ipg.uk.com/

Midwest Independent Publishers
Association
http://www.mipa.org

New Mexico Book Association
http://www.nmbook.org/

Publishers Association of the South
http://www.pubsouth.org

Publishers Marketing Association (PMA)
Jan Nathan
http://www.pma-online.org
For local affiliates, see
http://www.pma-online.org/
affiliat.cfm#affil

St. Louis Publishers Association
http://www.stlouispublishers.org

Small Publishers Association of
North America (SPAN)
Scott Flora
http://www.spannet.org/

Society for Scholarly Publishing
http://www.sspnet.org

Publicists/Marketing

These professionals provide a
number of services such as
scheduling you for radio-TV
appearances, writing your news
releases, introducing you to review
and sales sources, securing
distributors and wholesalers and/or
creating sales brochures. Contact
them for prices and services. For an
expanded listing of publicists, see
Literary Market Place.

AtlasBooks, a Division of
BookMasters, Inc.
Cathy Purdy
http://www.atlasbooks.com

Book Marketing Works
Brian Jud
http://www.bookmarketingworks.
com

Bradley's Guide to the Top National
TV Talk & Interview Shows
http://www.freepublicity.com/tv13

Cypress House
Cynthia Frank
http://www.cypresshouse.com

Direct Contact Media Services
Paul J. Krupin
http://www.imediafax.com
http://www.book-publicity.com

Free Radio Airtime (Radio publicity)
Alex Carroll
http://www.FreeRadioAirtime.com

Great Interviews Media Coaching &
Consulting Service
Matthew Gray
http://www.LoveLife.com/
GreatInterviews

Integrated Book Marketing
ibmarket@optonline.net

Ira Communications
Ira Streitfeld
iracom@cs.com

KSB Promotions
Kate Bandos
http://www.ksbpromotions.com

LCO-Levine Communications
Office
Michael Levine
http://www.LCOonline.com

MM Book Publicity
Maryglenn McCombs
http://www.maryglenn.com

One-On-One Book Marketing &
Promotion
Alan Gadney
onebookpro@aol.com

Phenix & Phenix
Marika Flatt
http://www.BookPros.com

Planned Television Arts
Rick Frishman
http://www.plannedtvarts.com

Promotion in Motion
IrwinZuckerPR@aol.com

PR/PR
Pam Lontos
http://www.prpr.net

Radio-TV Interview Report (RTIR)
Bradley Communications Corp.
Steve Harrison
http://www.FreePublicity.com/
info227.htm

Readers Radio Virtual Book Tours
Errol Smith
http://www.ReadersRadioNetwork.
com

Sherri Rosen Publicity
http://www.SherriRosen.com

Smarketing Agency
Ellen Reid
http://www.smarketing.com

To Press and Beyond
Gail Kearns, Penelope Paine
http://www.topressandbeyond.com

Shipping Services

Airborne
http://www.airborne.com

DHL
http://www.dhl.com

FedEx
http://www.FedEx.com

Purolator
http://www.purolator.com

UPS
http://www.ups.com

USPS
http://www.usps.gov

Speech Recognition Software

Dragon Naturally Speaking
http://www.nuance.com/

IBM ViaVoice (PC & Mac)
http://www-306.ibm.com/
software/voice/viavoice/

Web Site Design

American Author
Lars Clausen
http://www.americanauthor.com

BookMasters, Inc.
Cathy Purdy
http://www.bookmasters.com

Lightbourne, Inc.
Allison Wildman, Shannon Bodie,
Bob Swingle
http://www.lightbourne.com

Wholesalers

The most important are listed here.
For more, see the *American Book
Trade Directory* and *Literary Market
Place*, available at your public library.
You will also want a single national
distributor on an exclusive basis. (See
Distributor list above.)

Airlift Books (UK)
http://www.airlift.co.uk/perl/
index.pl

Ambassador Book Service
http://www.absbook.com

Baker & Taylor
Sue Tomae
Publisher Services Dept.
http://www.btol.com

Blackwell's Book Services
http://www.blackwell.com

Bookazine Corp., Inc.
http://www.bookazine.com

Book House, Inc.
http://www.thebookhouse.com

Brodart Company
http://www.brodart.com

Coutts Library Service
http://www.couttsinfo.com/en/
about/aboutus.html

DeVorss and Company
http://www.devorss.com

The distributors
http://www.thedistributors.com

Eastern Book Company
http://www.ebc.com

Emery-Pratt Co.
http://www.emery-pratt.com

Ingram Book Company
http://www.ingrambook.com

Midwest Library Service
http://www.midwestls.com

National Association of College
Stores (NACSCORP)
http://www.nacscorp.com

New England Mobile Book Fair
http://www.nebookfair.com/

New Leaf Distributing
http://www.newleaf.dist.com

Nutri-Books/Royal Publications
http://www.nutribooks.com/

Sunbelt Publications
http://www.sunbeltpub.com

YBP Library Services
(Formally Yankee Book Peddler)
http://www.ybp.com

Your book could bring you fame, fortune and free travel. Watch what you write. It could come back to reward you.

GLOSSARY

AAP—Association of American Publishers.

AAUP—Association of American University Presses.

ABA—American Booksellers Association.

ABI—Advance Book Information. Publishers supply information on their book to Bowker for inclusion in *Forthcoming Books* and *Books in Print*. This information is also referenced in other databases.

accounts receivable—Money owed a company by credit customers.

acknowledgments—A statement of gratitude for contributions, inspiration or an influence by others for a book.

acquisitions editor—The person in a publishing firm who acquires new manuscripts.

advance—An amount paid to the author on signing the contract. An advance is normally applied against (deducted from) royalties.

advance reading copy—A preliminary bound version of the book and cover for review and sales purposes, many times without final correction.

afterword—A final concluding section to a book, written by the author.

ALA—American Library Association.

American Booksellers Association—The trade association of nonchain retail bookstores in the U.S.

American Library Association—Largest library association in the U.S.

American National Standards (Z39 Standard) Committee—The committee responsible for standards for libraries, information science and publishing.

anthology—A collection of one or more authors published as a single work.

antiquarian bookseller—One who specializes in selling old or rare books.

appendixes—Part of the back matter of a book, usually containing relevant supplemental information for the reader, possibly organized by content.

artwork—Any illustrative matter other than straight text.

Association of American Publishers—The trade association of the largest book publishers in the U.S.

Association of American University Presses—The trade association of university presses.

author's alterations (AA)—Changes made by the author after the file has been sent to the printer.

back flap—The back inner flap of a dust jacket that often contains a biography of the author.

back list—Previously published books that are still in print and available from a publisher. Not front list books that are recently published.

back matter—Parts of the book that follow the main body of the text, such as the Appendix, Bibliography, Index, Glossary, etc. End matter.

back order—An order for books that are unavailable, which is held until the books become available.

bar code—The identification and price marking in bar format on books. The bar code for books is called Bookland EAN.

bastard title—Half title. Found on a page in front of the title page.

belt press—A large printing press that prints many pages in one pass.

best-seller—A top-selling book. There are several best-seller lists that draw sales figures from different markets.

bibliography—That part of the back matter listing books and materials consulted by the author in preparing the book, or that the author wishes to bring to the reader's attention.

binding—The processes following printing: folding, gathering, stitching, gluing, trimming and/or casing a book.

BISAC—Book Industry Systems Advisory Committee. A committee of the Book Industry Study Group (BISG).

bleed—Ink printed over the edge of the paper. The edge is trimmed off. Most magazines have covers with bleed.

blueline—What used to be given to publishers as the final proof of a book prior to it going to press. Today, the final proofs are one-off laser copies of the book with a perfect-bound blank cover.

blurb—A promotional announcement, phrase or advertisement.

body type—The majority of the type used in a book. Not a headline.

boldface—Type that is heavier than the text type with which it is used.

bond—A hard finish rag or sulphite paper used for stationery and forms.

book—A publication of 49 or more pages that is not a serial or periodical.

book fair—An event where publishers display their books.

booklet—A small book, usually with fewer than 48 pages.

book packager—A person or company that contracts with publishers to deliver contracted books.

book rate—See Media Mail and Special Standard Mail.

book trade—Book distributors, wholesalers and stores (chains, independent and online). Sometimes includes libraries.

bullets—Large black dots or other icons, that are used to set off items in a list.

C1S—Coated One Side. Usually refers to a book cover stock that is smooth on one side.

caption—The line of text accompanying an illustration.

cash basis—Accounting system. Not accrual.

case binding—Hardcover.

case bound—Hardcover or edition binding.

cataloging-in-publication data—Bibliographic information supplied by the Library of Congress that is printed on the copyright page. The CIP data helps libraries to shelve the book properly.

chapbook—A small book or pamphlet of poetry, popular tales, or ballads.

character—A letter, number, punctuation mark or space in printed matter.

check digit—A number used to validate other numbers in the preceding numerical field. The last number in an ISBN is a check digit.

checking copy—Finished book sent to prepublication (galley) reviewer.

clip art—Line drawings, screened pictures and illustrations designed to be copied and pasted into your file.

coated stock—Paper manufactured with a variety of surfaces that may be smooth, glossy or matte.

COD—Cash On Delivery. Where merchandise is paid for when delivered.

collating—Gathering of printed sheets into proper order for binding.

colophon—A listing of production details in the back matter.

color separation—A camera technique using different-colored lenses to draw out the three primary colors and black from a color illustration or photograph. The resulting negatives (also called film separations or sep negs) are used to make the printing plates.

composition—Typeset material. Typeset text ready to be pasted up.

continuity program—A standing order for succeeding volumes in a related program.

contrast—The degree of difference between the lightest and darkest parts of a picture.

co-op advertising—Where the publisher and the bookstore share the cost of local book advertising. The publisher pays the larger share.

co-op publishing—Where more than one person or company join to produce a book. Co-publishing.

copyediting—Editing of a manuscript for spelling, grammar, punctuation, accuracy and clarity.

copyright—The right to retain or sell copies of artistic works that you have produced.

copyright notice—The words placed on the copyright page, such as "Copyright © 2007, Dan Poynter."

crane—Prepublication galley.

credit memo—A statement showing money due a customer for returned merchandise.

crop marks—The lines used to define the desired limits of the area of a photograph or illustration to be reproduced. *See* trim marks.

dba—Doing business as. A sole proprietorship operated in another name.

dedication—A message in the front matter of the book in tribute to a person, cause or group.

defamation—Libel (written) or slander (spoken) that injures a person.

density—The relative darkness of an image area. In photography, the blackening or light-stopping ability of a photographic image, as numerically measured by a densiometer.

developmental editing—Assistance by an editor with the organization and approach to a book.

direct-mail advertising—Advertising matter mailed directly to a potential customer, via land (postal) or electronic mail (email).

disintermediation—Cutting out intermediaries, such as publishers, distributors, wholesalers and bookstores.

display ad—A print advertisement using graphics.

display type—Type that is larger than the text, as in a chapter headline.

distributor—A company that acts as your marketing (usually to one market such as bookstores), warehousing and shipping department. Not a jobber or wholesaler. Distributors are normally exclusive to a particular market, have traveling sales representatives and sell individual titles to wholesalers, jobbers, retail outlets and libraries.

dummy—A preliminary mock-up of a book folded to the exact size of the finished job.

dummy folio—"Working" page numbers added for identification purposes but changed before the book is printed.

dump—A display for books, usually made of cardboard. Also called a counter stand or floor stand (standee).

dust jacket—The thin paper wrap on a hardcover book.

eBook—Downloadable electronic (not printed) book.

editing—Changing, correcting, altering, polishing typed text into required form.

edition—All printings of a book that are a straight reprint. Once revisions are made, the book becomes a second edition.

el-hi—The elementary school/high school market.

email (e-mail)—Electronic messages over a computer network.

em dash—A dash (—) the width of a capital M.

en dash—A dash (–) the width of a capital N.

endpapers—The heavy sheets that fasten the pages of a hardcover book to the cover. End sheets.

epigraph—A page in the front matter where a quote or poem may be placed, setting the tone for the book.

epilogue—The last part of the text that brings the reader up-to-date.

errata—A loose sheet listing errors found in the printed book.

exclusive—1. A news or feature story printed by one media source substantially ahead of its competitors. 2. Sole distribution rights to specific markets given to a distributor.

ezine (e-zine)—Electronic magazine available on the Internet.

fair use—The allowable and legal use of a limited amount of copyrighted material without getting permission.

F&Gs—Folded and gathered signatures of a printed book ready for binding. F&Gs were formerly sent to the publisher for final approval prior to binding the print run.

first edition—The entire original printing from the same (unchanged) plates.

first serial rights—The exclusive right to serialize a book in a periodical.

flop—To flip over a photographic negative so the image will be reversed.

flush—To be even with, such as in "flush right" or "flush left," text against a margin.

flyer—A printed announcement. A flyer becomes a brochure when folded.

FOB—Free On Board. "FOB origin" means the addressee pays the shipping. "FOB destination" means the shipper pays the shipping costs. "FOB Santa Barbara" means the goods are delivered free as far as Santa Barbara; the addressee pays for transportation, if any, from there.

folio—The number on the page of a book.

font—The complete set of type in a single typeface, including characters, numbers and punctuation marks.

foreign rights—Subsidiary rights allowing the book to be published in other countries.

foreword—Introductory remarks about the book and its author found in the front matter. Not spelled "forward."

frontispiece—An illustration facing the title page.

front matter—All the pages in a book before the main text; the preliminary matter. The prelims, or front matter, include the Copyright Page, Title Page, Table of Contents, etc.

FTC—Federal Trade Commission.

fulfillment—The process of order-processing, picking, packing and shipping.

galleys—The prepublication copies of the book sent to some reviewers.

gang run (ganging)—Putting numerous unrelated jobs together for printing. Provides lower costs by economizing on setup charges.

ghostwriter—A professional writer who produces work for others.

glossary—A list of definitions found in the back matter.

glossy—A photograph with a shiny surface. Not matte (not dull).

gripper margin—The unprintable edge of the sheet of paper where the printing press or photocopier clamps the sheet to pull it through the printing machine. Often on top of the sheet and usually .25".

gutter—The space between columns of type, such as the inner margins in two facing pages of a book.

hairline—A very finely ruled line.

half title—A page, usually in front of the title page, where only the title appears. *See* bastard title.

halftone—A screened photograph. A tone pattern composed of dots of uniform density but varying in size. A reproduction of a photograph whereby the various tones (highlights and shadows) are translated into numerous tiny dots for printing.

halftone screen—A screen placed in front of the negative material in the process camera to break up a continuous tone image into dots of black and white to produce a halftone. There are two types: ruled glass screens and contact screens.

hardcover—A book bound in boards. Case bound.

headband—Reinforcing cloth at each end of the spine of a hardcover book.

headline—A large bold caption at the top of an article or advertisement.

hickey—A speck or blotch on a printed page.

highlights—The lightest (or whitest) portions of a photograph or artwork.

hot type—An older typesetting process using cast hot metal.

HTML—Hypertext Markup Language, used for documents on the Web.

hyperbole or hype—Exaggerated sales claims for a product or person.

IDs—Independent Distributor wholesalers (jobbers) who buy books and magazines in large quantities for resale to nonbookstore retail outlets such as newsstands, grocery stores, drugstores, hotels and airport shops.

illustration—Photographs and drawings. Artwork.

image area—The printable area of a page surrounded by margins.

imprint—The name under which a publisher prints a line of books. A publisher may have several imprints.

index—An A to Z listing in the back matter giving the location of specific material.

in print—Books that are currently available from publishers.

insertion order—A form used by advertising agencies to place advertising in various media.

interactive editing—editing of a book that considers the needs of eBooks, such as hyperlinks that take the reader to the Web or other parts of the book, formats of illustrations, etc.

International Standard Book Number—A unique number that identifies the binding, edition and publisher of a book. ISBNs are assigned by their publisher.

International Standard Serial Number—A number like an ISBN for serials/books published in a series. ISSNs are assigned by the Library of Congress.

inventory—Books on hand available for sale.

invoice—A bill.

ISBN—*See* International Standard Book Number.

ISSN—*See* International Standard Serial Number.

italics—Type with a right-hand slant. Used for quotations, titles and emphasis.

jobber—One who buys books in large quantities for resale to retailers and libraries. A rack-jobber supplies books and magazines to racks in retail outlets.

job printer—One who does not specialize in specific types of printing.

justification—Running lines of text so that the left and/or right margins are even.

kerning—Reducing space between letters.

layout—The overall appearance of a book.

leading—The amount of vertical spacing, measured in points, between lines of typeset text. Rhymes with "heading."

leaflet—Printed paper sheet folded in the center to produce four pages.

letterpress—Printing from raised type rather than from photographic plates.

libel—Written defamation.

library edition—A book with a reinforced binding.

Library of Congress—The national library serving the U.S. Congress.

Library of Congress Control Number—A unique title control number assigned by the Library of Congress to a given work. Often referred to now as the Preassigned Control Number, or PCN.

library rate—The special postal rate available for shipping books to or from libraries and educational institutions.

line art (line drawing)—A black-and-white illustration with no gray tones that does not require screening.

line shot—Any negative, print, copy or printing plate that is composed of solid image areas without halftone patterns.

list price—The suggested retail selling-price of merchandise.

LIT—A Microsoft reader file.

Literary Market Place (**LMP**)—The directory of the book publishing industry.

logo—A symbol or illustration used as an identifying mark by a business. Like a trademark.

lowercase—Small letters, not capitals.

mailing list server—An electronic mailing list server that sends messages to all the addresses on the list.

mail order—Fulfilling orders via the mail.

make-ready—All the printing press setup in preparation for a print run.

manuscript—The book (typed or handwritten) before it is typeset and printed.

margin—The white space around the copy on a page.

marketing plan—A publisher's total promotional plan for a book, including reviews, subsidiary rights, advertising and other customer contact.

mass customization—Using digital printing to place different names, text or images in each book.

mass-market paperback—The smaller, 4" x 7", cheaper editions usually sold next to magazines.

matte—A nonshiny, dull surface.

media—Print, broadcast, recording and other methods for delivering your message to the market.

media flyer—A brochure designed to be sent to talk shows.

Media Mail—The special postal rate available for shipping books.

monograph—A short report on a single subject.

multipurpose—Spinning off additional editions of the manuscript—hardcover, softcover, audio, eBook, etc.

negative—An image where the light areas of a subject appear dark and the dark areas appear light. Photographic material, film or a plate that contains such an image.

news release—An announcement sent to the media.

nth name—Incrementally selected names from a mailing list, such as every 10th name. Used in testing lists.

OCR—Optical Character Recognition. A device or computer software that can recognize (read) typewritten characters and convert them to electronic impulses for translation to output media language. An OCR reader can read a printed page into a computer for editing.

OEB—A file format for eBooks, "Open E Book."

opaque—Not admitting light. Painting out parts of negatives so they will not reproduce.

opinion-molders—People who lead thought, such as authors, editors, celebrities and other influential individuals.

orphan—A single word standing at the top of a page when copy has been set. *See* widow.

out of print—A book that is no longer available.

overrun—The books over the ordered amount. Because there are so many parts to a book, printers are allowed overruns and underruns of up to 10%.

packing slip—A document sent with a shipment of books itemizing the contents of the shipment.

page proof—A layout of the pages as they will appear in the book.

pagination—The numbering or order of pages in a book.

paperback—A softcover book.

PCN—Preassigned Control Number. The term for the Library of Congress Control Number when it is assigned prior to publication.

PDF—Portable Document Format produced by Adobe Acrobat. PDF is the file extension of the document name.

peer review—Manuscript review or editing by one or more experts in the subject field.

pen name—A pseudonym.

perfect binding—The standard glued-on cover seen on most softcover books. It has a squared-off spine on which the title and name of the author may be printed.

periodical—A periodically issued publication such as a magazine.

PI—Per inquiry advertising, where the media provide the space or time free and get a piece of each sale.

pica—A printing industry unit of measure equal to approximately 1/6 of an inch. There are 12 points to the pica. Usually used to measure width.

plagiarism—Copying the work of another and passing it off as one's own.

plate, printing—Usually the master device bearing the image to be printed. May be paper, plastic or metal.

plugging—A press condition whereby photographs appear muddy or characters fill in. Caused by poor plate burning, over-application of ink or incorrect ink/water balance.

POD—*See* print on demand.

point—A vertical measurement used in typesetting. One point equals 1/72 of an inch.

point-of-purchase display (POP)—A dump or rack of books.

positive—A photographic image in which the tones correspond to the original subject. A positive on paper is usually called a "print."

ppi—Pages per inch. Used to measure the thickness of paper.

PQN—*See* Print Quantity Needed.

preface—Introductory remarks by the author in the front matter. The preface gives the reason for writing the book and defines its aims and scope.

pre-galley—An early version of the book and cover used to be shown to other people in a publishing company.

premium—A book given away as part of a promotion.

press kit—A collection of publicity materials used to promote a book, usually presented in a cardboard folder with pockets.

press release—*See* news release.

print-on-demand—Producing books one at a time, as needed.

Print Quantity Needed—Digital (toner) printing. Not one at a time like POD. This printing process is cost-effective for quantities from 100 to 2,500 copies.

printer's error (PE)—Mistakes made by the printer in preparing for the press. Not author's alterations.

pro forma invoice—A full invoice that must be paid before the product is shipped.

proof—A digitally printed book representing what the printed book will look like, which is made for final author/publisher checking.

pseudonym—An assumed name used to conceal an author's identity. A pen name.

publication date—The date on which a book's promotion is high and books are available for purchase. A launch date usually set three to four months after the book is printed.

public domain—Material not protected by copyright.

publicist—One who prepares promotional materials and/or schedules media appearances.

Publishers Marketing Association (PMA)—A trade association that sponsors co-op promotions to help members sell books.

purchase order—A request for the purchase of merchandise, describing the merchandise, shipping instructions and other conditions of sale. A PO generally represents a promise to pay. Acceptance by the supplier constitutes a contract to supply the merchandise under specified terms.

quality paperback—A softcover or trade paper book.

quotation—An endorsement for a book.

quote—A price for printing.

ragged right—An uneven right-hand margin. Not justified.

recto—The right-hand page of a book.

reduction—A photographic process creating a small image.

register—The correct positioning of print on a page.

remaindering—The selling off of the remaining stock of books after sales fall off.

remnant space—Random advertising space in a periodical that has not been sold and is available at a reduced rate. Occurs usually in regional editions of national magazines.

reprint—1. To go back to press on the same book. 2. Printing the book in another version, such as a paperback version of a hardcover book.

returns—Unsold books that are returned to a publisher for credit.

reverse—To print an image white on black, rather than black on white.

review—An evaluation of a book, sometimes critical.

review copy—A complimentary copy of a book sent to reviewers and potential quality purchasers.

revised edition—The printing of a book after substantial changes to the contents. The ISBN should be different.

rights—An agreement to allow someone else to use the book, usually in another form. Examples are foreign rights, first serial rights and film rights.

royalties—Money paid to authors by publishers for the right to publish their work.

RFQ—Request For Quotation.

runaround—Where text is typeset around an illustration.

run-on printing—Continuing to print past the number ordered or quoted.

running heads—The book title or chapter title found at the top of the page in many books. See the top of this page.

saddle stitch—*See* stitch.

sales rep—An individual who presents books to stores and takes orders. A book traveler.

SASE—Self-addressed stamped envelope.

scoring—Creasing or pressing a line into paper so that it will fold more readily and more accurately.

screen—See halftone screen.

second serial rights—The nonexclusive right to serialize a book in a periodical.

serial—A publication issued in successive parts, usually at regular intervals.

serif—The "tails" on a type character that make it easier to read. The text in this book is set in a serif type.

sheet—Two printed pages, one on each side of a leaf of paper. If the sheet is folded to create four printed pages, it is called a leaflet.

sheet-fed press—A printing press that prints on sheets of paper, not rolls.

short discount—Less than 40%. Textbooks are often sold on a short discount.

shrink-wrapping—Thin transparent plastic wrapped around books to protect their condition. Good to be done in small quantities, such as groups of two or six books.

signature—A part of a book obtained by folding a large single sheet of paper into sections. A book signature may contain increments of 32 or 48 pages.

Smyth sewn—Where signatures are sewn together with thread prior to installing the cover on a book. Common with hardbound books.

spam—An unsolicited email message.

Special Standard Mail—Successor to Book Rate; now called Media Mail.

spine—The part of the book that connects the front to the back.

spine out—Displaying books on a shelf so that the spine shows. Not "face out."

spiral binding—Continuous wire binding.

Standard Address Number (SAN)—A number assigned to all organizations involved in buying, selling and lending books. The numbers are assigned by the ISBN agency at Bowker.

statement—A periodic (usually monthly) listing of invoices, credit memos and payments. Bookstores expect a monthly statement of account.

stet—A proofreading term to disregard editing notes and leave as is. From the Latin "to stand."

stitch—A staple. The staples seen in magazines and brochures are "saddle stitches."

STOP orders—A cash with order (Single Title Order Plan) used by bookstores.

subsidiary rights—Additional rights to publish the book in other forms. Examples are book club rights, foreign rights and serial rights.

subsidy press—A publisher who charges the author to publish a book. Subsidy presses have a bad reputation for editing, production quality and promotion. A "vanity press."

substantive editing—A deep edit that deals with the flow of ideas, approach and tone, organization of the book overall and within each chapter, with possible rewriting and clarifying of the text.

tear sheets—Ads, stories, etc., torn from the magazine they appeared in.

terms—Time, in days, allowed a customer for payment of an invoice. For example: Net 30 days.

testimonial—Book endorsement or blurb.

text—The main body of the page. Not the headlines.

tipping-in—The pasting into a book of extra sheets such as foldout maps.

title—1. A book or stock of the same book. 2. The name of the book.

title page—The right-hand page in the front matter that features the title, author's name and other crucial info.

title verso—The page opposite the title page, often the copyright page.

trade paperback—A quality paperback or softcover book.

trade publisher—One who publishes books primarily for the book trade (bookstores and libraries).

traveler, book—A sales rep.

trim size—The size of the page once trimmed to its final dimension.

turnaround—The time it takes for a job to be done, such as editing or typesetting.

uncorrected page proofs—A galley. A crane.

underrun—When a printer manufactures fewer copies than were ordered. *See* overrun.

unit cost—The cost to print each book.

vanity press—A subsidy press.

vendor—The supplier of goods or services.

verso—The left-hand page of a book.

web press—A fast printing press, using paper on rolls as opposed to sheets.

wholesaler—A company that buys books in quantities for resale to stores and libraries. Wholesalers handle all or most books, do not usually have sales reps and are not exclusive to special markets. Not a distributor.

widow—A single word standing as the last line of a paragraph in a typeset book. *See* orphan.

work for hire—Writing for which the writer does not retain ownership.

working title—A preliminary title used during manuscript preparation before the book is named.

XML—Extensible Markup Language lets Web developers create customized tags for presenting electronic information.

INDEX

Books are the compasses and telescopes and sextants and charts which other men have prepared to help us navigate the dangerous seas of human life.
—**Jesse Lee Bennett (1907–2000)**

COLOPHON

This book was completely produced using the New Model production system described within.

Writing and manuscript building
Manuscript preparation: MS-Word
Typesetting:
    Body text: Berling, 12 pt
    Headers: Gill Sans Light, 8 pt
    Chapter titles: Gill Sans Light, 32 pt
    Quotations: ITC Century Light Italic, 11.5 pt
    Stories: Gill Sans, 11 pt
    Caption: Gill Sans Bold, 11 pt

Prepress
Editing: Brainstorm Editorial, Robin Quinn
    quinnrobin@aol.com
Proofreading/Production Proofing: Brookes Nohlgren (booksbybrookes@earthlink.net)
    and Arlene Prunkle (info@penultimateword.com)
Book design: Bacall Creative, Patricia Bacall
    pbacall@bacallcreative.com
Typography: Creative Publishing, Ghislain Viau
    viaugh@colba.net
Production using QuarkXpress
Cover design: RH Graphic Design, Robert Howard
    rhoward@frii.com
Book Consultant: Ellen Reid's Book Shepherding, Ellen Reid
    ellen@bookshep.com

Conversion
QuarkXpress to PDF

Printing
Printing by McNaughton & Gunn, Ann Arbor, Michigan
    http://www.bookprinters.com from PDF file
Paper: 50# Domtar Opaque—Plainfield Smooth
Cover: 10 pt C1S, four-color, lay-flat gloss film lamination
Binding: Perfect-bound (adhesive, softcover)

Book trade distribution
National Book Network
    http://www.NBNbooks.com

*Have you ever heard anyone say, "Simon & Schuster,
I love their books. I buy everything they publish?"
Of course not. People want to know what the book is
about. Is this something they need to know? Who is the
author? Is he or she a credible person? No one ever
asks, "Who is the publisher?"*

PARAPUBLISHING.COM

WHERE AUTHORS AND PUBLISHERS GO
FOR ANSWERS

QUICK ORDER FORM

Fax orders: 805-968-1379. Send this form.

Telephone orders: Call 800-PARAPUB (800-727-2782) toll-free. Have your credit card ready.

Email orders: orders@ParaPublishing.com

Postal Orders: Para Publishing, Dan Poynter, PO Box 8206-380, Santa Barbara, CA 93118-8206, USA. Telephone: 805-968-7277

Please send the following books, disks or reports. I understand that I may return any of them for a full refund—for any reason, no questions asked.

_____

_____

_____

Please send more FREE information on:
❏ Other Books   ❏ Speaking/Seminars   ❏ Mailing Lists
❏ Consulting

Name: _____

Address: _____

City: _____ State: _____ Zip: _____

Telephone: _____

Email address: _____

Sales tax: Please add 7.75% for products shipped to California addresses.

Shipping by air
U.S.: $4.00 for first book or disk and $2.00 for each additional product.
International: $9.00 for first book or disk; $5.00 for each additional product (estimate).

PARAPUBLISHING.COM

QUICK ORDER FORM

Fax orders: 805-968-1379. Send this form.

Telephone orders: Call 800-PARAPUB (800-727-2782) toll-free. Have your credit card ready.

Email orders: orders@ParaPublishing.com

Postal Orders: Para Publishing, Dan Poynter, PO Box 8206-380, Santa Barbara, CA 93118-8206, USA. Telephone: 805-968-7277

Please send the following books, disks or reports. I understand that I may return any of them for a full refund—for any reason, no questions asked.

_____

_____

_____

Please send more FREE information on:
❏ Other Books   ❏ Speaking/Seminars   ❏ Mailing Lists
❏ Consulting

Name: _____

Address: _____

City: _____ State: _____ Zip: _____

Telephone: _____

Email address: _____

Sales tax: Please add 7.75% for products shipped to California addresses.

Shipping by air
U.S.: $4.00 for first book or disk and $2.00 for each additional product.
International: $9.00 for first book or disk; $5.00 for each additional product (estimate).

PARAPUBLISHING.COM

QUICK ORDER FORM

Fax orders: 805-968-1379. Send this form.

Telephone orders: Call 800-PARAPUB (800-727-2782) toll-free. Have your credit card ready.

Email orders: orders@ParaPublishing.com

Postal Orders: Para Publishing, Dan Poynter, PO Box 8206-380, Santa Barbara, CA 93118-8206, USA. Telephone: 805-968-7277

Please send the following books, disks or reports. I understand that I may return any of them for a full refund—for any reason, no questions asked.

_____

_____

_____

Please send more FREE information on:
❏ Other Books   ❏ Speaking/Seminars   ❏ Mailing Lists
❏ Consulting

Name: _____

Address: _____

City: _____ State: _____ Zip: _____

Telephone: _____

Email address: _____

Sales tax: Please add 7.75% for products shipped to California addresses.

Shipping by air

U.S.: $4.00 for first book or disk and $2.00 for each additional product.

International: $9.00 for first book or disk; $5.00 for each additional product (estimate).